CCNA IN 60 DAYS

Study Guide

Paul Browning (LLB Hons) CCNP, MCSE
Farai Tafa dual CCIE

ISBN: 978-0-9569892-1-5

Published by:
Reality Press Ltd.
Midsummer Court
314 Midsummer Blvd.
Milton Keynes
MK9 2UB
help@reality-press.com

LEGAL NOTICE
The advice in this book is designed to help you achieve the standard of the Cisco Certified Network Associate (CCNA) exam, which is Cisco's foundation internetworking examination. A CCNA is able to carry out basic router and switch installations and troubleshooting. Before you carry out more complex operations, it is advisable to seek the advice of experts or Cisco Systems, Inc.

The practical scenarios in this book are meant to illustrate a technical point only and should be used only on your privately owned equipment, never on a live network.

Acknowledgements

Thanks to all my classroom students at Networks Inc. in the UK, and all the thousands of students who have joined www.howtonetwork.net and www.in60days.net, for giving me regular feedback and ideas.

Contributors

Thanks to Tim Peel, CCNA, for his help in editing this book.

INTRODUCTION

My name is Paul Browning and, along with Farai, my job is to get you through your CCNA (or CCENT and ICND2) exam(s) in the next 60 days. Your job is to do what I tell you to do, when I tell you to do it. If you can do that, then in 60 days' time you will be a qualified Cisco CCNA engineer. If you skip days, lessons, or try to play catch-up by doing two or three days' work when you have time, you will fail, badly. Trust me, I've been teaching a long time and I know what I'm talking about.

Do any of the following problems sound familiar to you?

"I just don't know where to start studying. I feel overwhelmed by the information."

"I've bought all the CBT-style videos and books, and have even been on a course, but I don't feel ready to take the exam and I don't know if I ever will."

"I've been studying for a long time now, but I haven't booked the exam yet because I just don't feel ready."

I hear these comments every day from Cisco students on forums and via e-mails to my office. I've come to realise that the problem isn't the lack of quality training materials; that used to be the case in the late '90s, but now there are too many training manuals. The problem isn't the lack of desire to pass the exam. The problem is a lack of two things which mean the difference between success and obscurity—a plan and structure.

This is why personal trainers do so well. We can all exercise every day, go for a run, do push ups, and eat healthy food, but having a trainer means you don't have to think about it. You just turn up and do what he tells you to do and you get the results (unless you cheat). This is where I come in—you turn up at the time you agree to each day and do what I ask you to do. Don't argue with me, don't complain, don't make excuses as to why you can't do something. Just do it, as the Nike slogan goes.

ABOUT THE AUTHORS

Paul Browning, Author

I worked in the police force in the UK from 1988 to 2000. I was always on active duty and spent time as a detective and a sergeant. I got involved in IT in 1995 when I bought my first computer and had to get a friend to help me sort out the autoexec.bat file to get DOS working. Then I had to fix something inside the computer when it broke. I sort of enjoyed that so I paid to go on an A+ PC assembly course.

I volunteered to teach e-mail in the police station when that came in, around 1995, and that was fun too. I left the police force to work on a helpdesk in 2000 but quickly grew tired of the monotony of fixing the same problems. I studied hard and in a few months passed my MCSE and CCNA exams. I got a job with Cisco Systems in the UK in late 2000, where I was on the WAN support team.

We were all made redundant in 2002 and I found myself out of work because the IT bubble had burst by then. Frightened and desperate, I offered to teach a Cisco course at a local IT training centre and to my surprise, they agreed. I quickly had to write some notes and labs, which became a book I called *Cisco CCNA Simplified*.

The book gives readers all the information they need to pass the CCNA exam, as well as the ability to apply everything they have learned to the real world of Cisco networking. The book has sold many thousands of copies all over the world, and eventually it turned into an online course at www. howtonetwork.net, which now offers CCNP, as well as security and voice training.

With the notes I had written, I started my own Cisco training company, which taught CCNA and CCNP boot camps in the UK for a few years. I sold the company to a friend in 2008 so I could work on online training, which gave me more time with my family.

Farai Tafa, Technical Editor

Farai Tafa, CCIE 14811 RS/SP, is an internetwork engineer with over 10 years of experience in core IP routing, LAN and WAN switching, IP telephony, and wireless LAN implementation. He currently holds two Cisco CCIE certifications in the Routing and Switching and Service Provider tracks. His other certifications include CCVP, JNCIA, JNCIS, and ITILv3 Foundation.

Share the Love

Farai and I have sold thousands of books on Amazon but we get very few reviews. I know people are busy and forget, so can you please help us by posting a review on Amazon after you have had a chance to read through this book? Once you have done that, please e-mail us a screenshot of the posted review (with the title '60 Days Amazon Review' in the subject box) to howtonetworkhelp@gmail.com and we will send you a free CCNA exam worth $67 to thank you for taking the time to do it.

TABLE OF CONTENTS

CCNA in 60 Days

I thought I had finished all my CCNA-level writing, but after a few years, I could see one recurring problem. Many new members joined my www.howtonetwork.net site and started reading the theory, labs, and exams, and watching the lectures. They then posted on the forum, "Where the heck do I even begin?" Oh, dear. I offered some advice and tips but the same post came up time and time again.

I realised that people had a problem and I had a solution, so I created www.in60days.net, which offers a daily study task for the CCNA exam. At first, I told visitors to use their own CCNA manual and study topic X or Y on a certain day, but this wasn't enough for many people. They wanted a one-stop resource instead of having to use one site for labs, a book for theory, another site for lectures, and yet another one for exams; thus, the members-only section of the site was born. Each day, members get a lecture or two, labs, study notes, and a couple of study tasks.

The results have been amazing, with everyone who followed the plan popping out the other end as a CCNA. They achieved this either by taking the 30 day + 30 day two-exam route or by taking one exam at the end of 60 days. You don't need to be a member of www.in60days.net to use this book, by the way; the website is an additional resource you can use if you want the benefits of asking questions and watching lectures and labs as I configure them.

No doubt, there will be book updates and changes, as well as the odd error found. To check for these and access some cool study resources, please visit the website below:

www.in60days.net/book-updates

You can also post questions and comments on the site.

FAQS

Q. Is this book the same as your other CCNA book, *Cisco CCNA Simplified*?
A. Nope. I do have some of the text from that and some from my CCNP books in here, but most of it is new. I wanted to include other stuff and some more of my own comments and observations, so this book is an improvement on the others in many ways.

Q. I've done a few days now and no labs. Where are all the labs?
A. You can't do labs if you don't know the theory yet. You'll move from mostly theory to mostly labs as you get closer to the exams.

Q. Do I need to join www.in60days.net?
A. No. I designed this book to be a standalone resource. On the website, instead of text I do presentations on video and demonstrate all of the labs, but in the book I do it all in text format with figures. If you have the money to spare and like lectures then feel free to join, but you don't need to.

Q. Why don't you put the answers to the end-of-chapter questions after the questions?
A. I do everything to help you remember what you have learned. I guarantee that if I put the answers right after the questions, you would look at them and probably forget them. If you review the text again, you will remember them.

Q. Wasn't the online program free?
A. There is still a free version but it only tells you what to study each day. How you do it and what you use to study from is up to you.

Q. Why is some stuff in your cram guide but not in the theory?
A. Some stuff I just want to give you in the cram guide, but if I want to cover it in more detail, it will be in the book.

Q. Should I do the one-exam route or the two-exam route?
A. You can do either with this program. At the 30-day mark, you can take the CCENT exam or you can continue on to the ICND2 module and at the end take the CCNA exam.

Q. Which is best?
A. There is no best. It is cheaper to take one exam and get it over with, but there is more to cover. The two-exam route gives you more breathing space and you get a qualification after the first exam.

Q. How much time do I need to study each day?

A. Set aside two hours per day. Bear in mind that the average person watches five hours of TV every day and more on weekends.

Q. What if I miss a day?

A. You want to avoid that at all costs. Find a time when you can study every day. If you have to miss a day, then just pick up where you left off the next day.

Q. What if I have a question?

A. Feel free to post any questions you have on the free or members-only areas at www.in60days. net. The site starts with three free videos and then the last day shows you links to both parts of the site, free and members only. There is also a 'book updates' page at the link above.

Q. Can a person really pass in just 60 days? Cisco teaches the CCNA course over two years.

A. They do, but it is usually only one evening per week for two hours, with 20 to 30 students per class. The poor results speak for themselves on that program. My method is more intensive but it is also of very high quality.

Q. Do I need to buy anything else?

A. Not really. You need this book and some Cisco equipment. If you really want extra homework, check out my book called *101 Cisco CCNA Labs* from Amazon or on Kindle. You don't need to spend hundreds of bucks on CBT video programs. Trust me, you won't pass by watching some guy talking about TCP/IP! Members of the in60days site also get a lot more practise exams, but like I said, this book should do enough for you to pass the exam.

Q. I have more than two hours per day to spend on studying, so can I study more?

A. Sure. Study the same stuff again or do more labs. Don't study what you already know.

Q. What if I can't do two hours per day?

A. You will surely fail.

Q. Where are the troubleshooting labs?

A. They all are! You will no doubt make mistakes all the way through the labs and have to fix them in order to finish the lab. This is especially true with the challenge labs which have no solution provided.

HOW THE PROGRAM WORKS

The 60-day study program is a combination of learning through reading, review, cram, testing, and hands-on labs. You take in new information for the first few sessions and then start to review each lesson each day, as well as apply the lessons to live Cisco equipment. You will then begin to apply the theory to exam-style questions so you can apply your knowledge in the real exam.

You need to factor in two hours of study per day spread amongst the theory, labs, exams, and review. I've also built in free sessions for you to choose what you want to study. You start off with mainly theory and then build up to mainly labs and exams, plus review. You will review every lesson the next day and then come back to it again in other review days, as well as in labs and exams.

Take NAT, for example:

- Day 9—NAT
- Day 9—NAT labs
- Day 10—NAT review
- Day 20—NAT labs
- Days 24 through 27—Free study and NAT labs
- All days—NAT in the cram guide

In addition, there are NAT challenge labs and you study NAT every day in the cram guide. The same goes for many other subjects. Minor subjects such as CSMA/CD I refer to twice, but that is all. There is little chance this will come up in the exam, so there is little to remember. Same with SDM, which is in the syllabus but has never been asked in the exam, ever! There will be ample time to cover everything, as well as free study sessions where you can go over any weak areas. You keep working on your weak areas until there are none left.

You'll start off with some preparation sessions and please do not skip these. I can tell you for a fact that a person with a strong reason and desire to pass will always pass. A person who sort of, kind of likes the idea of passing the CCNA exam will soon give up when he sees the amount of work involved.

The preparation days will get you focused on the WHYs of wanting to pass. This will be the magnet which draws you towards your 60 daily study sessions and your final goal of becoming a Cisco CCNA engineer (and beyond, I hope).

This study guide is a mixture involving content from several sources, including:

- Original notes and ideas exclusive to this guide
- Some notes from my CCNA study guide, *Cisco CCNA Simplified*
- Farai Tafa's *CCNP Simplified* study guides
- Presentation notes from my in60days.net online program
- Extra notes/labs and explanations

If you have read any of the books above or have used the resources, some of it may seem familiar in places. The difference is I've brought everything together and have broken it down into daily study sessions. Over 90% of the content in this guide is completely new and original. We'll dip into the CCNP notes now and again when I want to add some extra detail for you, or sometimes you need to go a bit beyond CCNA level for stuff to make sense; otherwise, more questions are left hanging in the air, and we don't want that, do we?

I have included some bonus labs at the end of the book, so if you want to test your hands-on skills further, then please follow those. If you want some other review materials, please check out the free whitepapers section at www.howtonetwork.net.

ARE YOU READY?

The subjects below are covered in the CCNA exam syllabus. Often, exams are themed whereby they drill you hard on one or two subjects while other subjects are left alone. It is the luck of the draw. This course is designed to leave no gaps in your knowledge at all.

CCENT	CCENT	CCENT	CCENT	CCENT	CCENT	CCENT
Switching	IPv4	WAN	IOS	TCP	Routing	WLAN
Security*	Addressing	Basic Config*	Manage	DHCP*	Static*	Standards
Basic Config*	VLSM	Cables	Architecture	DNS	RIPv2*	Tshooting
Cables	NAT*			TCP/IP		Security
	Subnetting			OSI		
ICND2	**ICND2**	**ICND2**	**ICND2**	**ICND2**	**ICND2**	**ICND2**
Switching	IPv4	WAN	IOS		Routing	
STP/RSTP*	IPv6	Frame Relay*	ACLs*		OSPF*	
VLANs*	NAT*	PPP*	VPN		EIGRP*	
Trunking*	Summarisation		Router Security*			
VTP*						

As indicated in the chart above, the upper area outlines CCENT subjects and the lower area outlines ICND2 subjects. If you are taking the CCNA exam, questions pertaining to all of the subjects above could be asked in the exam. The asterisks denote subjects for which you may get hands-on labs in the actual exam set by Cisco. As you go along, please tick off each area you feel you fully understand. Of course, each area needs to be ticked before you attempt the exam!

The chart above is not a definitive guide, by the way; however, it represents my best effort at making sure the core stuff is covered for each exam. There is no guarantee that Cisco won't throw the odd low-ball at you!

YOUR STUDY PLAN

Here is the study plan in full so you can track your progress. Tick off each day as you go along. You can download a printable version at www.in60days.net/book-updates.

Day	Subject	Labs	Revision	Student Notes
1	Network Diagrams	-	-	
2	OSI & TCP	-	Network Diagrams	
3	Cables & Configs	-	OSI & TCP	
4	CSMA/CD	-	Cables & Configs	
5	Switching	Switch Basics	CSMA/CD	
6	Switching Tshoot	-	Switching	
7	Switch Security	Switch Sec	Switching Tshoot	
8	IP Addressing	IP Addressing	Switch Security	
9	NAT	NAT x 3	IP Addressing	
10	DHCP & DNS	DHCP	NAT	
11	VLSM	-	DHCP & DNS	
12	Router Arch	-	VLSM	
13	RIP & TCP/IP	RIPv2	Router Arch	
14	Static Routes	Static Routes	RIP & TCP/IP	
15	Network Security	-	Static Routes	
16	Wireless	-	Network Security	
17	WAN Basics	WAN	Wireless	
18	OSI Exam	Switching x 2	-	
19	Cables Exam	VLANs	Switching	
20	Subnet Exam	NAT x 3	IP Addressing	
21	Subnet Exam	DHCP	Switch Security	
22	Arch Exam	Static Routes	Router Arch	
23	VLSM Exam	RIPv2	VLSM	

Day	Subject	Labs	Revision	Student Notes
24	Exam	Choice	Choice	
25	Exam	Multi-tech	NAT/Choice	
26	Exam	Multi-switch	NAT/Choice	
27	Exam	Choice	Choice	
28	Exam	Choice	Choice	
29	Exam	Choice	Choice	
30	EXAM DAY	OR DAY OFF		
31	ACLs	ACLs	-	
32	ACLs 2	ACLs	ACLs	
33	ACLs 3	ACLs	ACLs	
34	Trunks & VLANs	VLANs	-	
35	STP	STP	VLANs	
36	RSTP	RSTP	STP & ACLs	
37	Summ & IPv6	STP	RSTP	
38	Router Sec	Router Sec	IPv6 & Summ	
39	EIGRP	EIGRP	Multi	
40	OSPF	OSPF	EIGRP	
41	Frame Relay	Frame Relay	OSPF	
42	PPP	PPP	Frame Relay	
43	Exam	PPP & NAT	NAT	
44	Exam	PPP & ACLs	ACLs	
45	Exam	Named ACLs	Switching (All)	
46	Exam	VLANs & STP	Crams	
47	Exam	EIGRP & ACLs	OSPF	
48	Exam	OSPF	EIGRP	
49	Exam	OSPF & ACLs	IPv6	
50	Exam	Multi-tech	-	
51	Exam	STP & VLANs	Choice	
52	Exam	OSPF & Sec	Choice	
53	Exam	EIGRP & ACLs	Choice	
54	Exam	OSPF & ACLs	Choice	
55	Exam	OSPF & NAT	Choice	
56	Exam	Multi	Choice	
57	Exam	Multi	Choice	
58	Choice	Choice	Choice	
59	Choice	Choice	Choice	
60	Choice	Choice	Choice	

PREPARATION DAY

You want to start studying today, I know. But would you start a marathon without a good pair of trainers on and a bottle of water? If you did, you would quit soon afterwards. I recently looked at the statistics of my free 60-day study videos on YouTube. Look at how people dropped off so quickly:

- Day 1—14353 views
- Day 2—4912 views
- Day 3—2526 views
- Day 41—264 views

It is quite sad, really, but it confirms my experience of teaching Cisco courses over the past 10 years. Cisco does not publish figures of how many start and then quit the Cisco Academy program but the drop-off rate is horrendous. Very few even attempt the exam at the end of two years, and with an international pass rate of around 50%, the outlook is grim! All that money and time down the drain, and if Cisco can't get you through the CCNA exam, then who can?

I can, for one!

Preparation day is all about you writing down your goals and motivation for this course. What follows is a printed version of the preparation day e-book available online at www.in60days.net. Please read it all and do all of the exercises.

How to Pass the CCNA Exam in 60 Days

The pencil icon below indicates an area where you need to fill in your response.

INTRODUCTION

Even though we have never met and I know nothing about you, I do know that if you are reading this, it's because you want to pass your Cisco CCNA exam and you can read English. Knowing this, I can tell you with some confidence that you can pass the exam.

Over the past 10 years, I have helped hundreds of people just like you pass their Cisco CCNA exam. They came from all walks of life as well—builders, gardeners, receptionists, the unemployed, people with several years of IT experience, and people with no IT experience whatsoever, apart from the ability to turn on a PC (and maybe turn it off). In fact, the CCNA exam got me out of a job I no longer loved and into a role with Cisco TAC. I have learned that anybody can pass the CCNA exam or do almost anything, but there is a catch. Would you like to know what it is?

You have to want it bad enough and be prepared to do the work.

No, that's it. We could all be super fit, attain degrees, start a business, or learn conversational Russian—if we really wanted to.

Allow me to tell you about a good friend of mine, Geoff Thompson. Geoff used to work in a factory in my old home town of Coventry in the UK. He worked 12-hour night shifts sweeping up dirt from the factory floor.

Geoff Receiving His BAFTA

He was broke and depressed at the thought of doing the same job for the next 35 years. What he really wanted to be was a writer. Not any old writer, though. He wanted to be a bestselling writer who not only wrote books but also wrote scripts for movies and dramas.

Geoff used to hide in the toilet in the factory and write while he was sitting on the toilet seat. His first book was about his experiences working as a doorman at a terribly violent nightclub situated in Coventry city centre. Geoff wrote the book by hand and then had his girlfriend and best friend help him type it up on a typewriter so he could submit it to publishers.

Ninety-nine rejection letters later, Geoff still could not find a publisher to take him on. He persisted, though, and eventually a start-up publishing company took a chance with him. His book became a bestseller, with over 300,000 copies sold, and it has been translated into many languages. It has also been made into a short film. Geoff has been a full-time writer now for the past 10 years and he has authored over 30 books. This allowed him to move out of his rented flat and into a five-bedroom luxury house.

Geoff is now working on scripts with movie directors, and his films are winning awards at film festivals all over the world. Geoff is the first to admit that he isn't anything special. He was plagued with doubts and fears, but he had a big dream and was willing to do the hard work to achieve it. You can learn more about Geoff at www.geoffthompson.com.

I shared Geoff's story because I firmly believe that if you want something, and you have a strong enough reason for doing it and are willing to put the work in, then you can have whatever you want.

I can say this with some confidence because this morning, while everyone in my estate was driving off to work, I was at home cuddling my beautiful baby daughter. I fed her and then while my partner went off to meet some fellow new mothers, I sat down to finish this e-book. In this short guide (or whatever you want to call it), I will tell you how to prepare yourself for the 'Pass the CCNA Exam in 60 Days' challenge. I want you to examine your reasons for wanting to pass the Cisco CCNA exam and ask yourself honestly whether you are willing to do what it takes. Doing the work is going to be pretty easy because I am going to take you by the hand and tell you what to do in minute detail.

There will be no shortcuts or cheats. You are going to learn the material and learn it well enough to pass the CCNA exam, and then apply what you have learned to a Cisco CCNA-level network role.

VILFREDO PARETO AND THE CCNA EXAM

Have you heard of the 80/20 rule? It was introduced by Italian economist Vilfredo Pareto, who found that 20% of effort yielded 80% of the results. This term has now been applied by personal development gurus and pseudo-scientists for many years now. It can be 90/10, 70/30, or whatever.

Looking at Pareto's principle in the context of CCNA studies, you'll find that out of every 100 people who embark upon a CCNA course, only 10% will take the CCNA exam. Read that again! Yes, you may be shocked at that statistic (and it is a real statistic). It doesn't matter if you have paid for a cheap and cheerful home study course, a weekend boot camp, or a two-week intensive course led by the world's top Cisco engineers. It even applies to the world-famous Cisco Networkers Academy (call them and ask for their results).

What I want to know is what are the 10% doing that the 90% are not? I could be flippant and say that the 90% aren't studying, but why not? In the UK, you can pay around $8000/£4000 for a two-week CCNA course. Why would anyone pay that amount of money (usually on credit cards or with a loan) only to fail the CCNA exam?

Well, let's not worry about the 90% for the moment. Let's work on you being one of the 10%, shall we?

HOW BAD DO YOU WANT IT?

I mentioned the fact that if you want something bad enough, you can have it. So long as the thing you want is achievable, then it can be done. I am probably about to annoy you but hopefully I am far enough away from you so you can't hit me. I am going to tell you the reason you have not passed the CCNA exam so far, if you have wanted to pass it for some time now, that is. The reason you have not passed it yet is because you don't want to.

Did that annoy you? It probably did. It annoyed me when I met a successful businessman a few years ago who told me I had not started my own company yet because I didn't want to. I had been telling him that it was a bad time, I was busy, I didn't have any money or experience, I hadn't decided what sort of business I wanted to run yet, I hadn't written a business plan...and so on and so forth. I had all the excuses. The truth is that I didn't actually start my first company until the boss of our company walked in and told all 42 of us that we were out of a job in 90 days. To make matters worse, the redundancy pay covered only half my monthly rent. All of a sudden, my excuses went out of the window and I took massive action. I still had no business plan or idea of what I wanted to do or how to do it, but I started anyway and learned as I went along.

Perhaps I can save you a lot of time now. I want you to take a few seconds and honestly ask yourself how badly you want to pass your CCNA exam. Search inside yourself and think of a number from 1 to 10 and circle it. Please do this now.

1　2　3　4　5　6　7　8　9　10

Here is the time saver. If you circled 7 or less, then don't bother picking up the books or going any further with this e-book or your CCNA studies at the moment. No, seriously, it is not possible to pass the CCNA exam with a half-hearted attitude. Unless you are some sort of savant or have a photographic memory, you will never pass. You will be one of the millions of people who each year embark upon a course of study and are doomed to fail.

Such people experience a moment of temporary excitement and order a set of books or book on a course on the Internet, but they never complete it. The books sit on the shelves or the membership starts, runs, and then expires. Why do you think all gyms now get you to sign up for at least 12 months on direct debit? They know that they will have a massive influx of members in the new year when people make resolutions, or leading up to summer when they know people will be on the beach taking off their t-shirts. After a month or two, 90% have stopped attending.

By the way, don't for a minute think that I am anything special. On my office shelf in front of me I have my *Learn Chinese* book staring at me, taunting me to pick it up. I have bought the best e-book on losing fat and gaining muscle ever written, and I have read it back to front six times and have made extensive notes. I just haven't tried doing any of the workouts or following the eating plans yet. Maybe next week, eh?

Ah, but give me my website www.howtonetwork.net and I will work on it from five in the morning until two the next morning. I will write articles and hire programmers to write cool study tools for it. I will take financial risks to help it grow, and I will phone strangers out of the blue to tell them about the site.

Do you want to know why I will do that but struggle to pick up a set of weights or eat a salad?

HOW YOUR MIND WORKS

As a species, we will always move towards pleasure and move away from pain. Yes, yes, I know I am stating the obvious, but bear with me because there is more to this than meets the eye.

The reason we avoid things we do not like is because when we think of them we think of pain. When I think about going for a run, I think of pain, and when I think about eating a pizza, I think about pleasure. This is a self-made neurological map in my brain, which I could in fact change.

If I imagined having a fit and healthy body every time I thought about going for a run, it would feel pleasurable and my pituitary gland would secrete endorphins, which would bond with cell receptors in my body, causing me to feel good.

If, every time I thought about pizza, I imaged a spare tyre of fat building round my midsection, causing my trousers to feel even tighter, my adrenal gland would release cortisol, causing me to feel awful. I would eat a salad then.

Of course, this isn't about pizza, is it? It is about changing how you perceive sitting down for two hours per day reading books and configuring Cisco routers and switches. And, of course, finally taking ownership for getting yourself through the Cisco CCNA exam.

FUTURE PACING

I am going to have to be tough on you now, my friend. Consider me that friend who has to give you kind but firm advice because you have been neglecting yourself for a while. You know he is a real friend if he tells you how he really feels.

I want you to pass your CCNA exam. No, I REALLY want you to pass it. I want you to feel proud of yourself and I want to celebrate your achievement with you. I could have picked any business, you know—project management, Internet marketing seminars, personal training, become a lawyer, or any number of other roles. I run a Cisco training business because I really love helping people like you achieve what you want out of your lives, using Cisco qualifications to allow that to happen.

When I was in the police force, I felt like I was helping people, but the paperwork and politics were dreadful. Every night, I was rolling around on the pavement, fighting with crack addicts who I knew would never be sent to prison because the prisons were too full. Every time we put somebody inside, we had to let somebody out early.

Here's a scenario for you. You walk into a car showroom just to have a look at your favourite model of car. You know, the one you've been dreaming of buying when you win the lottery. As you sit in the car, you grasp the steering wheel firmly and feel the top-quality leather hug your body in just the right places. The salesman spots his quarry (you) and before you know it, he is standing next to you, pretending to be your friend (as salesmen do) and asking you lots of questions about why you love this car. At some point, if he is a good salesman, he may say something like 'Can you imagine yourself driving down the road in this car?'

He has just future paced you. Future pacing involves putting your mind into the future, where some sort of scenario has played or is playing out. We all spend a lot of time with our minds bouncing between the past and the future, possibly feeling bad about things we said or did in the past (so we get to feel guilty all over again), or maybe worrying about the future (such as our finances, the supposed recession, or the next hurricane).

Now I want to future pace you. Not to sell you anything, well at least not anything you can buy. I want you to sell the CCNA to yourself.

Imagine sitting at the testing desk at your local Cisco testing centre. You click on the last question and a bar comes up on the screen. It tells you that you have achieved a great mark on your exam and you have passed. You are now a CCNA.

WOW! All that hard work, the hours of studying, the sacrifices have all been worth it. You get an interim certificate stamped before you leave and walk out into the open, feeling the warm sunshine on your face. Only 90 minutes earlier you had walked in feeling tense and nervous, wondering if you had done enough studying. If only I had done one more practise exam, you were thinking to yourself.

Once you learn to master your mind, you can master your destiny. I know it sounds all very Tony Robbins, but he is the guy living in a castle, flying a helicopter, and married to a model, so he must be doing something right. Right?

Grab your pen or pencil and answer the questions below.

How will you feel when you pass the CCNA exam? Where will you feel it?

_____

_____

_____

What will it prove to you about yourself when you pass the CCNA exam?

_____

_____

_____

Who will you tell when you pass it and what will they say to you?

_____

_____

_____

What will your work colleagues and boss think? Will it earn you more respect at work, and whom will it help to inspire?

_____

_____

_____

What differences will being a CCNA make to your life?

_____

_____

_____

What opportunities will open for you now that you are a CCNA?

_____

_____

_____

When I was studying, I knew I was going to pass. Maybe not the first time, but I knew I was going to be a CCNA because I couldn't imagine not being one! I was absolutely desperate to pass. I imagined being back home with my family, and I imagined doing a networking job, which is what I really wanted to do at the time. I imagined walking into work and sending out an e-mail to all my colleagues saying I was buying the cakes because I had passed my CCNA exam.

Please refer to the list above **every day** as you study for the CCNA exam. Without a strong reason to want to pass, you will find yourself being distracted or feeling unmotivated.

There is another ingredient you need to complete the enthusiasm pie: responsibility.

WHOSE FAULT IS IT ANYWAY?

Here is an extract from an e-mail I received this week:

> *'Hi Paul, I'm finding studying hard. I have a ton of decorating to do at home, I have to drive to work and back every day, there are lots of projects on at work at the moment, and I have to work extra hours and some weekends. My boss doesn't even pay me overtime.'*

I have this same e-mail every week from a different student. I swear that it must be a template passed around.

One fact I have found while running my own company, speaking to over a thousand students and trying to promote my company to hundreds of IT managers, is that everyone thinks they are busier than everyone else, and they only think about themselves (myself included). I hear it time and time again: 'I'm really busy at the moment, I have so much going on, and I'm fire fighting...'

I recently e-mailed a website owner with a view to doing some business together. The first line in his e-mail response was 'I'm a very busy person.' I felt like writing back, 'Oh, so it is YOU who is the busy person. I was wondering who it was. The rest of us sit around all day long doing nothing. What's it like to be so busy?'

People wear their 'busyness' like some sort of badge of honour. Just because they are working flat out all day long and feel like they have no free time does not mean they are busy. It means they don't know how to say 'no' to others, they are not planning their time, and they are not prioritising their tasks correctly.

Here's a famous story to illustrate what I mean. A man walking along a country lane sees another man chopping down a tree. This man had quite a lot of experience in felling trees and could clearly see that the axe needed to be sharpened. If it was, then the chopping time could be reduced from three hours to only an hour. He shouted over to the man chopping down the tree, 'Hey, why not sharpen that axe so you can chop down the tree faster?' The man stopped, wiped his brow of sweat, and shouted back, 'I don't have time to sharpen the axe because I'm too busy chopping down this tree!'

While I do not mean to sound unsympathetic to busy people, I'm afraid we all have the same 24 hours in the day. Richard Branson, Donald Trump, Bill Gates, me, and, most importantly, you.

The truth is that in my entire life I have never heard a successful person say the phrase 'I'm too busy.' People may tell me that they have several projects they are working on at the moment and do not want to take on another one, but that is very different from saying 'I'm too busy.' Saying that you are 'too busy' is taking responsibility for your life away from yourself and handing it over to your boss, wife, family, traffic, teachers, or whomever. I'm convinced that 'busyness' is a disease sweeping society at the moment and it is getting worse. In an age when we have more convenience than ever before, and more timesaving devices, we are becoming more and more time broke.

I hate to rant but 'I'm busy' will cripple your ability to pass the CCNA exam. Only this week I had yet another e-mail from a student who came on my CCNA course two years ago and who has not taken the exam yet because he has been 'too busy.' He told me the same thing two years ago when I called him a week after the course to see how his studying was progressing.

Since that time, Cisco has introduced SDM, wireless, security, IPv6, and lots of other things to the CCNA certification, so it is going to be even harder for him to pass. The boss who is giving this guy more work than he can handle is the same boss who will be making him redundant (with no qualifications) in a few weeks. He could have passed two years ago and got a nice networking role for more money and less overtime, with an extra $20,000 in the bank and an extra two hours per day with his family.

So what is my point? Here it is: When all is said and done, who is responsible for your success or failure in any endeavour?

Wife/Husband/Partner

Kids

Boss

Fate

Don't know

Not me

Me

Any answer other than 'me' renders you powerless.

ON CHANGE

I can tell you in a few seconds whether you are going to pass the CCNA exam by looking in your diary. If there isn't one to two hours in there every day for studying, then you will not pass. There are no shortcuts or secrets to success. You put in two hours for about 60 days and you pass. It is how I passed and how almost everyone else passes. Remember that I have been coaching CCNA students for several years now. I don't just teach my students and throw them out the door. They are all given study tools, exam strategies, cram guides, lab walkthroughs, and lots of other stuff. The sad truth is that many walk out of the door and do the same exact thing that they have done for weeks, months, and years before they came on the course: nothing.

Change is painful and change is difficult. This is why we do the same thing every day, like put a sock on the same foot first, sleep on the same side of the bed, park in the same space, eat the same meal at the same restaurant, and so on. To break the change we need a very strong reason for doing so, which gives us the motivation to go through with it.

SUMMER 2000

During the summer of 2000, I had left behind my career in the police force to pursue a career in IT. I was living in a tiny room in a house shared with three other IT helpdesk guys in a town called Reading. I was miles away from my wife and daughter, who I missed desperately. I was the oldest person on the helpdesk by several years, and I was desperately broke because I had taken a massive pay cut from my police salary.

Passing the CCNA exam was my ticket out of the helpdesk job and into a company closer to home, working with a network team and making good money.

How desperate, on a scale of 1 to 10, was I to pass the CCNA exam? If you guessed 10, you would be right. There was no way I could not pass it. I got up at 5:30 every morning and studied subnetting for two hours. I walked to work and during my lunch break studied for an hour. After work, I went back to my room and studied for another two hours.

I did this for six weeks and then I failed the exam. I was devastated but I was also desperate. I took it again two weeks later. The rest is history.

Here was the pain I was in. If I didn't pass, I was probably going to lose my house because I couldn't afford both my mortgage and rent for the room. I was missing my family. I was doing an insanely boring job with idiot salespeople screaming at me down the phone because they were too stupid to backup their documents and now their hard drive had crashed.

Here was the pleasure. Passing meant more money so I could afford to live with and support my family. It meant I could leave the helpdesk and get an exciting job in networking, which I felt really passionate about. It meant I could move back home and be with the people I loved.

Now let's start with the first exercise. Please don't just read this and put it off until later. There is no later. **Do it now**.

These questions may sound similar but they are different. That is, they are designed to access different parts of your neurology.

What will happen for you if you pass the CCNA exam?

_____

_____

_____

What will happen for you if you don't pass the CCNA exam?

_____

_____

_____

What won't happen for you if you don't pass the CCNA exam?

_____

_____

_____

What won't happen for you if you do pass the CCNA exam?

_____

_____

_____

Based upon your answers above, do you feel motivated (i.e., scoring 8 or above) to pass the CCNA exam?

Yes / No

By the way, if you read this and decide that you don't really want to pass it at the moment, that is fine. I'm not judging you. Live the life you want to live and be happy with your own choices. Maybe now is a bad time and you should leave studying until later.

ANOTHER STORY

Here is a story of a student who passed his CCNA exam. He booked on my CCNA course and then started to e-mail me questions as soon as his book arrived. He wanted to know which routers he needed to buy and then he was asking for clarification about certain parts of my CCNA study guide, *Cisco CCNA Simplified*.

He wanted to know whether it was enough to read the book over three times before coming on the course or whether he should read it a few more times. He was tight for time because he had to get up at 5:00 every morning to get to his factory job. He did 10-hour shifts and then worked in a bar to make extra money to send home to his family.

He would get home at midnight, study for two hours, and then get up for work again at 5 A.M. The best of it was that I never heard him complain that he was busy! He just got on with the job and did what he knew he had to do.

When he arrived on the course, he was the only student out of eight to have read the manual. The others, who were doing 8-hour workdays, said they had been far too busy to read it.

Three weeks after the course, this student had passed and the other seven hadn't. I still keep in touch with them all and from the other seven it is the same thing: busy at work, no time, have to mow the lawn, (insert more excuses here).

TIME STEALERS

So back to our 24 hours in the day. I'm guessing most of the time you have the same structure to your day, something like this:

Get up
Wash
Breakfast
Travel to work
Work
Break
Work
Travel home
Gym/Eat/TV/Family/Leisure
Sleep
Repeat until fade...

By the weekend, you may be tired, so you just want to relax and switch off. And who can blame you? After all, you have earned the rest because you worked hard. Well, actually the definition of hard work has changed over the years. It has gone from working 12-hour shifts down a coal shaft or picking cotton in a field for 14 hours to sitting on our butts at a desk for nine hours.

I know which one I would rather do. Now, instead of being physically exhausted at the end of the day, we are just mentally drained.

In your schedule, you have things you have to do and things you choose to do. The things you have to do may include the following:

Sleep
Travel to/from work
Eat
Look after your children
Work

The rest may have a certain degree of flexibility. You may even be able to fit in a little bit of study time during your working day if your job allows it. Here are the things you may be able to allocate study time to instead:

Gym/Eat/TV/Family/Leisure
Break

If you take away

Sleep—8 hours
Travel—1 to 2 hours
Work—8 hours

you are left with only a measly six hours during the day with which to allocate your study time. You may really want to spend some of that time with your family, at the gym, or doing something else.

One guy told me he simply didn't have the time to study. None, nada, not one minute. When I asked him whether he would be able to find the time if he was going to be given one million dollars when he passed the CCNA exam, he thought about it for a few seconds and said, 'Of course I would!'

Right. So the problem wasn't the lack of time, was it? He didn't think it was a priority to study and he did other things instead. If I had followed him for a few days, I absolutely guarantee you that this guy would be watching TV for at least two hours per day. He would also be spending time at work chatting to colleagues and surfing the web, and would probably sleep on the train home.

Let me ask you something. If it was only for two months, what things do you think you could either cut out altogether or cut down on so you could study and pass the CCNA exam?

> *Leisure*
> *Time with friends*
> *TV*
> *Relatives*
> *Fitness*
> *Surfing the web*
> *Reading books/newspapers*

If you were going to be paid $1 million when you passed, what things could you stop doing, or at least cut down on, for two months? Write a list now:

_____

_____

_____

_____

_____

The best way to fit in your study time is to study at the same time every day. I like to do it early in the morning while everyone else is asleep and the phone will not ring. You might like to do it late at night. You MUST diary in the time. If you tell yourself you will study when you have the time during the day, you will not study. I have done that with my workouts for months before I realised I wasn't having any workouts.

Here is a suggestion I gave to a student named Mike. He felt overwhelmed with his schedule, and after two years with the books on his shelves, he still had not gotten round to taking the CCNA exam.

After a while, I realised that he was never going to pass because he never put in any study time. He wanted to but he couldn't see where on Earth he was going to fit it in. Here was his daily schedule:

07:00	Wash/eat/leave home	
08:30	Start work	
13:00	Lunch at desk	No time for a break
18:00	Leave for home	Hit rush-hour traffic
19:30	Eat/family time	
20:30	Fall asleep in front of TV	
23:00	Fall into bed	

Mike's life was in a bit of a mess. He was rushing around at work and home and he felt time deprived. His diet was in a mess, he rushed out to work, he never took a work break, and he stayed late. By the time he got home, he was starving and irritable. The last thing he felt like doing was cramming in two hours of studying every day.

With a few simple ideas, we managed to turn his day around. I got Mike to try finishing work on time for a change first. The first time he went to leave, he was shot some strange looks, but he just explained that his wife was not very well and he had to get home to help with the kids. He left on time for the rest of the week, in fact, and people stopped asking why he was leaving on time. They just came to expect it.

Next, I got him to prepare a meal for work the night before. He packed some nice wholemeal sandwiches, fruit, and a flapjack for when he felt hungry. Now, instead of trying to work all day without food or rushing downstairs for a McDonald's, he felt he had energy to last the entire day. He also took the novel step of drinking water throughout the day and immediately his energy levels rose.

Mike also began to take a 15-minute coffee break in the morning and a full lunch break. He felt he deserved it since he worked hard all day long. He actually started to get far more done at work because he had more energy. During his lunch break, he began to study from his Cisco books.

Because he had more energy, he woke up earlier in the morning and began to study. He set his alarm but woke up before it, most days anyway. He spent an hour doing a couple of hands on Cisco labs, which he really enjoyed.

Best of all, Mike began to feel more in control of his life. By the time he got home (on time), he felt very energetic and awake. He got to spend quality time with his wife and children. By the time the children went to bed, he had time for one last study session. His wife was okay with that because she understood that when he passed the CCNA exam, he would be looking for a better-paid job closer to home. He was even talking about starting his own business, which was his dream.

Mike went to bed at 10 P.M., just after he had made his lunch for the next day. He didn't worry about his study plan for the next day. He knew he could tackle the next day's tasks because they were sitting in his e-mail inbox courtesy of the 'Pass Your CCNA in 60 Days' programme (Note—we no longer do the course via e-mail).

Here was Mike's new schedule:

06:00	Up and study	1 hour of studying
07:00	Wash/eat/leave home	Listen to CCNA audio in the car
08:30	Start work	WORK TIME
10:30	Coffee break	Cram guide for 15 minutes
13:00	Lunch	45 minutes of studying
17:00	Leave for home	Listen to CCNA audio
18:30	Eat/family time	FAMILY TIME
20:00	Study	45 minutes of studying
20:45	Time with wife	WIFE TIME
22:00	Off to bed	REST TIME

If you had told Mike that he could fit in two hours of study time every day, he would have laughed at you. Now, he is not only studying for more than two hours every day, he is also happier and healthier than ever before.

The best thing, though, is that when he passes the CCNA exam, he will have an extra 8 to 10 hours free every week to spend with his family, to go to the gym, or to take another certification exam.

GOAL SETTING 101

Don't tell me that you don't set goals because you do. You set a goal to read this e-book and you are doing just that. Your brain is a goal-seeking organism. It needs and wants goals. Goals help us grow.

The problem is that our brains are bored because we set the same old tired goals every day of every week—get to work on time, try to finish on time, make our money last until the next pay day, and so on. If you want to pass the CCNA exam, you will want to make that your number one goal, which will be easy if you don't have any other goals.

Here is how I recommend you do it:

- Step 1—Ask yourself, 'Is this something that I really want to do?' You may be reading this and thinking to yourself, 'I don't want to be a CCNA after all.'
  If you feel excited about passing the CCNA exam, then you know you are doing the right thing. I only say this because I have set a lot of goals but have never achieved them. One was having a six pack. The truth is that I am not really that bothered about not having one. So long as I am fit and healthy and doing my workouts, I like that. In the UK it is almost always raining, so when am I going to get to take off my t-shirt anyway?

- Step 2—Are you willing to do the work? Two hours per day for 60 days. Be honest with yourself. Are you going to do it or not? There is no 'let's see how I get on' or 'I'll try my best.' Rubbish! You are going to do it or not, and you already know what your answer is. If you are feeling excited in the pit of your stomach, you know you are going to do it.

- Step 3—Are you willing to follow a step-by-step study programme? I have actually done most of the hard work for you already. All you have to do is do what I say when I say to do it. If I tell you to do an access list video, don't go and watch a movie or call a friend for a chat!

- Step 4—Take one day at a time. Leave tomorrow for tomorrow. Open up today's study e-mail and do the tasks I sent you for the day.

GOAL WARNING

I had better warn you now that when you set a goal you will also encounter one or more challenges along the way. These are designed to divert you from achieving your goal. I don't know what these challenges will be, but they will come. It may be a big project at work where you are asked to work late, a family illness, invitations out to events, or friends calling you to invite you out to that movie you have been looking forward to for months.

Because every circumstance is different, I can't advise or tell you what you should do in response to these challenges. All I can tell you is that once you set the goal, you can expect some kind of challenges along the way. Your choice is to avoid, deal with, or delay dealing with that challenge and then move on with your studies.

If you have to deal with it then do so, and as quickly as possible, get back on track with your studies. Pick up where you left off and keep going.

AFFIRMATIONS

Do this and don't argue with me. Get a few small blank cards (postcard-sized) and your pen.

Write this on the first card:

'I really enjoy studying for my Cisco CCNA certification two hours per day. I am learning new things and proving to myself that I am disciplined and that I am the master of my own destiny.'

Write this on the next card:

'It is [insert your exam date here] and I feel so happy that I passed my Cisco CCNA exam with ease.'

Write this on the next card:

'I easily make time to study for my CCNA certification every day, and the old things which used to interrupt my day no longer happen anymore. It's amazing!'

Write this on the next card:

'Passing the CCNA exam is my number one goal. Nothing or no one is going to stop me.'

Read the cards three times per day—when you get up, in the afternoon, and before going to sleep. It will program your mind for success. It will become part of your subconscious that passing the CCNA exam is inevitable. You will also find you have more time and actually look forward to your study sessions. Studying will become a part of who you are.

Does it work? The week I started to use the affirmation 'I easily make $30,000 per month' I started to make that and more. Proof enough?

THE BUY-IN

If you are in a relationship, you are usually expected to invest time into it (if you want it to last, that is). A particular problem many male students have is that their partner will want to spend quality time with them at the end of the day, which, of course, is a reasonable request.

If you cannot fit two hours of studying into your day before you get home from work, then you are going to have to do it at home or get home late. If this is the case, you are going to need your partner's and your children's buy-in. If they do not understand why you are hidden in your spare room for hours every day, then they are going to resent it and possibly you as well.

Take some time to write a list of people who expect to spend quality time with you most evenings. When you have written the list, then write another list of reasons it is important to you that you pass the CCNA exam and how it will benefit them. For example, if it is your wife/husband or partner, he/she needs to know that having the CCNA qualification will mean a pay rise, another job closer to home, contracting and working four days per week, or whatever else will happen for you.

You will also need to plan a family treat for when you pass. Put a picture of the treat on your refrigerator and remind the family of it constantly. Eventually, your partner and children will be telling you to go into your room and study because they want the treat.

List the people whose buy-in you need.

_____

_____

_____

Write out what you are going to tell them to get their buy-in.

_____

_____

_____

Please take some time to explain that it is only for two months and that you will not be studying all night and day, just for two hours a day.

_____

_____

_____

STUDY INSTRUCTIONS

It is vital that you have two hours of quality study time every day. Fitting small bits in at work when the boss isn't there or while sitting in a coffee shop is fine, but quality study time with no interruptions is what you need.

Here is what I would like you to do to prepare for your study periods:

- Turn your mobile phone off.
- Unplug your home phone or send it to voicemail.
- Turn off your e-mail program.
- Tell colleagues, friends, or your children and partner not to interrupt you for two hours.
- Check your start time and mark your finish time.
- Study away from distractions, such as noise or outside-facing windows.
- Take a 10-minute break every hour to rest your mind.

You will have a study plan to follow telling you exactly what you need to do for your study period as part of the 'Pass Your CCNA Exam in 60 Days' programme.

DEALING WITH TIME STEALERS

I'm afraid that there are many people who think they are entitled to take as much of your time as they wish. Because you are being paid at work, then of course you belong to them, I'm afraid, but at the end of your work day, your time is your own.

Most people I meet tell me that they work longer hours at work for no extra pay because it is expected of them. Well, that has to change if you want to pass the CCNA exam. I've only experienced this with IT people, but there seems to be some sort of unwritten rule that says if you leave work at the end of the day, you are betraying or have no commitment to the company. In the police force, we were always paid when we worked overtime. I remember my first day working at Cisco, from 9 to 5. I got up to leave at 5:00 and the team leader asked me where the hell I was going. I told him I was going home to see my wife and family and I left. If I had stayed for free, it would have educated him to expect me to stay for free for the 'love of the job.' But that love was not reciprocated when they made 42 of us redundant and outsourced our jobs to India!

While others were working up to two hours per day for free, I was studying. When we were all made redundant, I was the one with the qualifications and they had nothing to show for their work. Nobody had even thanked them for all the days of extra work they had done. It was just expected.

People work longer hours for free usually out of fear—fear of criticism by their peers or boss. That is the very thing that locks people into a job for years. If you want to pass the CCNA exam, you are going to have to be brave and leave at the end of your workday.

If you are struggling to do that then it is either a courage issue or boundaries, and that needs working on. You can read an excellent book called *Boundaries* by Henry Cloud and John Townsend for more information, but I strongly encourage you to finish work on time and invest time in your personal development.

Friends and family can also be huge time stealers. I spoke to one student who said that he was constantly called by friends with computer problems who wanted free tech support. He was on the phone for up to two hours at a time helping friends install their broadband or recover lost files.

If you want to pass then you are going to have to get tough with time stealers. Those friends did not value that student's time, and in fact, they came to expect free tech support. Never mind the years it took this guy to learn PC assembly and troubleshooting or the two thousand bucks he spent on the course. This guy's friends were classic time stealers.

While I am not saying we shouldn't help our friends, I am saying that we should put ourselves first. What that student should do is start a small business and charge a special rate for his friends. He would then recover some of his learning costs and his friends would come to appreciate his time and efforts.

If this is a struggle for you, read the book *When I Say No I Feel Guilty*.

THE NEXT STEPS

For now, make sure you have access to Cisco routers and switches, a good quality study guide (such as *Cisco CCNA Simplified* or this one—authored by Farai and me), and a cram guide and you have set aside your study time, preferably every day.

I hope that this short document has helped you in some way. If it has worked then you are clear on why you want to pass the CCNA exam, you have got the buy-in of the people you need to support you, and you are focused on passing.

If it doesn't happen to you then I hope you are strong enough to take responsibility for your own situation in life. If you didn't take the exam, it was you who didn't book it, it was you who didn't say no to time stealers, and it was you who didn't do the work. As Wayne Dyer says, 'All blame is a waste of time.'

If you pass then I salute you. Welcome to the top 10% of the population who set the goal, did the work, and won the prize. You have earned it. Please let me know when you do pass and send over a photograph so you can be inducted into the CCNA Hall of Fame. You are a winner!

Drop me a line at help@howtonetwork.net.

PREPARATION DAY—PART 2

Next, we need to look at live rack equipment. Packet Tracer is a network emulation tool which all Cisco Academy students can access, but it seems to be around on various file sharing sites as well. It isn't as good as live equipment but it will do the job as far as the CCNA exam goes. In fact, I've done a few of the labs in the book using Packet Tracer to save time.

If you have your own Cisco routers and switches then this is the best solution. If you want to know what equipment to buy, please visit my site www.ccnahomelab.com, which explains this in detail.

If you don't have access to either of the above, then my site www.howtonetwork.net gives free vRack access to all members 24/7.

Network Devices

DAY 1 TASKS

- Read today's theory notes
- Read the CCENT cram guide

I presume no previous IT knowledge throughout this course, so today we will look at common devices you will encounter on a network. You won't really need to review this section much at all because the information is pretty easy to remember and is not very likely to come up in the exam.

Today you will learn about the following:

- Common network devices
- How networks are represented in diagrams
- LAN and WAN topologies

This lesson maps to the following CCNA syllabus requirements:

- Describe the purpose and functions of various network devices
- Select the components required to meet a network specification
- Interpret network diagrams
- Describe the components required for network and Internet communications

Common Network Devices

Network Switches

Only a few years ago, networks were still pretty small. This meant that you could simply plug all devices into a hub or a number of hubs. The job of the hub was to boost the signal on the network cable, if required, and then pass out the data on the wire to every other device plugged in. The problem with this, of course, is that the message was intended for only one network host, but it would be sent to tens or hundreds of other hosts connected to other hubs on the network. (Hubs will be covered in another lesson.)

Network switches are a more intelligent version of hubs. Switches use Content Addressable Memory (CAM) and therefore have the ability to remember which device is plugged into which port. Cisco manufactures switch models which are designed to work in small offices and all the way up to large enterprise networks consisting of thousands of devices.

We will explore this in more detail later, but, basically, switches can operate using the device MAC addresses of devices (known as Layer 2) and IP addresses (known as Layer 3), or they can perform more complex tasks, such as processing lists of permit/deny traffic or protocols (known as Layer 4), or a combination of all these layers and more. We cover where layers come from on Day 2.

Using a switch will allow you to divide your network into smaller, more manageable sections (known as segments). This will allow the teams who work inside your company to work on the same section of the network, which is useful because the devices will spend most of their time communicating with each other. Teams could easily be separated into functions, such as human resources, finance, legal, etc.

Each device will connect to an interface on the switch, which is referred to as a port.

FIG 1.1—Cisco 2960 Switch

Common network port speeds are 100Mbps and 1000Mbps (commonly referred to as 1Gbps). There are often fibre ports you can use to connect a switch to another switch. Each switch features management ports, which you can use to perform an initial configuration and general access for maintenance over the network.

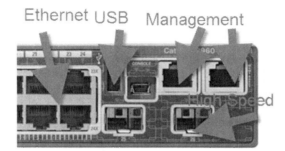

FIG 1.2—Switch Interface Types

You can also use IP telephones with your switches and, even better, the switch ports can provide power to these telephones. The basic network switch will be used to:

- Connect network devices
- Give access to network servers and routers
- Segment the network

Routers

As a Cisco engineer, you will spend a lot of time installing, configuring, and troubleshooting routers. For this reason, over half of the CCNA syllabus is dedicated to learning all about router configuration.

A router is a device used for networking. While network switches involve devices on a network, the router identifies which networks are where and the best way to reach them, and determines what to do if the network goes down.

Older models of routers only had ports, which were physically built into them and attached to the motherboard. This is still the case, but modern networks now require a router to perform functions for IP telephony, switching, and security, and to connect to several types of telecoms companies. For this reason, routers are also modular, which means you have the router chassis and empty slots into which you can connect a variety of routing or switching modules.

FIG 1.3—Cisco Router with a Blank Slot

The Cisco website has a lot of advice and information to explain which model of router will suit your business needs. There are also tools which will help you select the correct model and operating system.

How Networks Are Represented in Diagrams

All network engineers need a common method to communicate, despite which vendor they are using and which telecoms provider. If I had to describe my network topology to you for design or security recommendations, it would work much better if it were in an agreed format as opposed to something I had drawn by hand from memory.

The Cisco Certified Design Associate (CCDA) exam is where you will learn about network topologies in far more detail, but for the CCNA exam, you will need a basic understanding of these. This will allow Cisco to present network issues to you and ask you where you think the problem may lie.

Here are the common symbols for network devices you will encounter day to day. You can download these icons from the Cisco website if you type 'Cisco icons' in your browser's search engine.

Router

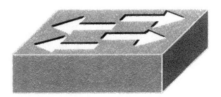

Switch (Layer 2)

Router with Firewall

Wireless Router

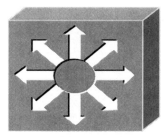

Multilayer Switch

The Cloud—Equipment Owned by the Telecoms Provider

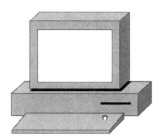

End Device—a PC

Serial Line

Ethernet Link

IP Telephone

Firewall

LAN and WAN Topologies

Topology refers to how network equipment is arranged in order to communicate. How this is done could be limited by the communication protocols the equipment uses, cost, geography, or other factors, such as the need for redundancy should the main link fail.

You should also note that there is often a difference between physical and logical topology. Physical topology is how the network appears when you look at it, whereas logical topology is how the network sees itself. The most common topologies are described below:

Point-to-Point

This topology is used mainly for WAN links. A point-to-point link is simply one in which one device has one connection to another device. You could add a secondary link connecting each device but if the device itself fails, then you lose all connectivity.

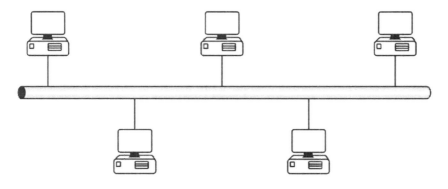

FIG 1.4—Point-to-Point Topology

Bus

This topology was created with the first Ethernet networks, where all devices had to be connected to a thick cable referred to as the backbone.

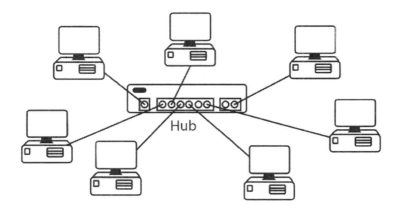

FIG 1.5—Bus Topology

Star

This is probably the most common topology you will encounter. Each network device is connected to a central hub or switch. If one of the cables to the devices fails, then only that device becomes disconnected, whereas with the bus topology, if that cable fails, the entire network fails. If the central hub or switch fails, of course, all of your devices lose network connectivity.

FIG 1.6—Star Topology

Ring

A ring topology uses a legacy connection method called a token ring, which went out of use several years ago.

FARAI SAYS: 'Believe it or not, it is still being used in some places in 2012!'

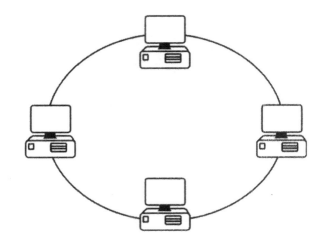

FIG 1.7—Ring Topology

A ring topology is used with Fiber Distributed Data Interface networks, which employ a dual-ring connection to provide redundancy should one ring fail.

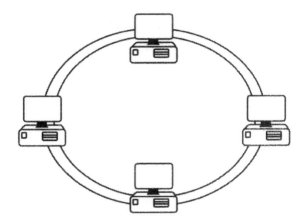

FIG 1.8—Dual-ring Topology

Mesh

When downtime is not an option a mesh topology can be considered. Full mesh networks provide a connection to each device from every other device. This solution is often used with WAN connections.

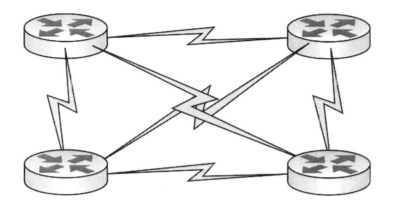

FIG 1.9—Full Mesh Topology

Typically, this type of solution will prove very costly. For this reason, partial mesh topologies can be considered. This means that there may be one or more 'hops,' or routers, to get to each device.

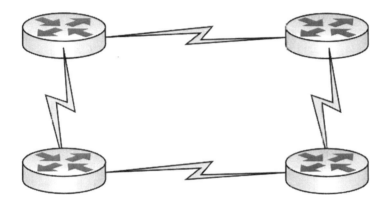

FIG 1.10—Partial Mesh Topology

Physical versus Logical

When you can see the network equipment, you are looking at the physical topology. This can be misleading because, although the network appears to be wired in a star fashion, it could, in fact, be working logically as a ring. A classic example of this is a ring network. Although the traffic circulates round the ring in a circular fashion, all of the devices plug into a hub. The ring is actually inside the token ring hub, so you can't see it from the outside, as illustrated in Figure 1.11 below:

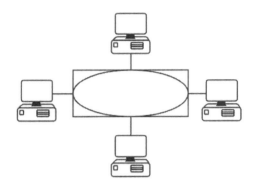

FIG 1.11—The Ring Is Inside the Hub

You may be asked to identify the different types of networks, both physically and logically. It is a good idea to remember that the physical topology is what you can see and the logical topology is what the network can see. This is summarised in Table 1.1 below:

Table 1.1—Physical versus Logical Topologies

Topology	Physical	Logical
Bus	Bus	Bus
Star	Star	Bus
Token Ring	Star	Ring
Point-to-Point	Bus	Bus
FDDI	Ring	Ring

DAY 1 QUESTIONS

1. Layer 2 addresses are also referred to as Layer _____ addresses.
2. Using a switch will allow you to divide your network into smaller, more manageable sections known as _____.
3. Common network port speeds are _____ Mbps and _____ Mbps.
4. A router can be thought of as a directory of _____.

Please re-check the FAQ for info on the answers. If you get really stuck please post on the book updates URL posted at the start of the book.

DAY 2

The OSI and TCP Models

DAY 2 TASKS
- Read today's theory notes
- Review yesterday's theory notes
- Read the CCENT cram guide

Today you will learn about the following:

- The OSI model
- The TCP model

This lesson maps to the following CCNA syllabus requirements:

- Identify and correct common network problems at Layers 1, 2, 3, and 7 using a layered model approach
- Describe the purpose and basic operation of the protocols in the OSI and TCP models

The OSI Model

Open Standards Interconnection (OSI) was created by the International Organization for Standardization (ISO).

With the technology boom came the rise of several giants in the fields of networking devices and software, including Cisco, Microsoft, Novell, IBM, HP, Apple, and others. Each vendor had their own cable types and ports and ran their own communication protocols. This caused major problems if you wanted to buy routers from one company, switches from another, and servers from yet another.

There were workarounds for these problems, such as deploying gateways on your network, which could translate between protocols, but such solutions created bottlenecks (slow portions of your network) and made troubleshooting very difficult and time consuming.

Eventually, vendors had to agree on a common standard which worked for everyone, and the free suite of protocols called Transmission Control Protocol/Internet Protocol (TCP/IP) was ultimately adopted by most. In the end, those vendors who failed to adopt TCP/IP lost market share and went bust.

The ISO created the OSI model to help vendors agree on a set of common standards with which they could all work. This involved dividing network functions into a set of logical levels or layers. Each layer would perform a specific set of functions, so, for example, if your company wanted to focus on network firewalls, they would work with other vendors' equipment.

The advantage was that each device was designed to perform a specific role well rather than several roles inadequately. Customers could choose the best device for their solution without being tied to one vendor. Troubleshooting became much easier because certain errors could be traced to a certain OSI layer.

The OSI layer divides all network functions into seven distinct layers. The layered model starts at Layer 7 and goes all the way down to Layer 1. The more complex functions, which are closer to the user, are at the top, moving down to network cable specifications at the bottom layer.

Table 2.1—The OSI Model

Layer #	Layer Name
7	Application
6	Presentation
5	Session
4	Transport
3	Network
2	Data Link
1	Physical

You can easily remember the names of the layers with the mnemonic 'All People Seem To Need Data Processing.' I would certainly get used to referring to each layer by its number because this is how real-world network technicians use the OSI.

As data is passed down from the top layers to the bottom for transportation across the physical network media, the data is placed into different types of logical data boxes. Although we often call these data boxes 'packets,' they have different names depending upon the OSI layer. The process of data moving down the OSI model is referred to as encapsulation. Moving back up and having these boxes stripped of their data is called de-encapsulation.

For the CCNA exam, you will be expected to understand the OSI model and which applications and protocols fit in which layer. They may also want you to apply your troubleshooting knowledge using the OSI layered approach. Let's examine each layer of the OSI, starting with Layer 7.

Layer 7—Application Layer

This layer is the closest layer to the end-user, you and me. The Application Layer isn't the operating system of the devices but usually provides services such as e-mail (SNMP and POP3), web browsing (using HTTP), and file transfer services (using FTP). The Application Layer determines resource availability.

Layer 6—Presentation Layer

The Presentation Layer presents data to the Application Layer. Multimedia works here, so think MP4, JPEG, GIF, etc. Encryption, decryption, and data compression also take place at this layer.

Layer 5—Session Layer

The role of the Session Layer is to set up, manage, and terminate sessions or dialogues between devices. These take place over logical links, and what is really happening is the joining of two software applications. SQL, RPC, and NFS all work at the Session Layer.

Layer 4—Transport Layer

The role of the Transport Layer is to break down the data from the higher layers into smaller parts, which are referred to as segments (at this layer). Virtual circuits are set up here, which are required before devices can communicate.

Before the data can be passed across the network, the Transport Layer needs to establish how much data can be sent to the remote device. This will depend upon the speed and reliability of the link from end-to-end. If you have a high-speed link but the end-user has a low-speed link, then the data will need to be sent in smaller chunks.

The three methods used to control data flow are as follows:

- Flow control
- Windowing
- Acknowledgements

Flow Control

If the receiving system is being sent more information than it can process, it will ask the sending system to stop for a short time. This normally happens when one side uses broadband and the other uses a dial-up modem. The packet sent telling the other device to stop is known as a source quench message.

FIG 2.1—Flow Control

Windowing

With windowing, each system agrees upon how much data is to be sent before an acknowledgment is required. This 'window' opens and closes as data moves along in order to maintain a constant flow.

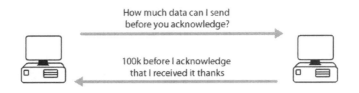

FIG 2.2—Windowing

Acknowledgements

When a certain amount of segments is received, the fact that they all arrived safely and in the correct order needs to be communicated to the sending system.

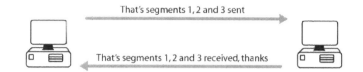

FIG 2.3—Acknowledgements

All of this is agreed upon during a process known as a three-way handshake. This is where you send a packet to establish the session. This first packet is called a synchronize (SYN) packet. Then the remote device responds with a synchronize acknowledgement (SYN-ACK) packet. The session is established in the third phase when you send an acknowledgement (ACK) packet. This is all done via the TCP service, which will be discussed in the next section (along with UDP).

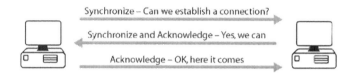

FIG 2.4—Three-way Handshake

The Transport Layer includes several protocols, and the most widely known are Transmission Control Protocol (TCP) and User Datagram Protocol (UDP), which are part of the TCP/IP suite of protocols. This suite is well known because it is the standard used on the Internet. TCP is known as a reliable connection-oriented protocol. It uses the three-way handshake, windowing, and other techniques to guarantee that your data gets to its destination safely. Many protocols use TCP, including Telnet, HTTPS, and FTP (although it sits at the Application Layer, it does use TCP).

UDP, on the other hand, is known as a connectionless protocol. It numbers each packet and then sends them to their destination. It never checks to see whether they arrived safely and will never set up a connection before sending the packet. Sometimes data is not that important and the application developer decides that you can always send the information again if it fails to get there.

Why is UDP used at all? TCP uses a lot of bandwidth on the network and there is a lot of traffic sent back and forth to set up the connection, even before the data is sent. This all takes up valuable time and network resources. UDP packets are a lot smaller than TCP packets and they are very useful if a really reliable connection is not that necessary. Protocols that use UDP include DNS and TFTP.

Layer 3—Network Layer

The Network Layer takes the segments from the Transport Layer and breaks them down into smaller units called packets. Most network engineers refer to data as packets, no matter what the OSI layer, which is fine; however, just remember that they are technically packets at the Network Layer.

The Network Layer must determine the best path to take from one network to another; for this reason, routers work at this layer. Routers use logical addressing here and TCP/IP addressing is called IP addressing, which will be covered in detail later.

Layer 2—Data Link Layer

The Data Link Layer chops packets down into smaller units referred to as frames. Layer 2 switches work at this layer and use hardware or MAC addresses, so they can switch traffic much faster because there is no need to check IP addresses and routing tables. WAN protocols work at Layer 2, including HDLC, ISDN, and PPP. The Ethernet also works at Layer 2.

In order to interface with the upper and lower levels, the Data Link Layer is further subdivided into the Logical Link Control (LLC) Sublayer and the Media Access Control (MAC) Sublayer. The LLC Sublayer interfaces with the Network Layer and the MAC Sublayer interfaces with the Physical Layer.

Layer 1—Physical Layer

Frames are converted into bits for placing on the wire at this layer. These bits consist of electrical pulses, which are read as 'on' or 'off' bits, or in binary 1s and 0s, respectively. Hubs work at this layer, and here is where you will find cable specifications, such as RJ45.

OSI Troubleshooting

Using a layered approach can be very effective when you're troubleshooting your network. The only decision from this point onwards is to determine which way you want to use the OSI stack, top-down or bottom-up.

I recommend bottom-up so you don't waste time looking at applications when the cause can often be found at the lower layers, such as loose or broken cables or incorrect IP addressing. If you start at the bottom layer and work your way up, you would do something like this:

- Layer 1—Are all the cables inserted into the ports correctly, or have they come loose? Are the cable ends bent or worn out? If cables are the problem, you will usually see an amber light showing on the device when it should be green. Has somebody forgotten to add the correct speed to the interface? Has the speed of the Ethernet port been correctly set? Has the interface been opened for use by the network administrator?

- Layer 2—Has the correct protocol been applied to the interface so it agrees with the other side, such as Ethernet/PPP/HDLC, etc.?
- Layer 3—Is the interface using the correct IP address and subnet mask?
- Layer 4—Is the correct routing protocol being used, and is the correct network being advertised from the router?

You will see how to apply these steps as you complete the labs in this book. Experts may argue that some Layer 4 issues are at Layer 3, some Layer 2 issues are actually at Layer 1, and so on. I prefer to focus on the fact that we are applying a layered troubleshooting method rather than debating about whether the correct issue is at the correct layer.

The TCP/IP, or DoD, Model

The TCP/IP model is now less often used or referred to; however, since Cisco left it in the CCNA syllabus, we need to consider it.

The TCP/IP model is a four-layered model created by an association known as DARPA. It is also known as the Department of Defense (DoD) model. The four layers top-down are as follows:

- 4—Application [Telnet/FTP/DNS/RIP]
- 3—Transport/Host-to-Host [UDP/TCP/ICMP]
- 2—Internet or Internetwork [IPSEC/IP]
- 1—Link/Network Interface [Frame Relay/Ethernet/ATM]

You may be asked how the TCP/IP model maps to the OSI model. This is illustrated below in Table 2.2:

Table 2.2—Mapping the TCP/IP Model to the OSI Model

Layer #	OSI	Data
7	Application	Application
6	Presentation	
5	Session	
4	Transport	Host to Host
3	Network	Internetwork
2	Data Link	Network Interface
1	Physical	

DAY 2 QUESTIONS

1. Name each layer of the OSI, from Layer 7 down to Layer 1.
2. The role of the Session Layer is to _____, _____, and _____ sessions or dialogues between devices.
3. What are the three methods used to control data flow at Layer 4?
4. The Transport Layer includes several protocols, and the most widely known are _____ and _____.
5. Why is UDP used at all if TCP/IP offers guaranteed delivery?
6. What is data referred to at each OSI layer?
7. In order to interface with the upper and lower levels, the Data Link Layer is further subdivided into which two sublayers?
8. What are the four TCP/IP layers from the top down?
9. How does the TCP/IP model map to the OSI model?

DAY 3

Cables and Media

DAY 3 TASKS

- Read today's theory notes
- Review yesterday's theory notes
- Read the CCENT cram guide

As a network engineer, you will be using a range of network cables and other media. You need to know which cables will work with which devices and interface for WAN, LAN, and management ports.

Today you will learn about the following:

- LAN cables
- WAN cables
- How to connect to a router
- Router modes
- How to configure a router

This lesson maps to the following CCNA syllabus requirements:

- Select the appropriate media, cables, ports, and connectors to connect switches to other network devices and hosts
- Describe the components required for network and Internet communications

LAN Cables

Ethernet Cables

Most cable-related network problems will occur on the Local Area Network (LAN) side rather than on the Wide Area Network (WAN) side due to the sheer volume of cables and connectors, and the higher frequency of reseating (unplugging and plugging in) the cables for device moves and testing.

Ethernet cables are used to connect your workstations to the switch, switch-to-switch and switch-to-router. The specifications and speeds have been revised and improved many times in recent years, which means you can soon expect today's standard speeds to be left behind for new and improved high-speed links right to your desktop.

The current standard Ethernet cable still uses eight wires twisted into pairs to prevent electromagnetic interference (EMI), as well as crosstalk, which is a signal from one wire spilling over into a neighbouring cable.

Cable categories, as defined by ANSI/TIA/EIA-568-A, include Categories 3, 5, 5e, and 6. Each one gives standards, specifications, and achievable data throughput rates, which can be achieved if you comply with distance limitations.

Category 3 cabling can carry data up to 10Mbps. Category 5 cabling is primarily used for faster Ethernet networks, such as 100BASE-TX and 1000BASE-T. Category 5e cabling uses 100-MHz-enhanced pairs of wires for running GigabitEthernet (1000Base-T). Finally, with Category 6 cabling, each pair runs 250 MHz for improved 1000Base-T performance. (1000 refers to the speed of data in Mbps, Base stands for baseband, and T stands for twisted pair.)

Duplex

When Ethernet networking was first used, data was able to pass on the wire in only one direction at a time. This is because of the limitations of the cables used at the time. The sending device had to wait until the wire was clear before sending data on it, without a guarantee that there wouldn't be a collision. This is no longer an issue.

Half duplex means that data can pass in only one direction at a time. Full duplex means that data can pass in both directions on the wire at the same time. This is achieved by using spare wires inside the Ethernet cable. All devices now run at full duplex unless configured otherwise.

Speed

You can leave the speed of the Ethernet port on your routers or switches as auto-negotiate or you can hard-set them to 10Mbps or 100Mbps.

To set the speed manually, you would configure the router as follows:

```
Router#config t
Router(config)#interface fast ethernet 0/0
Router(config-if)#speed ?
   10    Force 10 Mbps operation
   100   Force 100 Mbps operation
   auto  Enable AUTO speed configuration
```

The following command would allow you to view the router Ethernet interface settings:

```
Router#show interface fastethernet0
FastEthernet0 is up, line protocol is up
  Hardware is DEC21140AD, address is 00e0.1e3e.c179 (bia 00e0.1e3e.c179
  Internet address is 1.17.30.4/16
  MTU 1500 bytes, BW 10000 Kbit, DLY 1000 usec, rely 255/255, load 1/255
  Encapsulation ARPA, loopback not set, keepalive set (10 sec)
  Half-duplex, 10Mb/s, 100BaseTX/FX
```

Specifications for Ethernet cables by EIA/TIA dictate that the end of the cable presentation should be RJ45 male, which will allow you to insert the cable into the Ethernet port on your router/switch/PC.

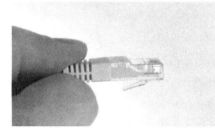

FIG 3.1—RJ45 Male End

FIG 3.2—RJ45 Female End

Straight Cables

Each Ethernet cable contains eight wires and each wire connects to a pin at the end. The position of these wires when they meet the pin determines what the cable can be used for. If each pin on one end matches the other side, then this is known as a straight-through cable. These cables can be used to connect your end device to an Ethernet port on your switch and your switch to your router. You can easily check if the wires match by comparing one side of the cable to the other.

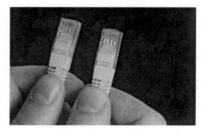

FIG 3.3—Comparing Cable Ends

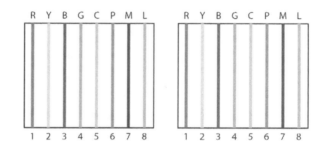

FIG 3.4—Cable Ends Match

Crossover Cables

By swapping two of the wires on the cable, it can now be used to connect a PC to a PC (without the use of a switch or a hub) or a switch to a switch. The wire on pin 1 on one end needs to connect to pin 3 on the other end, and pin 2 needs to connect to pin 6 on the other end. I have created my own colour scheme for the cables purely to illustrate my point. Red, yellow, blue, green, cyan, pink, magenta and lilac.

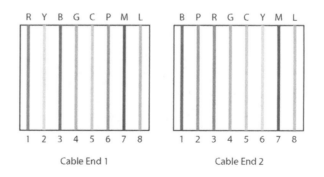

FIG 3.5—Pin 1 to Pin 3 and Pin 2 to Pin 6

Rollover Cables

All Cisco routers and switches have physical ports to connect to for initial set up and disaster recovery or access. These ports are referred to as console ports and you will regularly use these as a Cisco engineer. In order to connect to this port, you need a special type of cable called a rollover or console cable. It can sometimes be referred to as a flat cable because, as opposed to most round-bodied Ethernet cables, it is often flat along its body.

A rollover cable swaps all pins, so pin 1 on one end goes to pin 8 on the other end, pin 2 goes to pin 7, and so on.

FIG 3.6—A Typical Rollover Cable

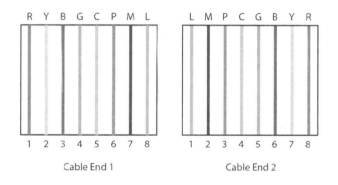

FIG 3.7—All Pins Swapped

Rollover cables usually have an RJ45 connection on one end and an 8-pin D-shaped connection on the other end, which is designed to connect to the COM port on your PC or laptop. The trouble is that devices no longer come with these ports, as they were so rarely supplied. You can now buy a DB8-to-USB converter cable from many electrical stores or online. They come with software drivers which will allow you to connect a logical COM port on your PC via a terminal program, such as PuTTY or HyperTerminal.

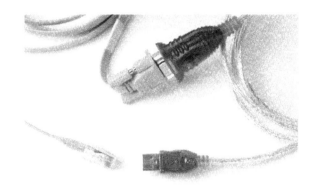

FIG 3.8—A COM-to-USB Converter Cable

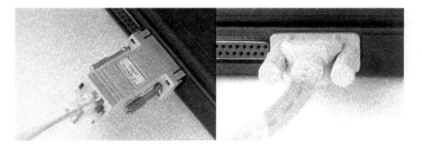

FIG 3.9—Connecting the Cable to the COM Port

FIG 3.10—Connecting the Cable to the Router or Switch Console Port

WAN Cables

Used for WAN connections, serial cables can come in several shapes, sizes, and specifications, depending upon the interface on your router and your connection type. ISDN uses different cables than Frame Relay or ADSL do, for example.

One common type of WAN cable you will use, especially if you have a home network to practise on, is a DB60. For this type of cable, you will have a data terminal equipment (DTE) end, which plugs into the customer equipment, and a data communication equipment (DCE) end, which determines the speed of the connection from the ISP.

FIG 3.11—A DB60 Cable

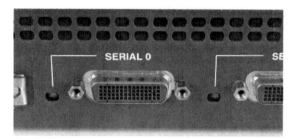

FIG 3.12—The DB60 Serial Interface

The most important thing to remember about DCE and DTE cables is that you need to apply a clock rate to the DCE end in order for the line to come up. Normally, your ISP would do this because they own the DCE end, but on a home lab or live rack, you own the DCE end. The command you would enter is clock rate 64000 (or whatever speed you like). You can type clock rate ? to see your options.

Please ensure that you understand the following commands before typing them out on a router. Firstly, to establish which router has the DCE cable attached, you need to type the show controllers command, followed by the interface number. You can see which interfaces you have on your router with the show ip interface brief command. You can actually shorten most commands, which is demonstrated in the output below. The shortened versions may not work in the exam, though, because the exam uses a router emulator (not a live router).

```
Router#sh ip int brie
Interface        IP-Address     OK? Method           Status Protocol
FastEthernet0/0 unassigned      YES unset  administratively down down
FastEthernet0/1 unassigned      YES unset  administratively down down
Serial0/1/0      unassigned     YES unset  administratively down down
Vlan1            unassigned       YES unset   administratively  down down
Router#show controllers s0/1/0
Interface Serial0/1/0
```

```
Hardware is PowerQUICC MPC860
DCE V.35, no clock
Router(config-if)#clock rate ?
Speed (bits per second
  1200
  2400
  4800
  9600
  19200
  38400
  56000
  64000          [output shortened]
```

Connecting to a Router

The first time you connect to a router or switch it can seem a little daunting. We have covered the console connection above, so once you connect this cable, you need to use a terminal emulation program on your PC or laptop. This will allow you to see router output and type in configuration commands.

HyperTerminal has been the default for many years, and you may need to use this still if you need to perform disaster recovery, but for now you can stick to PuTTY, which is very widely used. You can download PuTTY from **www.putty.org**. An old-fashioned connection using the COM port on a PC almost always uses a logical port on it labelled COM1 or COM2. You can see the facility to use this on PuTTY, which actually calls this the serial connection:

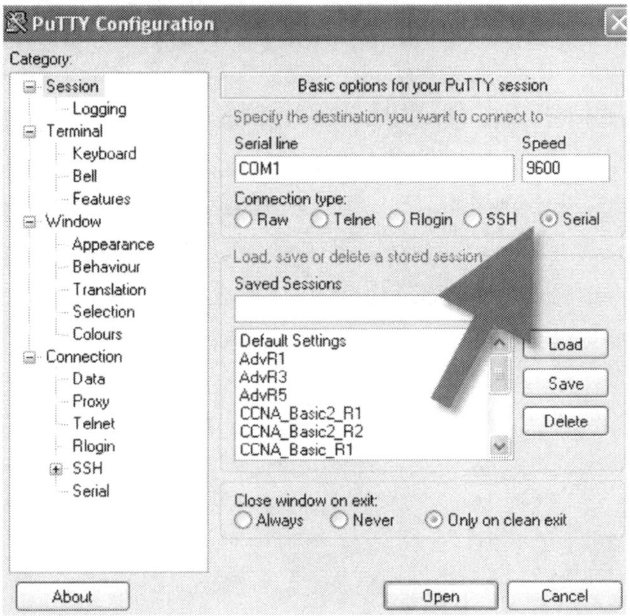

FIG 3.13—PuTTY Uses COM Ports for Serial Access

If you are using a USB-to-rollover cable, then you will have received a driver CD, which, when run, will give you a COM port number to use. You can find this port number in the Device Manager if you are using Windows:

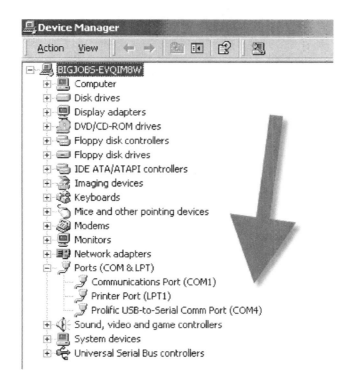

FIG 3.14—The Driver Has Assigned COM4 for Your Console Connection

If you are using HyperTerminal, you will also need to select more connection parameters, such as baud rate. You should choose the following:

- Bits per second: 9600
- Data bits: 8 is the default
- Parity: None is the default
- Stop bits: 1 is the default
- Flow control: must be None

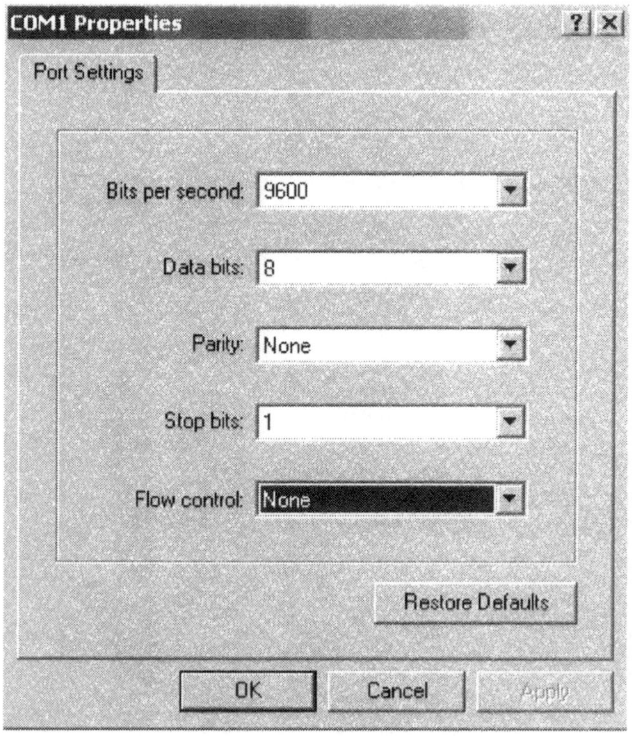

FIG 3.15—Setting Your HyperTerminal Settings

When you turn the router on, if you have selected the correct COM port AND plugged the rollover cable into the console port (instead of a different port by accident), you should see the router boot-up text. If you can't see any text, hit the Enter key a few times and then double-check your settings.

```
00:00:08: %LINK-3-UPDOWN: Interface Serial1, changed state to down
00:00:24: %LINEPROTO-5-UPDOWN: Line protocol on Interface Ethernet0, changed sta
te to down
00:00:24: %LINEPROTO-5-UPDOWN: Line protocol on Interface Ethernet1, changed sta
te to down
01:15:56: %LINK-5-CHANGED: Interface Ethernet0, changed state to administrativel
y down
01:15:56: %LINK-5-CHANGED: Interface Ethernet1, changed state to administrativel
y down
01:15:56: %LINK-5-CHANGED: Interface Serial0, changed state to administratively
down
01:15:56: %LINK-5-CHANGED: Interface Serial1, changed state to administratively
down
01:15:59: %LINEPROTO-5-UPDOWN: Line protocol on Interface Serial0, changed state
 to down
01:15:59: %LINEPROTO-5-UPDOWN: Line protocol on Interface Serial1, changed state
 to down
01:16:37: %SYS-5-RESTART: System restarted --
Cisco Internetwork Operating System Software
IOS (tm) 2500 Software (C2500-JS-L), Version 12.1(17), RELEASE SOFTWARE (fc1)
Copyright (c) 1986-2002 by cisco Systems, Inc.
Compiled Wed 04-Sep-02 03:08 by kellythw
Router>enable
Router#_
```

FIG 3.16—The Router Boot-up Text

The router may ask you if you want to enter initial configuration mode. Always type n or no because, otherwise, you will enter setup mode, which you don't want to do:

```
Would you like to enter the initial configuration dialog? [yes/no]:
% Please answer 'yes' or 'no'.
Would you like to enter the initial configuration dialog? [yes/no]: no
Press RETURN to get started!
Router>
```

With a different router model, you would see the following output:

```
Technical Support: www.cisco.com/techsupport
Copyright (c) 1986-2007 by Cisco Systems, Inc.
Conpiled Wed 18-Jul-07 04:52 by pt_team
        --- System Configuration Dialog ---
Continue with configuration dialog? [yes/no]: no
Press RETURN to get started!
Router>
```

Router Modes

In order to pass the CCNA exam, you will need to understand which router prompt you should be at to perform various actions. Whatever function you wish to perform, you will have to be in the correct mode (signified by the router prompt). This is the biggest mistake novice students make when they are having problems configuring the router and cannot find the right command to use. Make sure you are in the correct mode!

User Mode

The first mode you will be presented with when the router boots is known as User mode or User Exec mode. It has a very limited set of commands you can use with it, but it can be useful for looking at basic router elements. The default name of the router is 'Router' but this can be changed, as you will see later.

```
Router>
```

Privileged Mode

Typing enable at the User prompt takes you into the next mode known as Privileged mode or Privileged Exec mode. To get back to User mode, you simply type disable. To quit the session altogether, type logout or exit.

```
Router>enable
Router#
Router#disable
Router>
```

Privileged mode is very useful for looking at the entire configuration of the router, the statistics about how it is performing, and even which modules you have connected to the router. At this prompt, you would type `show` commands and troubleshoot with `debug` commands.

Global Configuration Mode

In order to configure the router, you have to be in Global Configuration mode. To get to Global Configuration mode, you simply type `configure terminal`, or `config t` for short, at the Privileged Exec prompt. Alternatively, just type `config` and the router will ask you which mode you would like to enter. The default is 'terminal' (the default options will be shown inside the square brackets [ ]). If you press Enter, the command inside the brackets will be accepted.

```
Router#config
Configuring from terminal, memory, or network[terminal]? ← press Enter
Enter configuration commands, one per line. End with CNTL/Z.
Router(config)#
```

Interface Configuration Mode

Interface Configuration mode allows you to enter commands for individual router interfaces, such as FastEthernet, Serial, etc. On a new router, all of the interfaces will be shut down by default, with no configuration present.

```
Router>enable
Router#config t
Enter configuration commands, one per line. End with CNTL/Z.
Router(config)#interface serial 0
Router(config-if)#
```

It is okay to read through this the first time, but it will make far more sense if you try out all of the commands on a real router as you read them. Remember to issue the `show ip interface brief` command to see which interfaces you have available. Your interface will probably not be Serial 0.

Line Configuration Mode

Line Configuration mode is used to make any changes to the console, Telnet, or auxiliary ports (if your router has these). You can control who can access the router via these ports, as well as put passwords or a security feature called 'access lists' on them.

```
Router#config t
Enter configuration commands, one per line. End with CNTL/Z.
Router(config)#line console 0
Router(config-line)#
```

You can also configure baud rates, exec levels, and more in Line Configuration mode.

Router Configuration Mode

In order to configure a routing protocol onto the router so it can dynamically build up a picture of the network, you will need to be in Router Configuration mode.

```
Router#config t
Enter configuration commands, one per line. End with CNTL/Z.
Router(config)#router rip
Router(config-router)#
```

Configuring a Router

There are no menus available on a router, and you cannot use a mouse to navigate between the different modes. It is all done via the command line interface (CLI). There is, however, some help in the form of the [?] keyword. If you type a question mark at the router prompt, you will be presented with a list of all the available commands.

Please note that you will only see the commands available for your mode. If you want to see interface configuration commands, you must be at the interface prompt.

```
Router#?
Exec commands:
access-enable    Create a temporary Access-List entry
access-profile   Apply user-profile to interface
access-template  Create a temporary Access-List entry
alps             ALPS exec commands
archive          manage archive files
bfe              For manual emergency modes setting
cd               Change current directory
clear            Reset functions
clock            Manage the system clock
cns              CNS subsystem
configure        Enter configuration mode
connect          Open a terminal connection
copy             Copy from one file to another
debug            Debugging functions (see also 'undebug')
delete           Delete a file
dir              List files on a
disable          Turn off privileged commands
disconnect       Disconnect an existing network connection
enable           Turn on privileged commands
erase            Erase a
exit             Exit from the EXEC
help             Description of the interactive help system
-- More --
```

If there is too much information to display on the screen, you will see the `-- More --` tab. If you want to see the next page, press the space bar. If not, hold down the Ctrl+Z keys together or press the letter Q to get back to the router prompt.

In addition, if you have started to type a command but forget what else you need to type in, using the question mark will give you a list of options available. The [?] keyword WILL work in the CCNA exam, but if you are using it, you didn't follow all my labs!

```
Router#cl? clear clock
```

If you begin to type out a command, so long as there is only one possible word or command available with that syntax, you can press the Tab key to have it completed for you.

```
Router#copy ru ← press the Tab key here
Router#copy running-config
```

The router has several modes from which to choose. This is to ensure you do not make changes to parts of the router configuration you do not intend to change. You can recognise which mode you are in by looking at the command prompt. For example, if you wanted to make some changes to one of the FastEthernet interfaces, you would need to be in Interface Configuration mode.

First, go into Global Configuration mode:

```
Router#config t
Router(config)#
```

Next, tell the router which interface you want to configure:

```
Router(config)#interface fastethernet 0
Router(config-if)#exit
Router(config)#
```

If you are not sure which way to enter the interface number, then use the [?] keyword. Do not worry about all of the choices you will be given. Most people only use the FastEthernet, Serial, and Loopback interfaces.

```
Router(config)#interface ?
Async              Async interface
BRI                ISDN Basic Rate Interface
BVI                Bridge-Group Virtual Interface
CTunnel            CTunnel interface
Dialer             Dialer interface
FastEthernet       IEEE 802.3u
Group-Async        Async Group interface
Lex                Lex interface
```

```
Loopback              Loopback interface
Multilink             Multilink-group interface
Null                  Null interface
Serial                Serial interface
Tunnel                Tunnel interface
Vif                   PGM Multicast Host interface
Virtual-Template      Virtual Template interface
Virtual-TokenRing     Virtual TokenRing interface
range                 interface range command

Router(config)#interface fastethernet ?
<0-0> FastEthernet interface number
Router(config)#interface fastethernet 0
```

Finally, the router drops into Interface Configuration mode:

```
Router(config-if)#
```

From here, you can put an IP address on the interface, set the bandwidth, apply an access list, and do a lot of other things.

If you ever need to exit out of a configuration mode, simply type exit. This takes you back to the next-highest level. To quit any sort of configuration mode, simply press Ctrl+Z together.

```
Router(config-if)#exit
Router(config)#
```

Or, if using Ctrl+Z:

```
Router(config-if)#^z
Router#
```

Loopback Interfaces

Loopback interfaces are not normally covered in the CCNA syllabus, but they are very useful in the real world and for practise labs. A Loopback interface is a virtual or logical interface that you configure, but it does not physically exist (so you will never see it on the router panel). The router will let you ping this interface, though, which will save you from having to connect devices to the FastEthernet interfaces in the labs.

An advantage of using Loopback interfaces is that they always remain up, if the router is working, because they are logical; they can never go down. You cannot put a network cable into the Loopback interface because it is a virtual interface.

```
RouterA#config t
RouterA#(config)#interface loopback 0
RouterA#(config-if)#ip address 192.168.20.1 255.255.255.0
```

```
RouterA#(config-if)#^z ← press Ctrl+Z
Router#
Router#show ip interface brief
Interface      IP-Address      OK?   Method      Status Protocol
Loopback0      192.168.20.1    YES   manual      up     up
```

Your output for this command will show all of the available interfaces on your router.

IN THE REAL WORLD: If you need to, you can shut down a Loopback interface with the shutdown command in Interface Configuration mode.

Loopback interfaces have to be given a valid IP address. You can then use them for routing protocols or for testing your router to see whether it is permitting certain traffic. You will be using them a lot throughout the course.

Editing Commands

It is possible to navigate your way around a line of configuration you have typed rather than deleting the whole line. The following keystrokes will move the cursor to various places around the line:

Keystroke	Meaning
Ctrl+A	Moves to the beginning of the command line
Ctrl+E	Moves to the end of the command line
Ctrl+B	Moves back one character
Ctrl+F	Moves forward one character
Esc+B	Moves back one word
Esc+F	Moves forward one word
Ctrl+P or up arrow	Recalls the previous command
Ctrl+N or down arrow	Recalls the next command
Ctrl+U	Deletes a line
Ctrl+W	Deletes a word
Tab	Finishes typing a command for you
Show history	Shows the last 10 commands entered by default
Backspace	Deletes a single character

It is fairly common to have a question on the above in the exam.

Configuring an IP Address on an Interface

In order for a router to communicate with other devices, it will need to have an address on the connected interface. Configuring an IP address on an interface is very straightforward, although you have to remember to go into Interface Configuration mode first.

Do not worry about where we get the IP address from at the moment; we will look at this later on.

```
Router>enable  ← takes you from User mode to Privileged mode
Router# config t  ← from Privileged mode to Configuration mode
Router(config)#interface serial 0  ← and then into Interface Configuration mode
Router(config-if)#ip address 192.168.1.1 255.255.255.0
Router(config-if)#no shutdown  ← the interface is opened for traffic
Router(config-if)#exit  ← you could also hold down Ctrl+Z keys together to exit
Router(config)#exit
Router#
```

A description can also be added to the interface, as shown in the following output:

```
RouterA(config)#interface serial 0
RouterA(config-if)#description To_Headquarters
RouterA(config-if)#^Z  ← press Ctrl+Z to exit
RouterA#show interface serial 0
Serial0 is up, line protocol is up
Hardware is HD64570
Description: To_Headquarters
Internet address is 12.0.0.2/24
MTU 1500 bytes, BW 1544 Kbit, DLY 20000 usec,
reliability 255/255, txload 1/255, rxload 1/255
Encapsulation HDLC, loopback not set
Keepalive set (10 sec)
Last input 00:00:02, output 00:00:03, output hang never [Output restrict-
ed...]
```

Show Commands

You can look at most of the settings on the router simply by using the show x command from Privileged mode, with 'x' being the next command, as illustrated in the following output:

```
Router#show ?
access-expression      List access expression
access-lists           List access lists
accounting             Accounting data for active sessions
adjacency              Adjacent nodes
aliases                Display alias commands
alps                   Alps information
apollo                 Apollo network information
```

```
appletalk        AppleTalk information
arap             Show AppleTalk Remote Access statistics
arp              ARP table
async            Information on terminal lines used as router interfaces
backup           Backup status
bridge           Bridge Forwarding/Filtering Database [verbose]
bsc              BSC interface information
bstun            BSTUN interface information
buffers          Buffer pool statistics
cca              CCA information
cdapi            CDAPI information
cdp              CDP information
cef              Cisco Express Forwarding
class-map        Show QoS Class Map
clns             CLNS network information
--More--
```

Some of the more common show commands and their meanings, along with an example, are listed below:

Show Command	Result
show running-configuration	Shows configuration in DRAM
show startup-configuration	Shows configuration in NVRAM
show flash:	Shows which IOS is in flash
show ip interface brief	Shows brief summary of all interfaces
show interface serial 0	Shows Serial interface statistics
show history	Shows last 10 commands entered

```
Router#show ip interface brief
Interface Address      OK?   Method   Status                 Protocol
Ethernet0 10.0.0.1     YES   manual   up                     up
Ethernet1 unassigned   YES   unset    administratively down  down
Loopback0 172.16.1.1   YES   manual   up                     up
Serial0   192.168.1.1  YES   manual   down                   down
Serial1   unassigned   YES   unset    administratively down  down
```

The method **tag indicates how the address has been assigned. It can state** unset, manual, NVRAM, IPCP, **or** DHCP.

Routers can recall commands previously entered at the router prompt—the default is 10 commands—which can be recalled by using the up arrow. Using this feature can save a lot of time and effort, as it prevents you from having to re-enter a long line. The show history command shows the buffer of the last ten commands.

```
Router#show history
show ip interface brief
show history
show version
show flash:
conf t
show access-lists
show process cpu
show buffers
show logging
show memory You can increase the history buffer with the terminal history
size command.

Router#terminal history ?
size Set history buffer size
<cr>
Router#terminal history size ?
<0-256> Size of history buffer
Router#terminal history size 20
```

DAY 3 QUESTIONS

1. The current standard Ethernet cable still uses eight wires twisted into pairs to _____ _____ _____.

2. _____ is when a signal from one Ethernet wire spills over into a neighbouring cable.

3. Which command would set the FastEthernet router interface speed to 10Mbps?

4. On a crossover cable, the wire on pin 1 on one end needs to connect to pin _____ on the other end and pin 2 needs to connect to pin _____.

5. Which cable would you use to connect a router Ethernet interface to a PC?

6. You can see which interfaces you have on your router with the show __ _____ _____ command.

7. Line Configuration mode lets you configure which ports?

8. A Loopback interface is a _____ or _____ interface that you configure.

9. The keyboard shortcut Ctrl+A does what?

10. The _____ keyboard shortcut moves the cursor back one word.

11. By default, the _____ _____ command shows the last 10 commands entered.

DAY 3 LAB—IOS COMMAND NAVIGATION

Topology

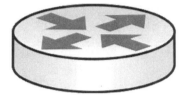

Purpose

Learn how to connect to a router via the console port and try out some commands.

Walkthrough

1. Use a console cable, along with Putty (free online if you search for 'Putty'), to connect to a router console port. Check out my 'Connect to a Cisco Router' video on YouTube if you get stuck: www. youtube.com/user/paulwbrowning

2. From the Router> prompt, enter the commands below, exploring various router modes and commands. If you are asked to enter setup mode, type no and hit enter. Please bear in mind that you will have a different router model to mine, so some output will differ.

```
Cisco IOS Software, 1841 Software (C1841-ADVIPSERVICESK9-M), Version
12.4(15)T1, RELEASE SOFTWARE (fc2)
Technical Support: www.cisco.com/techsupport
Copyright (c) 1986-2007 by Cisco Systems, Inc.
Compiled Wed 18-Jul-07 04:52 by pt_team


        --- System Configuration Dialog ---

Continue with configuration dialog? [yes/no]:no
Press RETURN to get started!

Router>enable
Router#show version
Cisco 1841 (revision 5.0) with 114688K/16384K bytes of memory.
Processor board ID FTX0947Z18E
M860 processor: part number 0, mask 49
2 FastEthernet/IEEE 802.3 interface(s)
2 Low-speed serial(sync/async) network interface(s)
191K bytes of NVRAM.
63488K bytes of ATA CompactFlash (Read/Write)
Configuration register is 0x2102
```

```
Router#show ip interface brief
Interface IP-Address  OK? Method Status                 Protocol

FastEthernet0/0  unassigned YES unset  administratively down down

FastEthernet0/1  unassigned YES unset  administratively down down

Serial0/0/0      unassigned YES unset  administratively down down

Serial0/1/0      unassigned YES unset  administratively down down

Vlan1            unassigned YES unset  administratively down down
Router#

Router#conf t
Enter configuration commands, one per line.  End with CNTL/Z.
Router(config)#interface serial 0/1/0 ← put your serial # here
Router(config-if)#ip address 192.168.1.1 255.255.255.0
Router(config-if)#interface loopback 0

Router(config-if)#ip address 10.1.1.1 255.0.0.0
Router(config-if)#^Z ← press Ctrl+Z keys together
Router#
Router#show ip interface brief
Interface  IP-Address OK? Method Status                 Protocol

FastEthernet0/0 unassigned  YES unset  administratively down down

FastEthernet0/1 unassigned  YES unset  administratively down down

Serial0/0/0      unassigned  YES unset  administratively down down

Serial0/1/0      192.168.1.1 YES manual administratively down down

Loopback0        10.1.1.1    YES manual up                      up

Vlan1            unassigned  YES unset  administratively down down

Router#show history
Router(config)#hostname My_Router
My_Router(config)#line vty 0 ?
  <1-15>  Last Line number
  <cr>
My_Router(config)#line vty 0 15 ← enter 4 if you have 0 to 4
My_Router(config-line)#
My_Router(config-line)#exit
My_Router(config)#router rip
My_Router(config-router)#network 10.0.0.0
My_Router(config-router)#
```

DAY 4

CSMA/CD

DAY 4 TASKS

- Read today's theory notes
- Review yesterday's theory notes
- Read the CCENT cram guide

Today we will look at how data is put onto the wire. This is more of a historical perspective because, as stated earlier, all wires on an Ethernet cable can be used now, permitting data to be sent in both directions at the same time (i.e., full duplex).

There are also references in the syllabus to Transmission Control Protocol/Internet Protocol (TCP/IP) as tools for troubleshooting, excluding their common services and ports. I've taken the liberty of adding this because many Cisco engineers haven't studied basic Microsoft or Network+ exams, so this may be their first experience with TCP/IP.

Today you will learn about the following:

- CSMA/CD
- TCP/IP

This lesson maps to the following CCNA syllabus requirement:

- Explain the technology and media access control method for Ethernet networks
- Verify device configuration and network connectivity using ping, Traceroute, Telnet, SSH, or other utilities
- Verify network status and router operation using basic utilities (including, ping, Traceroute, Telnet, SSH, ARP, and ipconfig) and show and debug commands

Carrier Sense, Multiple Access with Collision Detection

Carrier sense, multiple access with collision detection (CSMA/CD) can be broken down as follows: carrier sense means that the wire is listened to in order to determine whether there is a signal passing along it; multiple access simply means that more than one device is using the cables on the segment; and collision detection means that the protocol is running an algorithm to determine whether the frames on the wire have become damaged due to hitting another frame.

In Figure 4.1 below, you can see the switch port listening to the wire.

Is there a frame on the wire?

FIG 4.1—Port Listening to the Wire

If there is a collision on the wire, the algorithm runs and generates a random interval to wait for retransmit.

FARAI SAYS: 'Please note that modern Ethernet networks using switches with full-duplex connections no longer utilise CSMA/CD. It is still supported, but only for backwards compatibility.'

TCP/IP

TCP/IP is a complete suite of protocols and services which enable communication to take place over networks. Earlier competitors to TCP/IP, such as IPX/SPX, have all but died out due to their lack of adoption and ongoing development.

TCP/IP is a freely available and free to use set of standards maintained by the Internet Engineering Task Force (IETF), and it is used for end-to-end device connectivity. It has been developed and improved upon through submission of RFCs, which are documents submitted by engineers to convey new concepts or for peer review. One example is Network Address Translation (NAT) discussed in RFC 2663. IETF adopted some of these RFCs as Internet standards. You can learn more about the IETF and RFCs at the link below:

www.ietf.org/rfc.html

TCP/IP offers many services but many are outside the scope of the CCNA exam and will not be covered. I will also omit those covered in other sections, such as DNS and DHCP. The following sections outline the basics of TCP/IP.

Transmission Control Protocol (TCP)

TCP operates at the Transport Layer of the OSI model. It provides a connection-oriented service for reliable transfer of data between network devices. TCP also provides flow control, sequencing, windowing, and error detection. It attaches a 32-bit header to the Application Layer data, which is in turn encapsulated in an IP header. TCP is described in RFC 793. Common TCP ports include the following:

- FTP Data—20
- FTP Control—21
- SSH—22
- Telnet—23
- SMTP—25
- DNS—53 (also uses UDP)
- HTTP—80
- POP3—110
- NNTP—119
- NTP—123
- SNMP—161/162
- TLS/SSL—443

Internet Protocol (IP)

IP operates at the Network Layer of the OSI model. It is connectionless and responsible for transporting data over the network. IP addressing is a function of IP. IP examines the network layer address of every packet and determines the best path for that packet to take to reach its destination. IP is discussed in detail in RFC 791.

User Datagram Protocol (UDP)

UDP also operates at the Transport Layer of the OSI model. It transports information between network devices but, unlike TCP, no connection is established first. UDP is connectionless, gives best-effort delivery, and gives no guarantee the data will reach the destination. UDP is much like sending a letter with no return address. You know it was sent, but you never know if the letter got there.

UDP consumes less bandwidth than TCP does and is suitable for applications which do not need reliability or guarantees. Both TCP and UDP are carried over IP. UDP is described in RFC 768. Common UDP port numbers include the following:

- DNS—53
- TFTP—69

File Transfer Protocol (FTP)

FTP operates at the Application Layer and is responsible for reliably transporting data across a remote link. Because it has to be reliable, FTP uses TCP for data transfer.

You can debug FTP traffic with the `debug ip ftp` command.

FTP uses ports 20 and 21. Usually, a first connection is made to the FTP server from the client on port 21. A second data connection is then made either leaving the FTP server on port 20 or from a random port on the client to port 20 on the FTP server. You may wish to read more about active versus passive FTP for your own information, but it is unlikely this will be covered in CCNA-level exams.

Trivial File Transfer Protocol (TFTP)

For less reliable transfer of data, TFTP provides a good alternative. TFTP provides a connectionless transfer by using UDP port 69. TFTP can be difficult to use because you have to specify exactly the directory in which the file is located.

To use TFTP, you need to have a client (the router, in your case) and a TFTP server, which could be a router or a PC, or server on the network (preferably on the same subnet). You need to have TFTP software on the server so the files can be pulled off it and forwarded on to the client.

> **IN THE REAL WORLD:** Having a laptop or PC as a TFTP server containing backup copies of the startup configuration and IOS is a very good idea indeed.

TFTP is used extensively on Cisco routers to backup configurations and upgrade the router. The following command will carry out these functions:

```
RouterA#copy tftp flash:
```

You will be prompted to enter the IP address of the other host in which the new flash file is located:

```
Address or name of remote host []? 10.10.10.1
```

You will then have to enter the name of the flash image on the other router:

```
Source filename []? / c2500-js-1.121-17.bin
Destination filename [c2500-js-1.121-17.bin]?
```

You will be prompted to erase the flash on your router before copying, and then the file is transferred. When the router reloads, your new flash image should be present.

Other optional commands are `copy flash tftp` if you want to store a backup copy or `copy running config tftp` if you want to backup your running configuration file.

You can run a debug on TFTP traffic with the `debug tftp` command.

Simple Mail Transfer Protocol (SMTP)

SMTP defines how e-mails are sent to the e-mail server from the client. It uses TCP to ensure a reliable connection. SMTP e-mails are pulled off the SMTP server in different ways, and SMTP is used as an e-mail delivery service by most networks. POP3 is another popular way to do this. POP3 is a protocol that transfers the e-mail from the server to the client. SMTP uses TCP port 25.

Hyper Text Transfer Protocol (HTTP)

HTTP uses TCP to send text, graphics, and other multimedia files from a web server to clients. This protocol allows you to view web pages, and it sits at the Application Layer of the OSI model. HTTPS is a secure version of HTTP that uses Secure Sockets Layer (SSL) or Transport Layer Security (TLS) to encrypt the data before it is sent.

You can debug HTTP traffic with the `debug ip http` command. HTTP uses TCP port 80.

Telnet

Telnet uses TCP to allow remote connection to network devices. You will see more about Telnet in the labs. Telnet is not secure so many administrators are now using Secure Shell (SSH) to ensure a secure connection. Telnet is the only utility that can check all seven layers of the OSI model, so if you Telnet to an address, then all seven layers are working properly.

If you can't telnet to another device, it doesn't necessarily indicate a network problem. There could be a firewall or an access list blocking the connection, or Telnet may not be enabled on the device.

In order to telnet to a Cisco router, there must be a VTY password configured on the router. If you are trying to telnet to another device but cannot connect to it, you can enter Ctrl+Shift+6 together and then enter X to quit. To quit an active Telnet session, you can simply type `exit` or `disconnect`.

You can debug Telnet with the `debug telnet` command. Telnet uses TCP port 23. Secure Shell (SSH) is a secure alternative to telnet and uses TCP port 22.

Internet Control Message Protocol (ICMP)

ICMP is a protocol used to report problems or issues with IP packets (or datagrams) on a network. ICMP is a requirement for any vendor who wishes to use IP on its network. When a problem is experienced with an IP packet, the IP packet is destroyed and an ICMP message is generated and sent to the host that originated the packet.

As defined in RFC 792, ICMP delivers messages inside IP packets. The most popular use of ICMP is to send ping packets to test network connectivity of remote hosts. A ping command issued from a network device generates an echo request packet that is sent to the destination device. Upon receiving the echo request, the destination device generates an echo reply.

Because pings also have a time to live (TTL) field, they give a good indication of network latency (delay). The ping output below is from a desktop PC:

```
C:\>ping cisco.com
Pinging cisco.com [198.133.219.25] with 32 bytes of data:
Reply from 198.133.219.25: bytes=32 time=460ms TTL=237
Reply from 198.133.219.25: bytes=32 time=160ms TTL=237
Reply from 198.133.219.25: bytes=32 time=160ms TTL=237
Reply from 198.133.219.25: bytes=32 time=180ms TTL=237
Ping statistics for 198.133.219.25:
    Packets: Sent = 4, Received = 4, Lost = 0 (0% loss),
Approximate round trip times in milli-seconds:
Minimum = 160ms, Maximum = 460ms, Average = 240ms
```

In the output above, the ping packet is 32 bytes long, the time field reports how many milliseconds the response took, and the TTL is the time-to-live field (how many milliseconds before the packet expires).

The ping command on a Cisco router has a verbose facility that provides more granularity from which you can specify the source you are pinging, how many pings, and what size you send, along with other parameters. This feature is very useful for testing and is used several times in the accompanying lab scenarios, as illustrated in the output below:

```
Router#ping      ← press Enter here
Protocol [ip]:
Target IP address: 172.16.1.5
Repeat count [5]:
Datagram size [100]: 1200
Timeout in seconds [2]:
Extended commands [n]: yes
Source address:   ← you can specify a source address or interface here
Type of service [0]:
Set DF bit in IP header? [no]: yes
Data pattern [0xABCD]:
Loose, Strict, Record, Timestamp, Verbose[none]:
Type escape sequence to abort.
```

```
Sending 5, 1000-byte ICMP Echos to 131.108.2.27, timeout is 2 seconds:
U U U U U
Success rate is 0% percent, round-trip min/avg/max = 4/6/12 ms
```

Several notations represent the response the ping packet receives, as follows:

- ! —One exclamation mark per response
- . —One period for each timeout
- U —Destination unreachable message
- N —Network unreachable message
- P —Protocol unreachable message
- Q —Source quench message
- M —Could not fragment
- ? —Unknown packet type

You can terminate a ping session by holding down the Ctrl+Shift+6 keys (all together) and then the X key (on its own).

ICMP packet types are defined in RFC 1700. Learning all of the code numbers and names is outside the scope of the CCNA syllabus.

Many junior network engineers misuse the ping facility when it comes to troubleshooting. A failed ping could indicate a network issue or that ICMP traffic is blocked on the network. Because ping attacks are a common way to attack a network, ICMP is often blocked.

Traceroute

Traceroute is a very widely used facility which can test network connectivity and is a handy tool for measurement and management. Traceroute follows the destination IP packets by sending UDP packets with a small maximum TTL field and then listens for an ICMP time-exceeded response.

As the Traceroute packet progresses, the records are displayed for you hop by hop. Each hop is measured three times. An asterisk [*] indicates a hop has exceeded its time limit.

Cisco routers use the `traceroute` command, whereas Windows PCs use `tracert`, as illustrated in the output below:

```
C:\Documents and Settings\pc>tracert hello.com
Tracing route to hello.com [63.146.123.17]
over a maximum of 30 hops:
1 81 ms 70 ms 80 ms imsnet-c110-hg2-berks.ba.net [213.140.212.45]
```

```
 2  70 ms  80 ms  70 ms  192.168.254.61
 3  70 ms  70 ms  80 ms  172.16.93.29
 4  60 ms  81 ms  70 ms  213.120.62.177
 5  70 ms  70 ms  80 ms  core1-pos4-2.berks.ukore.ba.net [65.6.197.133]
 6  70 ms  80 ms  80 ms  core1-pos13-0.ealng.core.ba.net [65.6.196.245]
 7  70 ms  70 ms  80 ms  transit2-pos3-0.eang.ore.ba.net [194.72.17.82]
 8  70 ms  80 ms  70 ms  t2c2-p8-0.uk-eal.eu.ba.net [165.49.168.33]
 9 151 ms 150 ms 150 ms  t2c2-p5-0.us-ash.ba.net [165.49.164.22]
10 151 ms 150 ms 150 ms  dcp-brdr-01.inet.qwest.net [205.171.1.37]
11 140 ms 140 ms 150 ms  205.171.251.25
12 150 ms 160 ms 150 ms  dca-core-02.inet.qwest.net [205.171.8.221]
13 190 ms 191 ms 190 ms  atl-core-02.inet.qwest.net [205.171.8.153]
14 191 ms 180 ms 200 ms  atl-core-01.inet.net [205.171.21.149]
15 220 ms 230 ms 231 ms  iah-core-03.inet.net [205.171.8.145]
16 210 ms 211 ms 210 ms  iah-core-02.inet.net [205.171.31.41]
17 261 ms 250 ms 261 ms  bur-core-01.inet.net [205.171.205.25]
18 230 ms 231 ms 230 ms  bur-core-02.inet.net [205.171.13.2]
19 211 ms 220 ms 220 ms  buc-cntr-01.inet.net [205.171.13.158]
20 220 ms 221 ms 220 ms  msfc-24.buc.qwest.net [66.77.125.66]
21 221 ms 230 ms 220 ms  www.hello.com [63.146.123.17]
Trace complete.
```

The fields in the Traceroute output are as follows:

- ... —Timeout
- U —Port unreachable message
- H —Host unreachable message
- P —Protocol unreachable message
- N —Network unreachable message
- ? —Unknown packet type
- Q —Source quench received

Traceroute is a very useful command when you want to troubleshoot network connectivity issues.

Address Resolution Protocol (ARP)

Two types of addressing are used to identify network hosts—the IP (or Layer 3) address and the local (or data link) address. The data link address is also commonly referred to as the MAC address. Address resolution, as defined in RFC 826, is the process of the IOS determining the data link address from the network layer (or IP) address.

ARP resolves a known IP address to a MAC address. When a host needs to transfer data across the network, it needs to know the other host's MAC address. The host checks its ARP cache and if the MAC address is not there, it sends out an ARP broadcast message to find the host.

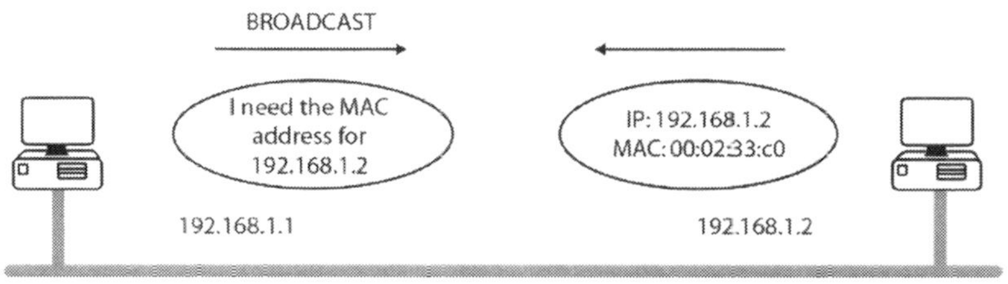

FIG 4.2—Host Broadcasts for Another Host's MAC Address

You can debug ARP with the `debug arp` command.

An ARP entry is required for communication across your network. You can see that a broadcast takes place if there is no ARP entry. It is also important to understand that ARP tables on routers and switches are flushed after a certain amount of time to conserve resources and prevent inaccurate entries.

On the router below, it has an ARP entry only for its own FastEthernet interface until its neighbour is pinged:

```
Router#show arp
Protocol  Address   Age (min)  Hardware Addr   Type   Interface
Internet  192.168.1.1    -     0002.4A4C.6801  ARPA   FastEthernet0/0

Router#ping 192.168.1.2

Type escape sequence to abort.
Sending 5, 100-byte ICMP Echos to 192.168.1.2, timeout is 2 seconds:
.!!!!
Success rate is 80 percent(4/5),round-trip min/avg/max = 31/31/31 ms

Router#show arp
Protocol  Address   Age (min)  Hardware Addr   Type   Interface
Internet  192.168.1.1          0002.4A4C.6801  ARPA   FastEthernet0/0
Internet  192.168.1.2    0     0001.97BC.1601  ARPA   FastEthernet0/0
Router#
```

Proxy ARP

Proxy ARP (see Figure 4.3 below) is defined in RFC 1027. Proxy ARP enables hosts on an Ethernet network to communicate with hosts on other subnets or networks, even though they have no knowledge of routing.

If an ARP broadcast reaches a router, it will not forward it (by default). Routers do not forward broadcasts, but if they do know how to find the host (i.e., they have a route to it), they will send their own MAC address to the host. This process is called proxy ARP and it allows the host to send off the data thinking it is going straight to the remote host. The router swaps the MAC address and then forwards the packet to the correct next hop.

The `ip proxy-arp` command is enabled on Cisco routers by default.

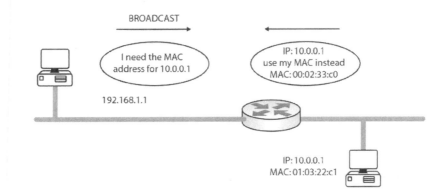

FIG 4.3—Router Uses Proxy ARP to Allow the Hosts to Connect

Reverse Address Resolution Protocol (RARP)

RARP maps a known MAC address to an IP address. Hosts such as diskless workstations (also known as thin clients) know their MAC address when they boot. They use RARP to discover their IP address from a server on the network.

Simple Network Management Protocol (SNMP)

SNMP is used for network management services. An SNMP management system allows network devices to send messages called traps to a management station. This informs the network administrator of any faults on the network, such as faulty interfaces, high CPU utilisation on servers, etc.

You can debug SNMP traffic with the `debug snmp` command. SNMP uses UDP ports 161 and 162.

Hyper Text Transfer Protocol Secure (HTTPS)

TLS, and the older protocol SSL, is used for secure communication over the Internet, which is carried out by means of cryptography. You will also find these used for e-mail and Voice over IP (VoIP). You will encounter SSL or TLS when surfing sites which begin with the URL https://. HTTP with TLS/SSL (HTTPS) uses port 443.

IP Configuration Command

Not actually a Cisco tool but part of your troubleshooting toolkit is the `ipconfig` command used at a Windows command prompt. You can use several switches with the `ipconfig` command, but perhaps the most commonly used command is `ipconfig /all`.

```
C:\WINDOWS\system32\cmd.exe                                           _ □ x

Microsoft Windows XP [Version 5.1.2600]
(C) Copyright 1985-2001 Microsoft Corp.

C:\Documents and Settings\TweakHound>ipconfig /all

Windows IP Configuration

        Host Name . . . . . . . . . . . . : mycomputersname
        Primary Dns Suffix  . . . . . . . :
        Node Type . . . . . . . . . . . . : Unknown
        IP Routing Enabled. . . . . . . . : No
        WINS Proxy Enabled. . . . . . . . : No

Ethernet adapter Local Area Connection:

        Connection-specific DNS Suffix  . :
        Description . . . . . . . . . . . : Intel(R) PRO/1000 CT Network Connect
ion
        Physical Address. . . . . . . . . : 00-00-00-00-00
        Dhcp Enabled. . . . . . . . . . . : No
        IP Address. . . . . . . . . . . . : 10.10.10.8
        Subnet Mask . . . . . . . . . . . : 255.255.255.0
        Default Gateway . . . . . . . . . : 10.10.10.1
        DNS Servers . . . . . . . . . . . : 000.000.00.0
                                            000.000.000.0
```

FIG 4.4—The ipconfig /all Command Output

Other switches you can use with the `ipconfig` command are as follows:

```
/?            Display this help message
/all          Display full configuration information
/release      Release the IP address for the specified adapter
/renew        Renew the IP address for the specified adapter
/flushdns     Purges the DNS Resolver cache
/registerdns  Refreshes all DHCP leases and re-registers DNS names
```

DAY 4 QUESTIONS

1. What does CSMA/CD stand for?
2. Give the port numbers for HTTPS, FTP, SNMP, Telnet, and SMTP.
3. Which service does ARP perform?
4. Which service does DNS perform?

DAY 5

Switching Concepts

DAY 5 TASKS

- Read today's theory notes
- Review yesterday's theory notes
- Complete today's lab
- Read the CCENT cram guide

Today is all about basic switching theory, as well as some initial switch configuration. You will spend most of your time as a Cisco engineer configuring and installing switches, so it's important to have a good level of switching knowledge.

Today you will learn about the following:

- The need for switches
- Basic switch configuration

This lesson maps to the following CCNA syllabus requirements:

- Explain the technology and media access control method for Ethernet networks
- Explain network segmentation and basic traffic management concepts
- Explain basic switching concepts and the operation of Cisco switches
- Perform and verify initial switch configuration tasks, including remote access management

The Need for Switches

Before switches were invented, every device on a network would receive data from every other device. Every time a frame was seen on the wire, the PC would have to stop for a moment and check the header to see whether it was the intended recipient. Imagine hundreds of frames going out on the network every minute. Every device would soon grind to a halt.

Figure 5.1 below shows all the devices on the network; note that they all have to share the same bandwidth because they are connected by hubs, which only forward frames.

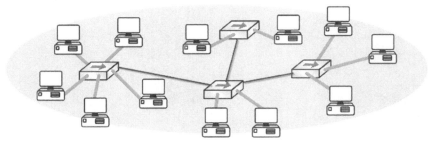

FIG 5.1—Every Device Listens to Every Other Device

The Problem with Hubs

I mentioned before that hubs are simply multiport repeaters. They take the incoming signal, clean it up, and then send it out of every port with a wire connected.

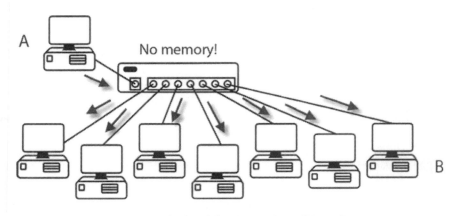

FIG 5.2—Hubs Send the Frame Out of Every Port

Hubs are dumb devices. They have no way of storing MAC addresses, so each time Device A sends a frame to Device B, it is repeated out of every port. Switches, on the other hand, contain a memory chip known as an application-specific integrated circuit (ASIC), which builds a table listing which device is plugged into which port. The table is held in Content Addressable Memory (CAM).

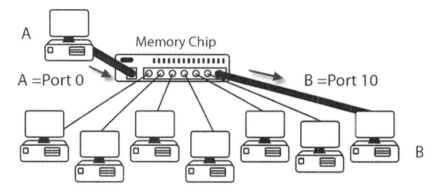

FIG 5.3—Switches Build a Table of MAC Addresses

When first booted, a switch has no addresses stored in its CAM table (Cisco exams also refer to this as the MAC address table.) Once frames start to pass, the table builds. If no frames pass through the port for a specified period of time, then the entry ages out. In the following example, no frame has been sent through the switch yet:

```
Switch#show mac-address-table
          Mac Address Table
-------------------------------------------
Vlan    Mac Address      Type        Ports
----    -----------      --------    -----
Switch#
```

There is no entry in the switch, but when you ping from one router to another (both attached to the switch), the table entry is built.

```
Router#ping 192.168.1.2
Type escape sequence to abort.
Sending 5, 100-byte ICMP Echos to 192.168.1.2, timeout is 2 seconds:
.!!!!
Success rate is 80 percent (4/5), round-trip min/avg/max = 62/62/63 ms
Switch#show mac-address-table
          Mac Address Table
-------------------------------------------
Vlan    Mac Address      Type        Ports
----    -----------      --------    -----
   1    0001.c74a.0a01   DYNAMIC     Fa0/1
   1    0060.5c55.da01   DYNAMIC     Fa0/2
```

This entry means that any frames destined for FastEthernet ports 0/1 or 0/2 on the switch will be sent straight out of the relevant port. Any other frames would mean the switch would have to do a one-off broadcast to see whether the destination devices were attached. You can see this with the period in the first of five pings above. The first ping times out whilst waiting for the switch to broadcast and receive a response from the destination router (80% success rate).

The `show mac-address-table` command is a very important one, so be sure to remember this both for the exam and for the real world.

Basic Switch Configuration

You will connect to a new switch via the console port, the same as any new router, because in order to connect via Telnet or SSH (more on these later), you will need to have at least a line or two of configuration on the switch already.

I know we haven't covered VLANs yet but for now, consider a VLAN to be a logical Local Area Network where devices could be anywhere on the network physically but, as far as they are concerned, they are all directly connected to the same switch. In the configuration below, by default, all ports on the switch are left in VLAN 1:

```
Switch#show vlan
VLAN Name                        Status     Ports
---- --------------------------  ---------  -------------------------------
1    default                     active     Fa0/1, Fa0/2, Fa0/3, Fa0/4
                                            Fa0/5, Fa0/6, Fa0/7, Fa0/8
                                            Fa0/9, Fa0/10, Fa0/11, Fa0/12
                                            Fa0/13, Fa0/14, Fa0/15, Fa0/16
                                            Fa0/17, Fa0/18, Fa0/19, Fa0/20
                                            Fa0/21, Fa0/22, Fa0/23, Fa0/24
```

If you want to add an IP address to the switch in order to connect to it over the network, you simply add an IP address to the VLAN; in this instance, it will be VLAN 1:

```
Switch#conf t
Enter configuration commands, one per line.  End with CNTL/Z.
Switch(config)#interface vlan 1
Switch(config-if)#ip add 192.168.1.3 255.255.255.0
Switch(config-if)#  ←  hold down Ctrl+Z keys now
Switch#show interface vlan 1
Vlan1 is administratively down, line protocol is down
  Hardware is CPU Interface, address is 0010.1127.2388 (bia
0010.1127.2388)
  Internet address is 192.168.1.3/24
```

You should also tell the switch where to send all IP traffic, because a Layer 2 switch has no ability to build a routing table:

```
Switch#conf t
Enter configuration commands, one per line.  End with CNTL/Z.
Switch(config)#ip default-gateway 192.168.1.1
Switch(config)#
```

If you have more than one switch on your network, you will want to change the default hostname so it can be identified more easily:

```
Switch(config)#hostname Switch1
Switch1(config)#
```

If you would like to telnet to the switch over the network, you need to enable this as well:

```
Switch1#conf t
Enter configuration commands, one per line.  End with CNTL/Z.
Switch1(config)#line vty 0 15
Switch1(config-line)#password cisco
Switch1(config-line)#login
```

VTYs are virtual ports on a router or switch used for Telnet or secure Telnet (SSH) access. They are closed until you add a password to them and the login command. You can often see ports 0 to 4, inclusive, or 0 to 15. One way to learn how many you have available is to type a question mark after the number zero, or use the show line command, as illustrated in the output below:

```
Router(config)#line vty 0 ?
  <1-15>  Last Line number
  <cr>Router#show line
  Tty Typ  Tx/Rx     A Modem  Roty AccO AccI   Lses  Noise  Overruns Int
*   0 CTY            -   -      -    -    -      0     0      0/0
    1 AUX 9600/9600  -   -      -    -    -      0     0      0/0       *
    2 VTY            -   -      -    -    -      2     0      0/0
    3 VTY            -   -      -    -    -      0     0      0/0
    4 VTY            -   -      -    -    -      0     0      0/0
    5 VTY            -   -      -    -    -      0     0      0/0
    6 VTY            -   -      -    -    -      0     0      0/0       -
```

For a more secure access method, you can permit only SSH traffic into the switch, which means the traffic will be encrypted. You will need a security image on your switch in order for this to work, as shown in the output below:

```
Switch1(config-line)#transport input ssh
```

Now, Telnet traffic will not be permitted into the VTY ports.

Please configure all of these commands on a switch. Just reading them will not help you recall them come exam day!

DAY 5 QUESTIONS

1. Switches contain a memory chip known as an _____, which builds a table listing which device is plugged into which port.
2. The _____-_____-_____ command displays a list of which MAC addresses are connected to which ports.
3. Which two commands add an IP address to the VLAN?
4. Which commands will enable Telnet and add a password to the switch Telnet lines?
5. How do you permit only SSH traffic into your Telnet lines?

DAY 5 LAB

Please log onto a Cisco switch and enter the commands from the previous section—Basic Switch Configuration.

DAY 6

Switch Troubleshooting

DAY 6 TASKS

- Read today's theory notes
- Review yesterday's theory notes
- Read the CCENT cram guide

In theory, once a device is configured and working it should stay that way, but, often, you will be working on a network which you didn't configure, or you will be working on a shift pattern supporting many unfamiliar networks on which changes have been made, causing one or more issues to the company.

Today you will learn about the following:

- Common switch issues

This module focuses on common switch issues and how to resolve them.

This lesson maps to the following CCNA syllabus requirements:

- Verify network status and switch operation using basic utilities (including ping, Traceroute, Telnet, SSH, arp, and IPconfig) and show and debug commands
- Identify, prescribe, and resolve common switched network media issues, configuration issues, auto negotiation, and switch hardware failures

Common Switch Issues

Can't Telnet to Switch

The first question is was Telnet ever working? If it was and is no longer, then perhaps somebody has made a change on the switch, reloaded it, and lost the configuration, or a device is now blocking Telnet traffic somewhere on the network:

```
Switch#telnet 192.168.1.1
Trying 192.168.1.1 ...Open

[Connection to 192.168.1.1 closed by foreign host]
```

The first thing to check is whether Telnet has actually been enabled on the switch (see below). Around 80% of errors on the network are due to silly mistakes or oversights, so never presume anything, and check out everything personally rather than relying on other people's words.

A simple show run command will reveal the switch configuration. Under the vty lines, you will see whether Telnet has been enabled. Note that you need to have the login or login local command under the vty lines and the password command, as shown below:

```
line vty 0 4
 password cisco
 login
line vty 5 15
 password cisco
 login
```

The login local command tells the switch or router to look for a username and password configured on it, as illustrated in the output below:

```
Switch1#sh run
Building configuration...
Current configuration : 1091 bytes!
version 12.1
hostname Switch1
username david privilege 1 password 0 football
line vty 0 4
 password cisco
 login local
line vty 5 15
 password cisco
 login local
[output truncated]
```

Can't Ping the Switch

Find out why the person wants to ping the switch in the first place. If you do want to ping a switch, there needs to be an IP address configured on it; in addition, the switch needs to know how to get traffic back out (the default gateway).

Can't Ping through the Switch

If a ping through the switch is unsuccessful, then check to ensure the end devices are in the same VLAN. Each VLAN is considered to be a network and for this reason must have a different address range to any other VLAN. In order for one VLAN to reach another, a router must route the traffic.

Interface Issues

By default, all interfaces are closed to traffic. In order to open them, the interface must be set with the no shut interface-level command:

```
Switch1(config)#int fast 0/3
Switch1(config-if)#no shut
```

Layer 2 interfaces can be set into three modes: trunk, access, or dynamic. Trunk mode lets the switch connect to another switch or a server. Access mode is for an end device, such as a PC or a laptop. Dynamic mode lets the switch detect which setting to select.

The default is usually dynamic desirable, but please check your model's settings. For the CCNA, you will be asked to configure a 2950 model switch. It will select the mode dynamically unless you hard-set it to trunk or access mode:

```
Switch1#show interfaces switchport
Name: Fa0/1
Switchport: Enabled
Administrative Mode: dynamic auto
```

The default can easily be changed, as shown in the output below:

```
Switch1#conf t
Enter configuration commands, one per line.  End with CNTL/Z.
Switch1(config)#int fast 0/1
Switch1(config-if)#switchport mode ?
  access    Set trunking mode to ACCESS unconditionally
  dynamic   Set trunking mode to dynamically negotiate access or  trunk mode
  trunk     Set trunking mode to TRUNK unconditionally
Switch1(config-if)#switchport mode trunk
%LINEPROTO-5-UPDOWN: Line protocol on Interface FastEthernet0/1, changed
state to down
Switch1(config-if)#^Z
```

```
Switch1#
%SYS-5-CONFIG_I: Configured from console by console
Switch1#show interfaces switchport
Name: Fa0/1
Switchport: Enabled
Administrative Mode: trunk
Operational Mode: trunk
```

More Interface Issues

Switch port default settings are auto detect duplex and auto detect speed. If you plug a 10Mbps device into a switch running at half duplex (if you could even find such a device), then the port should detect this and work. This isn't always the case, though, so the generic advice is to hard-set the switch port speed and duplex, as illustrated in the output below:

```
Switch1#show interfaces switchport
Name: Fa0/1
Switchport: Enabled
Administrative Mode: dynamic auto
Switch1#show interface fast 0/2
FastEthernet0/2 is up, line protocol is up (connected)
  Hardware is Lance, address is 0030.f252.3402 (bia 0030.f252.3402)
 BW 100000 Kbit, DLY 1000 usec,
     reliability 255/255, txload 1/255, rxload 1/255
  Encapsulation ARPA, loopback not set
  Keepalive set (10 sec)
  Full-duplex, 100Mb/s
Switch1(config)#int fast 0/2
Switch1(config-if)#duplex ?
  auto  Enable AUTO duplex configuration
  full  Force full duplex operation
  half  Force half-duplex operation

Switch1(config-if)#speed ?
  10    Force 10Mbps operation
  100   Force 100Mbps operation
  auto  Enable AUTO speed configuration
```

Hardware Issues

As with any electrical device, ports on a switch can fail or work only part of the time, which is harder to troubleshoot. Engineers often test the interface by plugging a known working device into another port on the switch. You can also bounce a port, which means to apply the shut command and then the no shut command to it. Swapping the Ethernet cable is also a common troubleshooting step.

Please check the documentation for your switch because, as well as featuring system and port LEDs, each port can display flashing or sold red, amber and green indicating normal function or port/system issues.

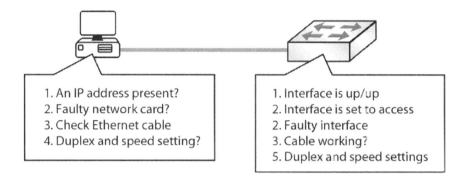

FIG 6.1—Common Switch Problems and Solutions

DAY 6 QUESTIONS

1. What is the most likely cause of Telnet to another switch not working?
2. In order for one VLAN to reach another, what must be in place?
3. A switch interface can be in which of three modes?
4. How do you set a switch to be in a specific mode?
5. Which commands will change the switch duplex mode and speed?

Switch Security

DAY 7 TASKS

- Read today's theory notes
- Review yesterday's theory notes
- Complete today's lab
- Read the CCENT cram guide

Switches and routers do not come with any security configuration. You need to add this depending upon your business requirements. The commands and procedures to secure your switch are pretty much the same as for your router.

Today you will learn about the following:

- Securing the switch

This lesson maps to the following CCNA syllabus requirement:

- Implement basic switch security (including port security, trunk access, management VLAN [other than VLAN 1], etc.)

Securing the Switch

Prevent Telnet Access
Telnet traffic sends the password in clear text, which means that it could easily be read on the configuration or by a network sniffer, if one was attached to your network.

Telnet is actually disabled by default (inasmuch that you need to set a password and, optionally, a username to get it working). However, if you still want to have remote access to the management ports, you can enable SSH traffic to the switch with the `transport input ssh` command, which was discussed earlier.

FARAI SAYS: '`transport input all` is enabled by default for all VTY lines; `transport input none` is enabled by default for other lines.'

Set an 'Enable Secret' Password

Global Configuration mode will permit a user to configure the switch or router and erase configurations, as well as reset passwords. You must protect this mode by setting a password or a secret password (which actually prevents the user getting past user mode). The secret password will be displayed on the routers running the configuration file, whereas the `enable secret` password will be encrypted.

You can actually have both a password and an enable secret password on your router and switch, which can cause confusion. Just set the enable secret password. The configuration file below illustrates how to issue a command without dropping back to Privileged mode by typing do before the command:

```
Switch1(config)#enable password cisco
Switch1(config)#do show run
Building configuration...
Current configuration: 1144 bytes
hostname Switch1
enable password cisco
```

FARAI SAYS: 'You can encrypt the `enable secret` password with the `service password-encryption` command, which will be covered later.'

You can erase most lines of configuration by issuing it again with the word no before the command. It is also worth noting that as Farai says, you can issue a `service password-encryption` command but this only offers weak (level 7) encryption whereas below, our secret password has strong (MD5) encryption :

```
Switch1(config)#no enable password
Switch1(config)#enable secret cisco
Switch1(config)#do show run
Building configuration...
Current configuration: 1169 bytes
hostname Switch1
enable secret 5 $1$mERr$hx5rVt7rPNoS4wqbXKX7m0 [strong level 5 password]
```

Change the Native VLAN

The native VLAN is used by the switch to carry specific protocol traffic, such as Cisco Discovery Protocol (CDP), VLAN Trunking Protocol (VTP), Port Aggregation Protocol (PAGP), and Dynamic Trunking Protocol (DTP) information. The default native VLAN is always VLAN 1; however, the native VLAN can be manually changed to any valid VLAN number (except for 0 and 4096, because these are in the reserved range of VLANs).

You can verify the native VLAN with the command (issued per interface) illustrated in the output below:

```
Switch#show interfaces fastethernet 0/1 switchport
Name: Fa0/1
Switchport: Enabled
Administrative Mode: trunk
Operational Mode: trunk
Administrative Trunking Encapsulation: dot1q
Operational Trunking Encapsulation: dot1q
Negotiation of Trunking: On
Access Mode VLAN: 1 (default)
Trunking Native Mode VLAN: 1 (default)
Voice VLAN: none
```

Having ports in VLAN 1 is considered a security vulnerability which allows hackers to gain access to network resources. To mitigate this problem, it is advisable to avoid putting any hosts into VLAN 1. You can also change the native VLAN on all trunk ports to an unused VLAN:

```
Switch(config-if)#switchport trunk native vlan 888
```

You can also prevent native VLAN data from passing on the trunk with the command below:

```
Switch(config-if)#switchport trunk allowed vlan remove 888
```

Change the Management VLAN

You can also add an IP address to the switch to allow you to telnet to it for management purposes. This is referred to as a switch virtual interface (SVI). It is a wise precaution to have this management access in a VLAN other than VLAN 1, as shown in the output below:

```
Switch(config)#vlan 3
Switch(config-vlan)#interface vlan 3

%LINK-5-CHANGED: Interface Vlan3, changed state to up
Switch(config-if)#ip address 192.168.1.1 255.255.255.0
```

Turn On Port Security

Switch ports can add another level of security to your network. You can specify a number of MAC addresses permitted through the port or hard-set a specific MAC address or range of addresses.

First, set security on the port:

```
Switch1(config)#int fast 0/1
Switch1(config-if)#switchport port-security
Switch1(config-if)#switchport port-security ?
  mac-address   Secure mac address
  maximum       Max secure addresses
  violation     Security violation mode
  <cr>
```

You can see from the output above that you can set a MAC address on the interface (or a maximum number of MAC addresses). This is also illustrated in Figure 7.1 below:

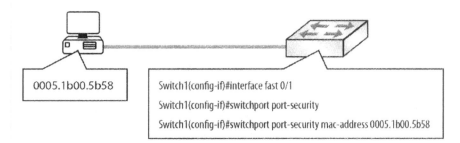

Fig 7.1—PC and Switch Connection

You can also set the action you want the port to take if there is a violation of your security settings, as shown in the output below:

```
Switch1(config-if)#switchport port-security violation ?
  protect    Security violation protect mode
  restrict   Security violation restrict mode
  shutdown   Security violation shutdown mode
```

- Protect—discard all frames with an unrecognized MAC.
- Restrict—drop packets with unknown MAC addresses when the number of secure MAC addresses reaches the administrator-defined maximum limit for the port.
- Shutdown—places a port in an errdisabled state (shut) when a port security violation occurs.

As a simple example, here is the MAC address of a router I have plugged into FastEthernet 0/1 on my switch:

```
Router#show int fast 0/0
FastEthernet0/0 is up, line protocol is up (connected)
  Hardware is Lance, address is 0001.c74a.0a01
```

Knowing this, I can hard-set the switch port to which it is connected:

```
Switch1(config)#int fast 0/1
Switch1(config-if)#switchport port-security
Switch1(config-if)#switchport port-security mac-address 0001.c74a.0a01
Switch1#show port-security int fast 0/1
Port Security              : Enabled
Port Status                : Secure-up
Violation Mode             : Shutdown
Aging Time                 : 0 mins
Aging Type                 : Absolute
SecureStatic Address Aging : Disabled
Maximum MAC Addresses      : 1
Total MAC Addresses        : 1
Configured MAC Addresses   : 0
Sticky MAC Addresses       : 0
Last Source Address:Vlan   : 0001.C74A.0A01:1
Security Violation Count   : 0
```

Now I plug a device with a MAC address ending in 2 into the port and it goes down:

```
%LINEPROTO-5-UPDOWN: Line protocol on Interface FastEthernet0/1, changed
state to down
Switch1#show port-security int fast 0/1
Port Security              : Enabled
Port Status                : Secure-shutdown
Violation Mode             : Shutdown
Aging Time                 : 0 mins
Aging Type                 : Absolute
SecureStatic Address Aging : Disabled
Maximum MAC Addresses      : 1
Total MAC Addresses        : 1
Configured MAC Addresses   : 1
Sticky MAC Addresses       : 0
Last Source Address:Vlan   : 0001.C74A.0A02:1
Security Violation Count   : 1
```

The administrator would now need to log into the switch and issue the no shut command for the interface (after attaching the device with the correct MAC address).

If you want to test this at home, you can change the MAC address on your router's FastEthernet interface with the mac-address command.

Turn Off CDP

Cisco Discovery Protocol (CDP) will be covered later on, but for now, you just need to know that it is on by default on most routers and switches universally and per interface, and its function is to discover attached devices. You may not want other Cisco devices to see information about your network devices, so you can turn this off, at least on the devices at the edge of your network which connect to other companies or your ISP.

> **FARAI SAYS:** 'CDP is not enabled by default on all platforms, such as ASR routers, for example.'

In the output below, you can see how a router connected to my switch is able to see basic information when I issue the `show cdp neighbor detail` command:

```
Router#show cdp neighbor detail
Device ID: Switch1
Entry address(es):
Platform: Cisco 2950, Capabilities: Switch
Interface: FastEthernet0/0, Port ID (outgoing port): FastEthernet0/2
Holdtime: 176
Version :
Cisco Internetwork Operating System Software
IOS (tm) C2950 Software (C2950-I6Q4L2-M), Version 12.1(22)EA4, RELEASE
SOFTWARE(fc1)
Copyright (c) 1986-2005 by Cisco Systems, Inc.
Compiled Wed 18-May-05 22:31 by jharirba
advertisement version: 2
Duplex: full
Router#
The command below will turn off CDP for the entire device:
Switch1(config)#no cdp run
To turn off CDP for a particular interface, issue the following command:
Switch1(config)#int fast 0/2
Switch1(config-if)#no cdp enable
```

Add a Banner Message

A banner message will show when a user logs into your router or switch. It won't offer any actual security but it will display a warning message of your choice. In the configuration below, I chose the letter Y as my delimiting character, which tells the router I've finished typing my message:

```
Switch1(config)#banner motd Y
Enter TEXT message.  End with the character 'Y'.
KEEP OUT OR YOU WILL REGRET IT Y
Switch1(config)#
```

When I telnet to the switch from my router, I can see the banner message. The mistake was choosing Y as the delimiting character because it cuts off my message:

```
Router#telnet 192.168.1.3
Trying 192.168.1.3 ...Open
KEEP OUT OR
```

Set a VTP Password

This hasn't been covered yet, but VTP ensures that accurate VLAN information is passed between the switches on your network. In order to protect these updates, you should add a VTP password on your switch, as illustrated in the output below:

```
Switch1(config)#vtp domain 60days
Changing VTP domain name from NULL to 60days
Switch1(config)#vtp password cisco
Setting device VLAN database password to cisco
Switch1(config)#
```

Restrict VLAN Information

By default, switches permit all VLANs across the trunk links. You can change this by specifying which VLANs can pass, as illustrated in the following output:

```
Switch1(config)#int fast 0/4
Switch1(config-if)#switchport mode trunk
Switch1(config-if)#switchport trunk allowed vlan ?
  WORD    VLAN IDs of the allowed VLANs when this port is in trunking mode
  add     add VLANs to the current list
  all     all VLANs
  except  all VLANs except the following
  none    no VLANs
  remove  remove VLANs from the current list
Switch1(config-if)#switchport trunk allowed vlan 7-12

Switch1#show interface trunk
Port        Mode          Encapsulation  Status       Native vlan
Fa0/4       on            802.1q         trunking     1
Port        Vlans allowed on trunk
Fa0/4       7-12
```

Update the IOS

Many administrators don't realise that Cisco regularly updates IOS versions per device in order to add improvements, plug security vulnerabilities, and fix known bugs. For this reason, it is important to keep your Switch IOS and Router IOS up to date.

DAY 7 QUESTIONS

1. Why would you choose SSH access over Telnet?
2. What are your three options for port security?
3. Your three options upon violation of your port security are protect, _____, and _____.
4. How would you hard-set a port to accept only MAC 0001.c74a.0a01?
5. Which command turns off CDP for a particular interface?
6. Which command turns off CDP for the entire router or switch?
7. Which command adds a password to your VTP domain?
8. Which command would permit only VLANs 10 to 20 over your interface?

DAY 7 LAB—BASIC SWITCH SECURITY

Topology

Please note that your switch will need to have a security image which permits basic security settings.

Purpose

Learn how to apply basic security settings to a Cisco switch.

Walkthrough

1. Connect a PC or laptop to your switch. In addition, set up a console connection for your configuration. The port to which you connect your PC will be the one you configure security settings on in this lab. I have chosen FastEthernet 0/1 on my switch.

2. Log into the VTY lines and set up telnet access referring to a local username and password.

```
Switch#conf t
Enter configuration commands, one per line.  End with CNTL/Z.
Switch(config)#line vty 0 ?
  <1-15>  Last Line number
  <cr>
Switch(config)#line vty 0 15
Switch(config-line)#?
Switch(config-line)#login local
Switch(config-line)#exit
Switch(config)#username in60days password cisco
Switch(config)#
```

3. Add an IP address to VLAN 1 on the switch (all ports are in VLAN 1 automatically). Additionally, add the IP address 192.168.1.1 to your PC's FastEthernet interface.

```
Switch(config)#interface vlan 1
Switch(config-if)#ip address 192.168.1.2 255.255.255.0
Switch(config-if)#no shut
%LINK-5-CHANGED: Interface Vlan1, changed state to up
%LINEPRCTO-5-UPDOWN: Line protocol on Interface Vlan2, changed state to up
Switch(config-if)#^Z  ←  press Ctrl+Z keys
Switch#
```

```
Switch#ping 192.168.1.1  ←  test connection from switch to PC
Type escape sequence to abort.
Sending 5, 100-byte ICMP Echos to 192.168.1.1, timeout is 2 seconds:
.!!!!
Success rate is 80 percent (4/5), round-trip min/avg/max = 31/31/32 ms

Switch#
```

4. Test Telnet by telnetting from your PC to your switch.

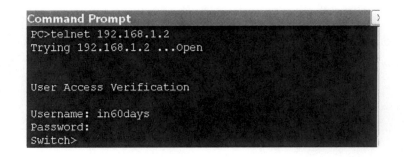

5. Your IT manager changes his mind and wants only SSH access, so change this on your VTY lines. Only certain models and IOS versions will support the SSH command.

```
Switch(config)#line vty 0 15
Switch(config-line)#transport input ssh
```

6. Now telnet from your PC to the switch. Because only SSH is permitted, the connection should fail.

7. Set port security on your switch for the FastEthernet port. It will fail if you have not hard-set the port to access (as opposed to dynamic or trunk).

```
Switch(config)#interface fast 0/1
Switch(config-if)#switchport port-security
Command rejected: FastEthernet0/1 is a dynamic port.

Switch(config-if)#switchport mode access
Switch(config-if)#switchport port-security
Switch(config-if)#
```

8. Hard-set the MAC address from your PC to be permitted on this port. You can check this with the `ipconfig/all` command on your PC command line. Then check the port security status and settings.

```
Switch(config-if)#switchport port-security mac-address 0001.C7DD.CB18
Switch(config-if)#^Z
Switch#show port-security int fast 0/1
Port Security            : Enabled
Port Status              : Secure-up
Violation Mode           : Shutdown
Aging Time               : 0 mins
Aging Type               : Absolute
SecureStatic Address Aging : Disabled
Maximum MAC Addresses    : 1
Total MAC Addresses      : 1
Configured MAC Addresses : 0
Sticky MAC Addresses     : 0
Last Source Address:Vlan : 0001.C7DD.CB18:1
Security Violation Count : 0
```

9. Change the MAC address on your PC, or if you can't do this, plug another device into the switch port. This should make the port shut down due to a breach in the security settings. The screen-shot below shows where you would change the MAC address in Packet Tracer.

10. You should see your FastEthernet port go down immediately.

```
Switch#
%LINK-5-CHANGED: Interface FastEthernet0/1, changed state to administra-
tively down

%LINEPROTO-5-UPDOWN: Line protocol on Interface FastEthernet0/1, changed
state to down
```

```
%LINEPROTO-5-UPDOWN: Line protocol on Interface Vlan1, changed state to
down

Switch#
%SYS-5-CONFIG_I: Configured from console by console

Switch#show port-security interface fast 0/1
Port Security              : Enabled
Port Status                : Secure-shutdown
Violation Mode             : Shutdown
Aging Time                 : 0 mins
Aging Type                 : Absolute
SecureStatic Address Aging : Disabled
Maximum MAC Addresses      : 1
Total MAC Addresses        : 0
Configured MAC Addresses   : 0
Sticky MAC Addresses       : 0
Last Source Address:Vlan   : 0001.C7DD.CB19:1
Security Violation Count   : 1
```

NOTE: Please repeat this lab until you understand the commands and can type them without looking at the walkthrough (and the same for all the other labs in this book). I also recommend you follow the router security lab in Day 38.

DAY 8

IP Addressing

DAY 8 TASKS

- Read today's theory notes
- Review yesterday's theory notes
- Complete today's lab
- Read the CCENT cram guide
- Spend 15 minutes on the subnetting.org website

Welcome to what many people find to be one of the hardest areas of the CCNA syllabus to understand. In order to understand IP addressing for the CCNA exam, we must cover binary mathematics and the hexadecimal numbering system, classes of addresses, powers of two and rules such as subnet zero, and broadcast and network addresses, as well as formulas to work out subnets and host addresses.

Don't worry, though; this is a process, not a one-off event, so follow my notes and then feel assured that we will be coming back to review these concepts many times.

Today you will learn about the following:

- IP addressing (using binary and hexadecimal)
- Using IP addresses
- Subnetting
- Easy subnetting
- Network design

This lesson maps to the following CCNA syllabus requirements:

- Describe the need and role of addressing in a network
- Create and apply an addressing scheme to a network
- Assign and verify valid IP addresses to hosts, servers, and networking devices in a LAN environment
- Calculate and apply an addressing scheme, including VLSM IP addressing design, to a network

Annoyingly, Cisco has put some VLSM requirements into the CCENT and the ICND2 exams. More emphasis on this seems to be in the ICND2 exam, but you need to prepare yourself for questions in both exams equally. VLSM will be covered on Day 11, but you need to understand IP addressing and subnetting first.

IP Addressing

All devices on a network need some way to identify themselves as a specific host. Early networks simply used a naming format, and a server on the network kept a map of MAC addresses to host names. Tables quickly grew very large and with this grew issues such as consistency and accuracy. IP addressing effectively resolved this issue.

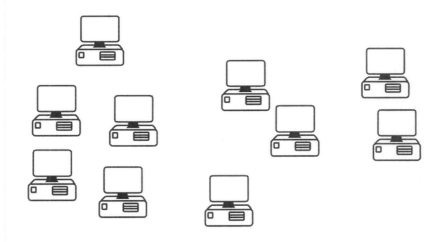

FIG 8.1—Device Naming Tables Became Too Cumbersome

IP Version 4

IP version 4 (IPv4) was devised to resolve the device naming issue. IPv4 uses binary to apply an address to network devices. IPv4 addresses use 32 binary bits divided into four groups of eight (octets). The following is an example of an IPv4 address in binary:

11000000.10100011.11110000.10101011

which we would see in decimal as:

192.163.240.171

Each binary bit represents a decimal number and you can use or not use the number by placing a 1 or a 0, respectively, in the relevant column. The eight columns are as follows:

128	64	32	16	8	4	2	1
1	1	0	0	0	0	0	0

In the chart above, you can see that we are using only the first two decimal numbers (those with 1s beneath them), which produces the value 128 + 64 = 192.

Binary

In order to understand how IP addressing works, you need to understand binary mathematics (sorry). Computers and networking equipment do not understand decimal. We use decimal because it is a numbering system using 10 digits, invented by a caveman centuries ago when he realised he had 10 digits on his hands that could be used for counting dinosaurs as they walked past his cave.

Computers and networking equipment can only understand electrical signals. Since an electrical signal is either on or off, the only numbering system that will work is binary. Binary uses only two numbers, a 0 or a 1. A 0 means there is no electrical pulse on the wire and a 1 means that there is a pulse on the wire.

Any number can be made up from binary values. The more binary values you add, the larger the number can become. For every binary value you add, you double the next number (e.g., 1 to 2 to 4 to 8 to 16, and so on into infinity), starting at the right and moving left. With two binary digits, you can count up to 3. Just place a 0 or a 1 in the column to decide whether you want to use that value.

Let's start with only two binary values in columns 1 and 2.

2	1
0	0

0 + 0 = 0

2	1
0	1

0 + 1 = 1

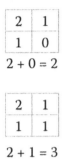

2	1
1	0

2 + 0 = 2

2	1
1	1

2 + 1 = 3

If you use eight binary bit places (an octet), you can get any number from 0 up to 255. You can see that the numbers start from the right and move across to the left.

128	64	32	16	8	4	2	1

If you add a 0 to each of these columns, you have a value of 0 in decimal.

128	64	32	16	8	4	2	1
0	0	0	0	0	0	0	0

If you add a 1 to each of these columns, you have a value of 255 in decimal.

128	64	32	16	8	4	2	1
1	1	1	1	1	1	1	1

Don't believe me?

128 + 64 + 32 + 16 + 8 + 4 + 2 + 1 = 255

So logic dictates that you can actually make any number from 0 to 255 by placing a 0 or a 1 in various columns, for example:

128	64	32	16	8	4	2	1
0	0	1	0	1	1	0	0

32 + 8 + 4 = 44

IP addressing and subnetting are based upon the fundamentals above. Table 8.1 below summarises what you know so far. Pay special attention to this table because the values can be used for any subnet mask (more on that later).

Table 8.1—Binary Values

Binary	Decimal
10000000	128
11000000	192
11100000	224
11110000	240
11111000	248
11111100	252
11111110	254
11111111	255

Make up some of your own binary numbers to ensure you understand this concept fully.

Hexadecimal

Hexadecimal (or hex) is an alternative numbering system. Rather than counting in 2s or by 10, 16 numbers or characters are used. Hex starts at 0 and goes all the way up to F, as illustrated below:

0 1 2 3 4 5 6 7 8 9 A B C D E F

Each hexadecimal digit actually represents four binary digits, as shown below in Table 8.2:

Table 8.2—Decimal, Hex, and Binary Digits

Decimal	0	1	2	3	4	5	6	7
Hex	0	1	2	3	4	5	6	7
Binary	0000	0001	0010	0011	0100	0101	0110	0111

Decimal	8	9	10	11	12	13	14	15
Hex	8	9	A	B	C	D	E	F
Binary	1000	1001	1010	1011	1100	1101	1110	1111

Converting from binary to hex to decimal is fairly simple, as shown in Table 8.3 below:

Table 8.3—Conversion of Binary to Hex to Decimal

Decimal	13	6	2	12
Hex	D	6	2	C
Binary	1101	0110	0010	1100

Hex is a more manageable counting system for humans than binary but close enough to binary to be used by computers and networking equipment. Any number can be made using hex, as it can use binary or decimal; just count in multiples of 16 instead, for example:

1 x 16 = 16

16 x 16 = 256

256 x 16 = 4096

...and so on.

Hex	4096	256	16	1
			1	A

Counting in hex, therefore, goes 0 1 2 3 4 5 6 7 8 9 A B C D E F 10 11 12 13 14 15 16 17 18 19 1A 1B 1C 1D 1E 1F 20 21 22 etc. to infinity. 1A (above), for example, is an A in the 1 column and a 1 in the 16 column: A = 10 + 16 = 26.

When converting binary to hex, it makes the task easier if you break the octet into two groups of four bits. So 11110011 becomes 1111 0011. 1111 is 8 + 4 + 2 + 1 = 15, and 0011 is 2 + 1 = 3. 15 is F in hex and 3 is 3 in hex, giving us the answer F3. You can check Table 8.2 to confirm this.

Hex to binary is carried out using the same process. For example, 7C can be split into 7, which is 0111 in binary, and C (12 in decimal), which is 1100 in binary. The answer, then, is 01111100.

Converting Exercise

Here are some examples for you to try. Write out the charts above for working out hex and binary (i.e., for hex, a 1 column, then a 16 column, then a 256 column, and so on).

1. Convert 1111 to hex and decimal.
2. Convert 11010 to hex and decimal.
3. Convert 10000 to hex and decimal.
4. Convert 20 to binary and hex.
5. Convert 32 to binary and hex.
6. Convert 101 to binary and hex.
7. Convert A6 from hex to binary and decimal.
8. Convert 15 from hex to binary and decimal
9. Convert B5 from hex to binary and decimal.

It would be useful in the exam to write out Table 8.2 to help you work out any binary to hex to decimal conversions.

The rule for using IP addressing is that each address on the network must be unique to that host (i.e., it can't be shared). Some addresses can't be used for hosts. This will be covered in more detail later, but for now know that you can't use an address which is reserved for the entire network, a broadcast address, or addresses reserved for testing. In addition, three groups are reserved for use on internal networks to save addresses.

Because of the rapid growth of network sizes, each IP address must be used in conjunction with a subnet mask. The subnet mask is there to tell the network devices how to use the numbers in the IP address. The reason for this is that some of the addresses available for hosts on your network can actually be used to chop the network down into smaller chunks or subnets.

An example of an IP address with a subnet mask is 192.168.1.1 255.255.255.240.

Address Classes

You need to know this and you don't! I know I'm not helping much, but address classes are actually only significant historically, so as a new Cisco engineer, you might become confused when you look at the old rules and try to apply them to new methods of network design.

We still refer to groups of IP addresses as classes, but with the introduction of subnet masking and VLSM, they are actually no longer applicable to network design. Address classes are useful to know, though, because they show us which parts of the IP address we can and can't use for our mini-networks (subnets).

When IPv4 was first invented, addresses were divided into classes. The classes of addresses were then allocated to companies on an as-needed basis. The bigger the company, the bigger the address class. The address classes were assigned letters, A through E. A Class A address was reserved for the biggest networks. A Class A address can be numbered from 1 to 126 in the first octet. The reason for this is that the first bit on the first octet must be 0. If you have 0 in the first octet, then the remaining values can only go from 1 to 126, for example:

00000001 = 1
01111111= 126

You can't have an address of all 0s on a network. If you actually add the other three octets, then you can see Class A addresses in full, for example:

10.1.1.1
120.2.3.4
126.200.133.1

These are all Class A addresses because they are within the range of 1 to 126. 127 is not a permitted number for IP addresses; 127.0.0.1 is actually an address used to test whether TCP/IP is working on your device.

A Class B address must have the first two bits of the first octet set to 10. This means that the first octet can only use the numbers 128 to 191, for example:

10000000 = 128
10111111 = 191

For Class C addresses, the first three bits on the first octet must be set to 110, giving us addresses 192 to 223, for example:

11000000 = 192
11011111 = 223

Class D addresses are used for multicasting (directed broadcasts), and Class E addresses are for experimental use only.

Subnet Mask Primer

I mentioned earlier that part of the address identifies the network and part of it identifies the host on the network. Subnet masks establish which parts are which. The difficulty is that it isn't always easy to establish which is which by just looking at the subnet mask. This requires practise, and for the more difficult addresses, you must work them out by hand (or cheat by using a subnet calculator).

Even if you are not chopping your network into smaller parts, you must still apply a subnet mask to every address used. Each network class comes with a default subnet mask, for example:

Class A = 255.0.0.0
Class B = 255.255.0.0
Class C = 255.255.255.0

When the binary bits are turned on, the network knows that this number is to be used for the network, not for a host on the network, as illustrated below:

192	168	12	2
255	255	255	0
Network	Network	Network	Host

The address above means that 192.168.12 is the network and 2 is a host on that network. Furthermore, any address starting with 192.168.12 is on the same network. You can see from the number on the first octet and the default subnet mask that this is a Class C network.

Remember the rule I mentioned earlier: You can't use the network numbers for hosts, so the numbers below cannot be used on devices:

10.C.0.0
192.168.2.0
174.12.0.0

The other rule is that you can't use the broadcast address on each network or subnet. A broadcast address goes to all devices on the network, so, logically, it can't be used for devices. A broadcast address is one in which all the host bits are active, or turned on:

10.255.255.255
192.168.1.255

In the examples above, each binary bit is turned on for the host portion.

Using IP Addresses

Next up, the practicalities of using IP addresses—which ones can be used and which ones can't be used?

You know that there has been a huge explosion in the use of computers over the past two decades. A PC used to be a very expensive item which few people could afford; therefore, they were reserved for use by well-funded companies only. Today, nearly every house contains one or more computers.

The problem, of course, is that IPv4 was devised when only a limited number of devices were being used and there was no anticipation of this situation changing. As addresses were being allocated, it was realised that at the current rate of growth, we would quickly run out of available addresses.

Private IP Addresses

One of several solutions was to reserve some classes of addresses for anybody to use, so long as that address wasn't used over the Internet. This range of addresses is known as private IP addresses, and this solution was created by two RFCs, 1918 and 4193. RFC stands for Request for Comments and is a means for engineers to submit ideas for networking methods, protocols, and technology advancements.

The ranges of private addresses are as follows:

10.x.x.x—any address starting with a 10
172.16.x.x to 172.31.x.x—any address starting with 172.16 to 172.31, inclusive
192.168.x.x—any address starting with 192.168

Subnetting

Subnetting allows you to steal bits of an IP address which were traditionally used for hosts on the network. You can now carve smaller networks from your larger network space, and these smaller networks are referred to as subnetworks, or subnets for short.

If you apply the default subnet masks to the three usable address classes, you will see the portions of the address you can't use for carving out subnets, as illustrated in the chart below:

A—255	0	0	0
Can't Use	Can Use	Can Use	Can Use
B—255	255	0	0
Can't Use	Can't Use	Can Use	Can Use
C—255	255	255	0
Can't Use	Can't Use	Can't Use	Can Use

For example, if you take a Class C network with the default subnet mask:

IP Address	192	168	1	0
Subnet Mask	255	255	255	0
In Binary	11111111	11111111	11111111	00000000

and steal some of the available host bits on the last octet:

IP Address	192	168	1	0
Subnet Mask	255	255	255	192
In Binary	11111111	11111111	11111111	11000000

you get two stolen bits on the last octet. This gives you the following subnets, each with 62 hosts:

Network	Network	Network	Subnet	Hosts	Broadcast Address
192	168	1	0	1–62	63
192	168	1	64	65–126	127
192	168	1	128	129–190	191
192	168	1	192	193–254	255

With the bigger network, you could have used host numbers 1 to 254, so you have less available host numbers to use here but the trade-off is more networks. The chart below shows how the four subnets were determined:

128	64	32	16	8	4	2	1	Subnet
0	0	0	0	0	0	0	0	**0**
0	1	0	0	0	0	0	0	**64**
1	0	0	0	0	0	0	0	**128**
1	1	0	0	0	0	0	0	**192**

Delving into binary math, you can see that using the first two bits of the host address lets you use the binary combinations 00, 01, 10, and 11, and writing these out in full, as you see in the subnets column, gives you the subnets 0, 64, 128, and 192. To clarify this further, the first two rows in grey are subnet numbers and the remaining six rows are for use by host numbers on each subnet.

If you feel your head spinning right about now, this is normal. It takes a while for all of this to finally click, I'm afraid.

Easy Subnetting

Come exam day, or when troubleshooting a subnetting issue on a live network, you will want to get to your answer quickly and accurately. For this reason, I devised an easy way to subnet, which is the subject of my Subnetting Secrets website (www.subnetting-secrets.com) and an Amazon Kindle book by the same name. You won't need either of these, to be honest, as I cover what you need to know in this book.

A very useful resource I've created is www.subnetting.org, which gives you free challenge questions to solve around subnetting and network design.

Classless Inter-Domain Routing

Classless Inter-Domain Routing (CIDR) was created by the Internet Engineering Task Force as a method to allocate blocks of IP addresses and to route IP packets. The main feature of CIDR we will examine here is using slash address notation to represent subnet masks. This is important because it saves time, it is used in the real world, and, if that isn't enough, you will be given exam questions involving CIDR addresses.

With CIDR, instead of using the full subnet mask, you write down the number of binary bits used. For 255.255.0.0, for example, there are two lots of eight binary bits used, so this would be represented with a /16. For 255.255.240.0, there are eight plus eight plus four binary bits used, giving you /20.

When you refer to subnet masks or network masks in the context of internetworking, you would say 'slash sixteen' or 'slash twenty' to work colleagues and they would know that you are referring to a CIDR mask.

The Subnetting Secrets Chart

I'm about to save you many weeks of subnetting frustration. My Subnetting Secrets cheat chart has been used by thousands of CCNA and CCNP students all over the world to pass exams and ace technical interviews for networking roles.

Seriously. Until I stumbled across the easy way while studying for my CCNA several years ago, students were forced to write out network addresses in binary or go through painful calculations in order to get to the correct answer.

In order to write out the Subnetting Secrets chart, you will need a pencil and paper. You need to be able to write it out from memory because in your exam you will be given a whiteboard to use for any working out. You can also use pen and paper in any technical interviews.

On your paper, on the top right, write the number 1, and then to the left of that double it to 2, then 4, then 8, and keep doubling up to number 128. This is one binary octet:

128	64	32	16	8	4	2	1

Under the 128 and going down, write out the number you would get if you put a tick in the first box (the 128 box). Then the next number below that will be what you would get if you ticked the next box (64), and the next (32), and the next (16), and so on until you had ticked all eight boxes:

128
192
224

240
248
252
254
255

If you put together both parts, you will have the upper portion of the Subnetting Secrets cheat sheet:

Bits	128	64	32	16	8	4	2	1
Subnets								
128								
192								
224								
240								
248								
252								
254								
255								

The top row will represent your subnet increment and the left column your subnet mask. Using this part of the chart, you could answer any subnetting question in a few seconds. If you want to add the part of the chart which tells you how to answer any design question, such as 'How many subnets and hosts will subnet mask X give you,' just add a 'powers of two' section.

One column will be 'powers of two' and one 'powers of two minus two.' The minus two is to cover the two addresses you can't use, which are the subnet and the broadcast addresses on the subnet. You start with the number 2 and double it as many times as you need to in order to answer the question.

Bits	128	64	32	16	8	4	2	1
Subnets								
128								
192								
224								
240				**For working out which subnet a host is in**				
248								
252								
254								
255								

	Subnets	Hosts -2					
2			**For working out how many subnets and how many hosts per subnet**				
4							
8							
16							
32							
64							

You will probably learn best by jumping straight into an exam-style question:

Which subnet is host 192.168.1.100/26 in?

Well, you know that this is a Class C address and the default mask is 24 binary bits, or 255.255.255.0. You can see that instead of 24 there are 26 bits, so 2 bits have been stolen to make subnets. Simply write down your Subnetting Secrets cheat sheet and tick two places along the top row. This will reveal in what amount your subnets go up.

You can then tick down two places on the subnets column to reveal the actual subnet mask.

Bits	128	64	32	16	8	4	2	1
Subnets	✔	✔						
128	✔							
192	✔							
224								
240								
248								
252								
254								
255								
	Subnets	Hosts -2						
2								
4								
8								
16								
32								
64								

Now you know two things: subnets will go up in increments of 64 (you can use 0 as the first subnet value) and your subnet mask for /26 ends in 192, so, in full, it is 255.255.255.192:

192.168.100.0 is your first subnet
192.168.100.64 is your second subnet
192.168.100.128 is your third subnet
192.168.100.192 is your last subnet

You can't go any further than your actual subnet value, which is 192 in this example. But remember that the question is asking you to find host 100. You can easily see that the subnet ending in 64 is where host 100 would lie because the next subnet is 128, which is too high.

Just for completeness, I will add the host addresses and the broadcast addresses. You can quickly work out the broadcast address by taking the next subnet value and subtracting 1:

Subnet	First Host	Last Host	Broadcast
192.168.100.0	192.168.100.1	192.168.100.62	192.168.100.63
192.168.100.64	192.168.100.65	192.168.100.126	192.168.100.127
192.168.100.128	192.168.100.129	192.168.100.190	192.168.100.191
192.168.100.192	192.168.100.193	192.168.100.254	192.168.100.255

Consider the IP addresses to be values of anything from 0 to 255. Much like an odometer in a car, each number rolls up until it rolls back to 0 again, but the next box rolls over 1. Below are two sample octets. I jump up when we get to 0 2 to save space:

Octet 1	Octet 2
0	0
0	1
0	2 (jump up)
0	255
1	0
1	1
1	2

If you wanted to use the design part of the chart, you could. There is no need to for this question, but to see how it works, you just tick down two places in the subnets column because you stole 2 bits. From 8 bits in the last octet, that leaves you 6 bits for hosts, so tick down six places in the Hosts column to reveal that you get 64 minus 2 bits per subnet, or 4 subnets and 62 hosts per subnet:

Bits	128	64	32	16	8	4	2	1
Subnets	✔	✔						
128	✔							
192	✔							
224								
240								
248								
252								
254								
255								
	Subnets	Hosts -2						
2	✔	✔						
4	✔	✔						
8		✔						
16		✔						
32		✔						
64		✔						

Ready for another question? Of course you are.

Which subnet is host 200.100.2.210/25 in?

Same drill as before. You know this is a Class C address, and that to get from 24 to 25 bits, you need to steal 1 bit. Tick one across the top row and one down the left column:

Bits	128	64	32	16	8	4	2	1
Subnets	✔							
128	✔							
192								
224								
240								
248								
252								
254								
255								

Therefore, your mask will be 255.255.255.128, and your subnets will go up in increments of 128. You can't actually steal less than 1 bit for a Class C address; this will give you only two subnets:

200.100.2.0

and

200.100.2.128

You can already answer the question because you can see that host 210 will be in the second subnet. Just to demonstrate, I will write out the host and broadcast addresses again:

Subnet	First Host	Last Host	Broadcast
200.100.2.0	200.100.2.1	200.100.2.126	200.100.2.127
200.100.2.128	200.100.2.129	200.100.2.254	200.100.2.255

Next question: Which subnet is 172.16.100.11/19 in?

You need to add 3 to 16 (the default Class B mask) to get to 19. Tick across three places on the top row of the chart to get the subnet increment and down three on the left column to get the subnet mask. You don't need the lower portion of the chart for these types of questions.

Bits	128	64	32	16	8	4	2	1
Subnets	✔	✔	✔					
128	✔							
192	✔							
224	✔							
240								
248								
252								
254								
255								

Your subnet mask is 255.255.224.0 and you are subnetting on the third octet because the first two are reserved for the network address/default subnet mask.

Your subnets will be as follows:

172.16.0.0

172.16.32.0

172.16.64.0

172.16.96.0*

172.16.128.0

172.16.160.0

172.16.192.0

172.16.224.0

In the exam, please stop once you get to one subnet past the one your host is in, because going one past will make sure you have the right subnet. You are looking for host 100.11 on the 172.16 network; the asterisk in the list of subnets above denotes the subnet that the host number resides in.

If, for some reason, in the exam they asked you to identify the host addresses and broadcast address (for extra points), you can easily add these. I will put them in for the first few subnets:

Subnet	First Host	Last Host	Broadcast
172.16.0.0	172.16.0.1	172.16.31.254	172.16.31.255
172.16.32.0	172.16.32.1	172.16.63.254	172.16.63.255
172.16.64.0	172.16.64.1	172.16.95.254	172.16.95.255
172.16.96.0	172.16.96.1	172.16.127.254	172.16.127.255

In the exam, they may well try to trick you by adding broadcast addresses as options for host addresses, or even subnet addresses for host addresses. This is why you need to be able to identify which is which. You will also come across the same issue on live networks, where other engineers have tried to add the wrong address to an interface.

Next question: Which subnet is host 172.16.100.11/29 in?

As you can see by now, you can use any mask you wish with most any subnet. I could have asked you about the address 10.100.100.1/29, so don't let the fact that you have a Class A address with subnet bits going into the second, third, or fourth octet put you off.

You need to steal 13 bits for the subnet mask but the subnetting chart has only eight places. Since you are looking at the easy way to subnet, just focus on the part of the chart which the remaining numbers spill over into. If you drew another chart next to the one you had just filled up, you would have five places filled up (8 + 5 = 13 bits):

Bits	128	64	32	16	8	4	2	1
Subnets	✔	✔	✔	✔	✔			
128	✔							
192	✔							
224	✔							

240	✔								
248	✔								
252									
254									
255									

From the chart above, you can see that the subnet mask is 255.255.255.248. The 255 in the third octet is there because you filled it up whilst moving over into the fourth octet. The subnets are also going up in increments of 8.

You could start off with 172.16.0.0, but the problem with that is it would take quite some time to count up in multiples of 8 before you got to 172.16.100.11 this way, and the exam is a timed one. Therefore, you need to fast track the counting process.

If you start counting up in increments of 8, you would get the following:

    172.16.0.0
    172.16.0.8
    172.16.0.16, and you could keep counting up to
    172.16.1.0
    172.16.1.8, and keep counting up to
    172.16.20.0
    172.16.20.8

This would take a very long time because there are over 8,000 subnets (2 to the power of 13 gives you 8192, and you can check this using the design section of the Subnetting Secrets cheat sheet).

Let's presume that each third octet is going up one digit at a time (which it is). Why not jump up to 172.16.100.x to start with?

    172.16.100.0
    172.16.100.8*
    172.16.100.16

From the above, you can see which subnet host 11 is in, and if you were asked to work out the broadcast address, it would look like the chart below:

Subnet	First Host	Last Host	Broadcast
172.16.100.0	172.16.100.1	172.16.100.6	172.16.100.7
172.16.100.8	172.16.100.9	172.16.100.14	172.16.100.15
172.16.100.16	172.16.100.17	172.16.100.22	172.16.100.23

That is enough subnetting for now. We will revisit this subject many times over. For some network design examples, please check www.in60days.net/book-updates.

Remember also that there are a few subnetting resources available for you to use:

www.subnetting.org—subnetting question generator

www.youtube.com/user/paulwbrowning—my YouTube channel with free videos

Please also refer to the book update link at the start of the book for some examples of network design using the lower part of the chart.

DAY 8 QUESTIONS

1. Convert 192.160.210.177 into binary.
2. Convert 10010011 into decimal.
3. What is the private range of IP addresses?
4. Write out the subnet mask from CIDR /20.
5. Write out the subnet mask from CIDR /13.
6. 192.168.1.100/26 gives you which available subnets?
7. 172.16.100.11/19 means your subnets will go up in increments of how many?

DAY 8 LAB—IP ADDRESSING ON ROUTERS

Topology

Purpose

Learn how to get used to configuring IP addresses on routers and pinging across a Serial interface.

Walkthrough

1. Start off by establishing your Serial interface numbers, as they may differ from mine in the diagram above. Also, please establish which side has the DCE cable attached because this side will require the `clock rate` command.

```
Router>en
Router#sh ip interface brief
Interface   IP-Address  OK? Method Status                Protocol
FastEthernet0/0 unassigned  YES unset  administratively down down
FastEthernet0/1 unassigned  YES unset  administratively down down
Serial0/1/0     unassigned  YES unset  administratively down down
Vlan1           unassigned  YES unset  administratively down down
Router#
Router#show controllers serial 0/1/0

M1T-E3 pa: show controller:
PAS unit 0, subunit 0, f/w version 2-55, rev ID 0x2800001, version 2
idb = 0x6080D54C, ds = 0x6080F304, ssb=0x6080F4F4
Clock mux=0x30, ucmd_ctrl=0x0, port_status=0x1
line state: down
DCE cable, no clock rate
```

2. Add a hostname and IP address to one side. If this side is the DCE, add the clock rate.

```
Router#conf t
Enter configuration commands, one per line.  End with CNTL/Z.
Router(config)#hostname RouterA
RouterA(config)#interface s0/1/0
RouterA(config-if)#ip add 192.168.1.1 255.255.255.0
RouterA(config-if)#clock rate 64000
RouterA(config-if)#no shut
%LINK-5-CHANGED: Interface Serial0/1/0, changed state to down
RouterA(config-if)#
```

3.   Add an IP address and hostname to the other router. Also, bring the interface up with the no shut command.

```
Router>en
Router#conf t
Enter configuration commands, one per line.  End with CNTL/Z.
Router(config)#hostname RouterB
RouterB(config)#int s0/1/0
RouterB(config-if)#ip address 192.168.1.2 255.255.255.0
RouterB(config-if)#no shut
%LINK-5-CHANGED: Interface Serial0/1/0, changed state to down
RouterB(config-if)#^Z
RouterB#
%LINK-5-CHANGED: Interface Serial0/1/0, changed state to up
```

4.   Test the connection with a ping.

```
RouterB#ping 192.168.1.1

Type escape sequence to abort.
Sending 5, 100-byte ICMP Echos to 192.168.1.1, timeout is 2 seconds:
!!!!!
Success rate is 100 percent (5/5), round-trip min/avg/max = 31/31/32 ms
```

NOTE: If the ping doesn't work, then double-check to make sure that you have added the clock rate command to the correct router. Ensure that the cable is inserted correctly and use the show controllers serial x/x/x command, inputting your own interface number.

DAY 9

Network Address Translation

DAY 9 TASKS

- Read today's theory notes
- Review yesterday's theory notes
- Complete today's labs
- Read the CCENT cram guide
- Spend 15 minutes on the subnetting.org website

Network Address Translation (NAT) is another strange subject, because Cisco has broken down NAT requirements between the CCENT and the ICND2 syllabuses. For the CCENT exam, you are asked to configure NAT using Security Device Manager (SDM), but SDM has never been tested in the actual CCNA exam and is now end-of-life so although I list it as part of the syllabus, we don't include it.

Today you will learn about the following:

- NAT basics
- Configuring and verifying NAT
- NAT troubleshooting

This lesson maps to the following CCNA syllabus requirements:

- Explain the basic uses and operation of NAT in a small network connected to one ISP
- Enable NAT for a small network with a single ISP and connection using SDM, and verify operation using CLI and ping
- Configure NAT for given network requirements using SDM (including CLI/SDM)
- Troubleshoot NAT issues

NAT Basics

Imagine for a moment networks running on colours instead of using IP addresses. There is an unlimited supply of the colours blue and yellow but the other colours are in short supply. Your network is divided into many users using the colours blue and yellow because they are free to use. The blue users need to get out to the web fairly regularly, so you buy a few green tokens which your router can use to swap for the blue users' tokens when they need to reach hosts on the web.

Your router would be doing this:

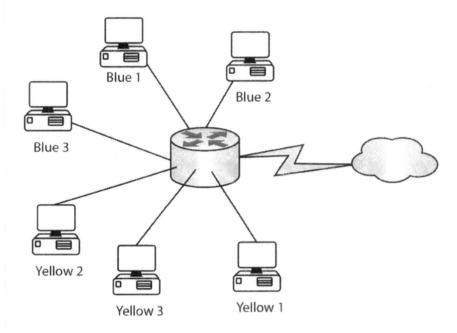

FIG 9.1—Inside Tokens Swapped for Outside Tokens

Inside Tokens	Outside Tokens
Blue 1	Green 1
Blue 2	Green 2
Blue 3	Green 3

When each of the blue devices has finished with the outside connection, the green token can be released for use by another blue device. The benefits to this are outside devices can't see your internal token IDs and you are helping conserve the limited amount of green tokens available for use on the Internet.

As you can see, NAT not only protects your network IP addresses but also is another method of address conservation. NAT is performed on routers or firewalls, so, instead of colours, you would see something like this:

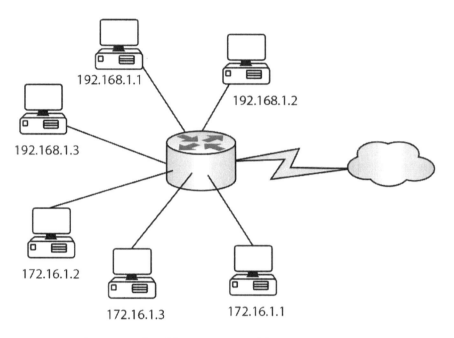

FIG 9.2—Inside Addresses Swapped for Outside Addresses

Inside Addresses	Outside Addresses
192.168.1.1	200.100.1.5
192.168.1.3	200.100.1.7

There are three ways to configure NAT on your router, depending upon your particular requirements. You will need to know all three for the CCNA exam.

In order to configure NAT, you need to tell the router which interfaces are on the inside and outside of your NAT network. This is because you could actually swap internal addresses for a pool of NAT addresses, or, at the very least, a single NAT address, and perform NAT between two Ethernet interfaces on your router.

Having said that, for the exam and in the real world, you will usually translate private Internet addresses into routable addresses on the Internet. You will see this on your home broadband router, which will usually give your laptop an IP in the 192.168.1 range but then have a routable address on the interface to the ISP.

NAT enables hosts on private networks to access resources on the Internet or other public networks. NAT is an IETF standard that enables a LAN to use one set of IP addresses for internal traffic, typically private address space as defined in RFC 1918, and another set of addresses for external traffic, typically publicly registered IP address space.

NAT converts the packet headers for incoming and outgoing traffic and keeps track of each session. The key to understanding NAT and, ultimately, troubleshooting NAT problems is having a solid understanding of NAT terminology. You should be familiar with the following NAT terms:

- The NAT inside interface
- Inside local address
- Inside global address
- The NAT outside interface
- Outside local address
- Outside global address

In NAT terminology, the inside interface is the border interface of the administrative domain controlled by the organisation. This does not necessarily have to be the default gateway used by hosts that reside within the internal network.

The inside local address is the IP address of a host residing on the inside network. In most cases, the inside local address is an RFC 1918 address (i.e., non-routable, such as 192.168.x.x or 172.16.x.x). This address is translated to the outside global address, which is typically an IP address from a publically assigned or registered pool. It is important to remember, however, that the inside local address could also be a public address.

The inside global address is the IP address of an internal host as it appears to the outside world. Once the inside IP address has been translated, it will appear as an inside global address to the Internet public or to any other external network or host.

The outside interface is the boundary for the administrative domain that is not controlled by the organisation. In other words, the outside interface is connected to the external network, which may be the Internet or any other external network, such as a partner network, for example. Any hosts residing beyond the outside interface fall outside the local organisation's administration.

The outside local address is the IP address of an outside, or external, host as it appears to inside hosts. Finally, the outside global address is an address that is legal and can be used on the Internet. Both outside local addresses and outside global addresses are typically allocated from a globally routable address or network space.

To clarify these concepts further, Figure 9.3 below shows the use of the addresses in a session between two hosts. NAT is enabled on the intermediate gateway:

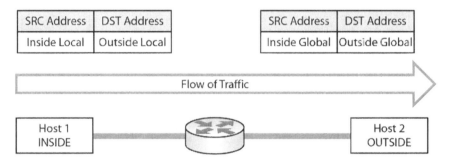

FIG 9.3—Understanding NAT Inside and Outside Addresses

NAT inside and outside addressing is a classic exam question, so come back to this concept a few times.

Configuring and Verifying NAT

The configuration and verification of Network Address Translation with Cisco IOS software is a straightforward task. When configuring NAT, perform the following:

- Designate one or more interfaces as the internal (inside) interface(s) using the `ip nat inside` interface configuration command.
- Designate an interface as the external (outside) interface using the `ip nat outside` interface configuration command.
- Configure an Access Control List (ACL) that will match all traffic for translation. This can be a standard or an extended named or numbered ACL.
- Optionally, configure a pool of global addresses using the `ip nat pool <name> <start-ip> <end-ip> [netmask <mask> | prefix-length <length>]` global configuration command. This defines a pool of inside global addresses to which inside local addresses will be translated.
- Configure NAT globally using the `ip nat inside source list <ACL> [interface|pool] <name> [overload]` global configuration command.

The following example shows you how to configure basic NAT with Cisco IOS software. You can see that the configuration has used the `description` and `remark` features available to help administrators more easily manage and troubleshoot their networks:

```
R1(config)#interface FastEthernet0/0
R1(config-if)#description 'Connected To The Internal LAN'
R1(config-if)#ip address 10.5.5.1 255.255.255.248
R1(config-if)#ip nat inside
R1(config-if)#exit
R1(config)#interface Serial0/0
R1(config-if)#description 'Connected To The ISP'
R1(config-if)#ip address 150.1.1.1 255.255.255.248
R1(config-if)#ip nat outside
R1(config-if)#exit
R1(config)#access-list 100 remark 'Translate Internal Addresses Only'
R1(config)#access-list 100 permit ip 10.5.5.0 0.0.0.7 any
R1(config)#ip nat pool INSIDE-POOL 150.1.1.3 150.1.1.6 prefix-length 24
R1(config)#ip nat inside source list 100 pool INSIDE-POOL
R1(config)#exit
```

Following this configuration, the show ip nat translations command can be used to verify that translations are actually taking place on the router, as illustrated below:

```
R1#show ip nat translations
Pro Inside global   Inside local   Outside local   Outside global
icmp 150.1.1.4:4    10.5.5.1:4     200.1.1.1:4     200.1.1.1:4
icmp 150.1.1.3:1    10.5.5.2:1     200.1.1.1:1     200.1.1.1:1
tcp  150.1.1.5:159 10.5.5.3:159    200.1.1.1:23    200.1.1.1:23
```

You actually have three choices when it comes to configuring NAT on your router:

1. Swap one internal address for one external address [Static NAT]
2. Swap many internal addresses for two or more external addresses [Dynamic NAT]
3. Swap many internal addresses for many external ports [Port Address Translation]

Static NAT

You would want to swap one specific address for another address when you have a web server (for example) on the inside of your network. If you keep using dynamic addressing, then there is no way routing will work, because the inbound packet has no routing table entry (this is why you will add a static route in your NAT labs).

FARAI SAYS: 'You would use static NAT for any server that needs to be reachable via the Internet, such as e-mail or FTP.'

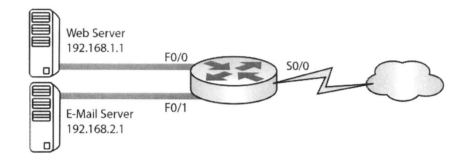

FIG 9.4—Static NAT in Use

Inside Addresses	Outside NAT Addresses
192.168.1.1	200.1.1.1
192.168.2.1	200.1.1.2

For the network above, your configuration would be as follows:

```
Router(config)#interface f0/0
Router(config-if)#ip address 192.168.1.1 255.255.255.0
Router(config-if)#ip nat inside
Router(config)#interface f0/1
Router(config-if)#ip address 192.168.2.1 255.255.255.0
Router(config-if)#ip nat inside
Router(config)#interface s0/0
Router(config-if)#ip nat outside
Router(config-if)#exit
Router(config)#ip nat inside source static 192.168.1.1 200.1.1.1
Router(config)#ip nat inside source static 192.168.2.1 200.1.1.2
```

The ip nat inside/outside command tells the router which are the inside NAT interfaces and which are the outside NAT interfaces. The ip nat inside source command defines the static translations, of which you could have as many as you wish, so long as you paid for the public IP addresses. The vast majority of configuration mistakes I fixed whilst at Cisco were missing ip nat inside and outside statements! You might see questions in the exam where you have to spot configuration mistakes.

I strongly recommend that you type the commands above onto a router. You will do many NAT labs in this book, but the more you type whilst you read the theory section, the better the information will stick in your head.

Dynamic NAT or NAT Pool

You will often need to use a group, or pool, of routable addresses. One-to-one NAT mapping has its limitations, of course, expense and extensive lines of configuration on your router to name two. Dynamic NAT allows you to configure one or more groups of addresses to be used by your internal hosts.

Your router will keep a list of the internal addresses to external addresses, and eventually the translation in the table will time out. You can alter the timeout values but please do so on the advice of a Cisco TAC engineer.

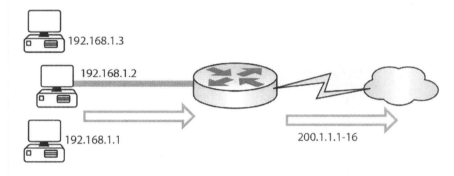

192.168.1.3

192.168.1.2

192.168.1.1

200.1.1.1-16

FIG 9.5—Internal Addresses to a NAT Pool of Routable Addresses

If you issued a `show ip nat translations` command on the router when the inside hosts have made outside connections, you would see a chart containing something like this:

Inside Addresses	Outside NAT Addresses
192.168.1.3	200.1.1.11
192.168.1.2	200.1.1.14

In Figure 9.5 above, you have internal addresses using a pool of addresses from 200.1.1.1 to 16. Here is the configuration file to achieve it. I have left off the router interface addresses for now:

```
Router(config)#interface f0/0
Router(config-if)#ip nat inside
Router(config)#interface s0/1
Router(config-if)#ip nat outside
Router(config)#ip nat pool poolname 200.1.1.1 200.1.1.16 netmask
255.255.255.0
Router(config)#ip nat inside source list 1 pool poolname
Router(config)#access-list 1 permit 192.168.1.0 0.0.0.255
```

The access list is used to tell the router which addresses it can and cannot translate. The subnet mask is actually reversed and is called a wildcard mask, which will be covered later. All NAT pools need a name, and in this example, it is simply called 'poolname.' The source list is referring to the access list.

NAT Overload/Port Address Translation

IP addresses are in short supply, and if you have hundreds or thousands of addresses which need to be routed, it could cost you a lot of money. In this instance, you can use NAT overload, also referred to as Port Address Translation (PAT). PAT cleverly allows a port number to be added to the IP address as a way of uniquely identifying it from another translation using the same IP address. There are over 65,000 ports available per IP address.

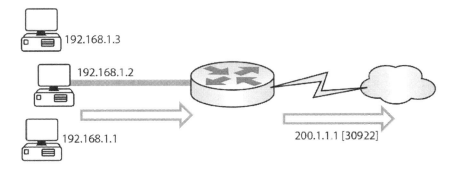

FIG 9.6—NAT Overload

The show ip nat translations table this time would show the IP addresses and port numbers:

Inside Addresses	Outside NAT Addresses (with Port Numbers)
192.168.1.1	200.1.1.1:30922
192.168.2.1	200.1.1.2:30975

To configure PAT, you would carry out the exact same configuration as for dynamic NAT, but you would add the keyword [overload] to the end of the pool:

```
Router(config)#interface f0/0
Router(config-if)#ip nat inside
Router(config)#interface s0/1
Router(config-if)#ip nat outside
Router(config)#ip nat pool poolname 200.1.1.1 200.1.1.1 netmask
255.255.255.0
Router(config)#ip nat inside source list 1 pool poolname overload
Router(config)#access-list 1 permit 192.168.1.0 0.0.0.255
```

This should be pretty easy to remember!

> **FARAI SAYS:** 'Using PAT with more than one IP is a waste of address space because the router will use the first IP and increment port numbers for each subsequent connection. This is why PAT is typically configured to overload to the interface.'

Troubleshooting NAT

Nine out of ten times, the router administrator has forgotten to add the `ip nat outside` or `ip nat inside` command to the router interfaces. In fact, this is almost always the problem! The next most frequent mistakes include the wrong access list and a misspelled pool name (it is case sensitive).

You can debug NAT translations on the router by using the `debug ip nat [detailed]` command, and you can view the NAT pool with the `show ip nat translations` command.

DAY 9 QUESTIONS

1. NAT converts the _____ headers for incoming and outgoing traffic and keeps track of each session.
2. The _____ address is the IP address of an outside, or external, host as it appears to inside hosts.
3. How do you designate inside and outside NAT interfaces?
4. Which `show` command displays a list of your NAT table?
5. When would you want to use static NAT?
6. Write the configuration command for NAT 192.168.1.1 to 200.1.1.1.
7. Which command do you add to a NAT pool to enable PAT?
8. NAT most often fails to work because the _____ command is missing.
9. Which `debug` command shows live NAT translations occurring?

DAY 9 LAB 1—STATIC NAT

Topology

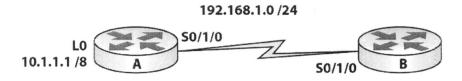

192.168.1.0 /24

Purpose

Learn how to configure static NAT.

Walkthrough

1. Add IP address 192.168.1.1 255.255.255.0 to Router A and change the hostname to Router A. Add IP address 192.168.1.2 255.255.255.0 to Router B. Add a clock rate to the correct side and ping from A to B or from B to A. Check the previous labs if you need a reminder.

2. You need to add an IP address to Router A to simulate a host on the LAN. You can achieve this with a Loopback interface.

    ```
    RouterA#conf t
    Enter configuration commands, one per line.  End with CNTL/Z.
    RouterA(config)#interface loopback 0
    RouterA(config-if)#ip add 10.1.1.1 255.0.0.0
    RouterA(config-if)#
    ```

3. For testing, you need to tell Router B to send any traffic to any network back out towards Router A. You will do this with a static route.

    ```
    RouterB#conf t
    Enter configuration commands, one per line.  End with CNTL/Z.
    RouterB(config)#ip route 0.0.0.0 0.0.0.0 serial 0/1/0
    RouterB(config)#
    ```

4. Test to see whether the static route is working by pinging from the Loopback interface on Router A to Router B.

    ```
    RouterA#ping
    Protocol [ip]:
    Target IP address: 192.168.1.2
    Repeat count [5]:
    Datagram size [100]:
    Timeout in seconds [2]:
    Extended commands [n]: y
    ```

```
Source address or interface: 10.1.1.1
Type of service [0]:
Set DF bit in IP header? [no]:
Validate reply data? [no]:
Data pattern [0xABCD]:
Loose, Strict, Record, Timestamp, Verbose[none]:
Sweep range of sizes [n]:
Type escape sequence to abort.
Sending 5, 100-byte ICMP Echos to 192.168.1.2, timeout is 2 seconds:
Packet sent with a source address of 10.1.1.1
!!!!!
Success rate is 100 percent (5/5), round-trip min/avg/max = 31/31/32 ms

RouterA#
```

5. Configure a static NAT entry on Router A. Using NAT, translate the 10.1.1.1 address to 172.16.1.1 when it leaves the router. You also need to tell the router which is the inside and outside NAT interface.

```
RouterA#conf t
Enter configuration commands, one per line.  End with CNTL/Z.
RouterA(config)#int loopback 0
RouterA(config-if)#ip nat inside
RouterA(config-if)#int ser 0/1/0
RouterA(config-if)#ip nat outside
RouterA(config-if)#
RouterA(config-if)#ip nat inside source static 10.1.1.1 172.16.1.1
RouterA(config)#
```

6. Turn on NAT debugging so you can see the translations taking place. Then issue another extended ping (from L0) and check the NAT table. Your output may differ from mine due to changes in IOS.

```
RouterA#debug ip nat

IP NAT debugging is on
RouterA#
RouterA#ping
Protocol [ip]:
Target IP address: 192.168.1.2
Repeat count [5]:
Datagram size [100]:
Timeout in seconds [2]:
Extended commands [n]: y
Source address or interface: 10.1.1.1
Type of service [0]:
```

```
Set DF bit in IP header? [no]:
Validate reply data? [no]:
Data pattern [0xABCD]:
Loose, Strict, Record, Timestamp, Verbose[none]:
Sweep range of sizes [n]:
Type escape sequence to abort.
Sending 5, 100-byte ICMP Echos to 192.168.1.2, timeout is 2 seconds:
Packet sent with a source address of 10.1.1.1

NAT: s=10.1.1.1->172.16.1.1, d=192.168.1.2 [11]
!
NAT*: s=192.168.1.2, d=172.16.1.1->10.1.1.1 [11]

NAT: s=10.1.1.1->172.16.1.1, d=192.168.1.2 [12]
!
NAT*: s=192.168.1.2, d=172.16.1.1->10.1.1.1 [12]

NAT: s=10.1.1.1->172.16.1.1, d=192.168.1.2 [13]
!
NAT*: s=192.168.1.2, d=172.16.1.1->10.1.1.1 [13]

NAT: s=10.1.1.1->172.16.1.1, d=192.168.1.2 [14]
!
NAT*: s=192.168.1.2, d=172.16.1.1->10.1.1.1 [14]

NAT: s=10.1.1.1->172.16.1.1, d=192.168.1.2 [15]
!
Success rate is 100 percent (5/5), round-trip min/avg/max = 31/46/110 ms

RouterA#
NAT*: s=192.168.1.2, d=172.16.1.1->10.1.1.1 [15]

RouterA#show ip nat translations
Pro   Inside global    Inside local    Outside local     Outside global
icmp 172.16.1.1:10 10.1.1.1:10     192.168.1.2:10    192.168.1.2:10
icmp 172.16.1.1:6  10.1.1.1:6      192.168.1.2:6     192.168.1.2:6
icmp 172.16.1.1:7  10.1.1.1:7      192.168.1.2:7     192.168.1.2:7
icmp 172.16.1.1:8  10.1.1.1:8      192.168.1.2:8     192.168.1.2:8
icmp 172.16.1.1:9  10.1.1.1:9      192.168.1.2:9     192.168.1.2:9
---   172.16.1.1         10.1.1.1        ---               ---

RouterA#
```

7. Bear in mind that the router will clear the NAT translation soon afterwards in order to clear the NAT address(es) for use by other IP addresses.

```
NAT: expiring 172.16.1.1 (10.1.1.1) icmp 6 (6)

NAT: expiring 172.16.1.1 (10.1.1.1) icmp 7 (7)
```

DAY 9 LAB 2—NAT POOL

Topology

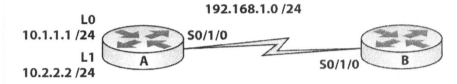

L0
10.1.1.1 /24

L1
10.2.2.2 /24

192.168.1.0 /24

S0/1/0

A

S0/1/0

B

Purpose

Learn how to configure a NAT pool (dynamic NAT).

Walkthrough

1. Add IP address 192.168.1.1 255.255.255.0 to Router A and change the hostname to Router A. Add IP address 192.168.1.2 255.255.255.0 to Router B. Add a clock rate to the correct side and ping from A to B or from B to A. Check the previous lab if you need a reminder.

2. You need to add two IP addresses to Router A to simulate a host on the LAN. You can achieve this with two Loopback interfaces. They will be in different subnets but both start with a 10 address.

    ```
    RouterA#conf t
    Enter configuration commands, one per line.  End with CNTL/Z.
    RouterA(config)#interface loopback 0
    RouterA(config-if)#ip add 10.1.1.1 255.255.255.0
    RouterA(config-if)#int l1  ← short for Loopback 1
    RouterA(config-if)#ip address 10.2.2.2 255.255.255.0
    RouterA(config-if)#
    ```

3. For testing, you need to tell Router B to send any traffic to any network back out towards Router A. You will do this with a static route.

    ```
    RouterB#conf t
    Enter configuration commands, one per line.  End with CNTL/Z.
    RouterB(config)#ip route 0.0.0.0 0.0.0.0 serial 0/1/0
    RouterB(config)#
    ```

4. Test to see whether the static route is working by pinging from the Loopback interface on Router A to Router B.

    ```
    RouterA#ping
    Protocol [ip]:
    Target IP address: 192.168.1.2
    Repeat count [5]:
    ```

```
Datagram size [100]:
Timeout in seconds [2]:
Extended commands [n]: y
Source address or interface: 10.1.1.1
Type of service [0]:
Set DF bit in IP header? [no]:
Validate reply data? [no]:
Data pattern [0xABCD]:
Loose, Strict, Record, Timestamp, Verbose[none]:
Sweep range of sizes [n]:
Type escape sequence to abort.
Sending 5, 100-byte ICMP Echos to 192.168.1.2, timeout is 2 seconds:
Packet sent with a source address of 10.1.1.1
!!!!!
Success rate is 100 percent (5/5), round-trip min/avg/max = 31/31/32 ms

RouterA#
```

5. Configure a NAT pool on Router A. For this lab, use 172.16.1.1 to 10. Any address starting with 10 will be a NAT. Remember that you MUST specify the inside and outside NAT interfaces or NAT won't work.

```
RouterA#conf t
Enter configuration commands, one per line.  End with CNTL/Z.
RouterA(config)#int 10
RouterA(config-if)#ip nat inside
RouterA(config)#irt 11
RouterA(config-if)#ip nat inside
RouterA(config-if)#int ser 0/1/0
RouterA(config-if)#ip nat outside
RouterA(config-if)#exit
RouterA(config)#ip nat pool 60days 172.16.1.1 172.16.1.10 netmask
255.255.255.0
RouterA(config)#ip nat inside source list 1 pool 60days
RouterA(config)#access-list 1 permit 10.1.0.0 0.255.255.255
RouterA(config)#access-list 1 permit 10.2.0.0 0.255.255.255
RouterA(config)#
```

The `ip nat pool` command creates the pool of addresses. You need to give the pool a name of your own choosing. The `netmask` command tells the router which network mask to apply to the pool.

The `source list` command tells the router which access list to look at. The ACL tells the router which networks will match the NAT pool.

6. Turn on NAT debugging so you can see the translations taking place. Then issue extended pings (from L0 and L1) and check the NAT table. Your output may differ from mine due to changes in IOS. You want to see two addresses from the NAT pool being used.

```
RouterA#debug ip nat

RouterA#ping
Protocol [ip]:
Target IP address: 192.168.1.2
Repeat count [5]:
Datagram size [100]:
Timeout in seconds [2]:
Extended commands [n]: y
Source address or interface: 10.1.1.1
Type of service [0]:
Set DF bit in IP header? [no]:
Validate reply data? [no]:
Data pattern [0xABCD]:
Loose, Strict, Record, Timestamp, Verbose[none]:
Sweep range of sizes [n]:
Type escape sequence to abort.
Sending 5, 100-byte ICMP Echos to 192.168.1.2, timeout is 2 seconds:
Packet sent with a source address of 10.1.1.1

NAT: s=10.1.1.1->172.16.1.1, d=192.168.1.2 [26]
!
NAT*: s=192.168.1.2, d=172.16.1.1->10.1.1.1 [16]

NAT: s=10.1.1.1->172.16.1.1, d=192.168.1.2 [27]
!
NAT*: s=192.168.1.2, d=172.16.1.1->10.1.1.1 [17]

NAT: s=10.1.1.1->172.16.1.1, d=192.168.1.2 [28]
!
NAT*: s=192.168.1.2, d=172.16.1.1->10.1.1.1 [18]

NAT: s=10.1.1.1->172.16.1.1, d=192.168.1.2 [29]
!
NAT*: s=192.168.1.2, d=172.16.1.1->10.1.1.1 [19]

NAT: s=10.1.1.1->172.16.1.1, d=192.168.1.2 [30]
!
Success rate is 100 percent (5/5), round-trip min/avg/max = 17/28/32 ms

RouterA#
NAT*: s=192.168.1.2, d=172.16.1.1->10.1.1.1 [20]

RouterA#ping
Protocol [ip]:
Target IP address: 192.168.1.2
Repeat count [5]:
```

```
Datagram size [100]:
Timeout in seconds [2]:
Extended commands [n]: y
Source address or interface: 10.2.2.2
Type of service [0]:
Set DF bit in IP header? [no]:
Validate reply data? [no]:
Data pattern [0xABCD]:
Loose, Strict, Record, Timestamp, Verbose[none]:
Sweep range of sizes [n]:
Type escape sequence to abort.
Sending 5, 100-byte ICMP Echos to 192.168.1.2, timeout is 2 seconds:
Packet sent with a source address of 10.2.2.2

NAT: s=10.2.2.2->172.16.1.2, d=192.168.1.2 [31]
!
NAT*: s=192.168.1.2, d=172.16.1.2->10.2.2.2 [21]

NAT: s=10.2.2.2->172.16.1.2, d=192.168.1.2 [32]
!
NAT*: s=192.168.1.2, d=172.16.1.2->10.2.2.2 [22]

NAT: s=10.2.2.2->172.16.1.2, d=192.168.1.2 [33]
!
NAT*: s=192.168.1.2, d=172.16.1.2->10.2.2.2 [23]

NAT: s=10.2.2.2->172.16.1.2, d=192.168.1.2 [34]
!
NAT*: s=192.168.1.2, d=172.16.1.2->10.2.2.2 [24]

NAT: s=10.2.2.2->172.16.1.2, d=192.168.1.2 [35]
!
Success rate is 100 percent (5/5), round-trip min/avg/max = 31/31/32 ms

RouterA#
NAT*: s=192.168.1.2, d=172.16.1.2->10.2.2.2 [25]

RouterA#show ip nat trans
Pro  Inside global Inside local  Outside local      Outside global
icmp 172.16.1.1:16 10.1.1.1:16  192.168.1.2:16     192.168.1.2:16
icmp 172.16.1.1:17 10.1.1.1:17  192.168.1.2:17     192.168.1.2:17
icmp 172.16.1.1:18 10.1.1.1:18  192.168.1.2:18     192.168.1.2:18
icmp 172.16.1.1:19 10.1.1.1:19  192.168.1.2:19     192.168.1.2:19
icmp 172.16.1.1:20 10.1.1.1:20  192.168.1.2:20     192.168.1.2:20
icmp 172.16.1.2:21 10.2.2.2:21  192.168.1.2:21     192.168.1.2:21
icmp 172.16.1.2:22 10.2.2.2:22  192.168.1.2:22     192.168.1.2:22
icmp 172.16.1.2:23 10.2.2.2:23  192.168.1.2:23     192.168.1.2:23
icmp 172.16.1.2:24 10.2.2.2:24  192.168.1.2:24     192.168.1.2:24
icmp 172.16.1.2:25 10.2.2.2:25  192.168.1.2:25     192.168.1.2:25

RouterA#
```

DAY 9 LAB 3—NAT OVERLOAD

Repeat Lab 2. This time, when referring to the pool, add the `overload` command to the end of the configuration line. This instructs the router to use PAT. Leave off `loopback 1`. Please note that as Farai says, in the real world, your pool will usually have only one address or you will overload your outside interface.

```
RouterA(config)#ip nat inside source list 1 pool 60days overload
```

I've done some of the previous labs using Cisco Packet Tracer for convenience, so you will often see different output to mine. Here is a sample output from a PAT lab. You will see that the router is adding a port number to each translation. Unfortunately, you see a similar number at the end of the NAT pool labs, which is an annoyance of PT.

```
RouterA#show ip nat tran
Inside global Inside local    Outside local   Outside global
10.0.0.1:8759 172.16.1.129:8759 192.168.1.2:8759 192.168.1.2:8759
```

DAY 10

DHCP and DNS

DAY 10 TASKS

- Read today's theory notes
- Review yesterday's theory notes
- Complete today's lab
- Read the CCENT cram guide
- Spend 15 minutes on the subnetting.org website

Dynamic Host Configuration Protocol (DHCP) is used by hosts to gather initial configuration information, which includes parameters such as IP address, subnet mask, and default gateway, upon boot up. Since each host needs an IP address to communicate in an IP network, DHCP eases the administrative burden of manually configuring each host with an IP address. As with NAT (and other topics), the syllabus mentions SDM but this has been retired.

Domain Name System (DNS) maps hostnames to IP addresses, enabling you to type www.in60days. net into your web browser instead of the IP address of the server on which the site is hosted.

Today you will learn about the following:

- DHCP operations
- Configuring DHCP
- Troubleshooting DHCP issues
- DNS operations
- Configuring DNS
- Troubleshooting DNS issues

This lesson maps to the following CCNA syllabus requirements:

- Configure, verify, and troubleshoot DHCP and DNS operations on a router (CLI/SDM)
- Describe and verify DNS operations

DHCP Operations

DHCP simplifies network administrative tasks by automatically assigning IP information to hosts on a network. This information can include IP addresses, subnet masks, and default gateways and is usually assigned when the host boots up.

When the host first boots up, if it has been configured to use DHCP (which most hosts are), it will send a broadcast message asking for IP information to be allocated. The broadcast will be heard by the DHCP server and the information will be relayed.

FARAI SAYS: 'This is assuming that they are on the same subnet. If they are not, then see the `ip helper-address` command below.'

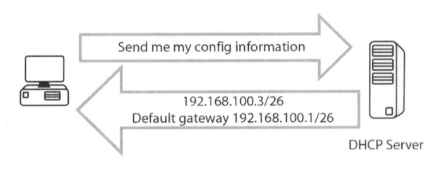

FIG 10.1—Host Requests IP Configuration Information

DHCP actually uses UDP ports 67 and 68 to communicate over the network, and, of course, actual servers are usually used as DHCP servers, although routers can also perform this role, if required. Routers can also be configured to obtain their IP address from a DHCP server, if required, although this is rarely done. The command to configure this is:

```
Router(config-if)#ip address dhcp
```

DHCP states for clients are as follows:

1. Initialising
2. Selecting
3. Requesting
4. Bound

5. Renewing

6. Rebinding

DHCP servers can be configured to give an IP address to a host for a specified period called the lease time. This can be for hours or days. You can and should reserve IP addresses which cannot be allocated to hosts on the network. These IP addresses will already be in use on router interfaces or for servers. If you fail to do this, you may see duplicate IP address warnings on your network because the DHCP server has allocated your address to a host.

The full DHCP request and assign process can be seen in Figure 10.2 below:

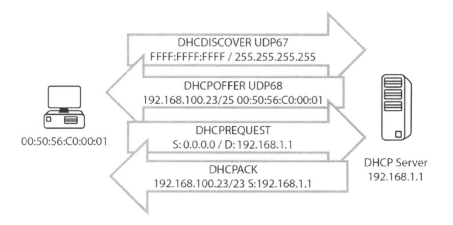

FIG 10.2—DHCP Request and Allocation Process

Configuring DHCP

If you do need to configure DHCP on your router, then follow these steps:

1. Exclude addresses (servers/gateways).

```
ip chcp excluded-address <starting address> <ending address>
```

2. Configure the pool.

```
ip chcp pool <name>
```

3. Configure network number/pool mask.

```
network <network> <mask>
```

4. Specify the default gateway IP address.

```
default-router <address 1...address 8>
```

5. Add DNS server address, if required, and lease time.

```
R1(config)#ip dhcp excluded-address 10.1.1.1 10.1.1.9
R1(config)#ip dhcp excluded-address 10.2.2.1
R1(config)#ip dhcp pool POOL-A
R1(dhcp-config)#network 10.1.1.0 /24
R1(dhcp-config)#default-router 10.1.1.1
R1(dhcp-config)#dns-server 172.16.1.252 172.16.1.253 172.16.1.254
R1(dhcp-config)#netbios-name-server 172.16.1.253 172.16.1.254
R1(dhcp-config)#lease 8 0 0
R1(dhcp-config)#exit
R1(config)#ip dhcp pool POOL-B
R1(dhcp-config)#network 10.2.2.0 255.255.255.248
R1(dhcp-config)#default-router 10.2.2.1
R1(dhcp-config)#dns-server 172.16.1.254
R1(dhcp-config)#lease 0 8 0
R1(dhcp-config)#exit
```

The lease values above are 0 days, 8 hours, and 0 minutes. Several of the options above are optional, such as the default router and NetBIOS name server, but they have been added so you can see the range of configuration commands available. Please do try out these commands on your router.

Troubleshooting DHCP Issues

As with NAT, DHCP issues are almost always due to an error in the configuration (jokingly referred to as a Layer 8 issue, meaning somebody messed up).

The `service dhcp` command is turned on by default, but sometimes it has been manually disabled by a network administrator for some reason. (I've seen network administrators call Cisco with urgent routing issues on their network after they entered the `no ip routing` command on their router—seriously!)

DHCP packets need to be permitted through your router if you are using a server on another subnet to administer DHCP configurations. DHCP uses broadcast messages as part of its process (which routers won't forward), so the IP address of the DHCP server needs to be added to the router to allow it to forward the broadcast message as a unicast packet. The command `ip helper-address` achieves this. This is another exam-favourite question!

You can also use the following `debug` commands as part of your troubleshooting process:

```
debug ip dhcp server events
debug ip dhcp server packet
```

Please ensure that you type out ALL of these commands onto a router. There is no way on Earth that you will remember them by reading them on a page. Try out the configurations, make mistakes, post questions, break it on purpose (not on a live network), and fix it again.

DNS Operations

DNS maps hostnames to IP addresses (not the other way around). This allows you to browse a web address from your web browser instead of the server IP address.

DNS uses UDP port 53.

Configuring DNS

If you want to permit your router to find a DNS server on the web, then use the command `ip name-server 1.1.1.1`, or the relevant IP address of the server.

You can also set a hostname to the IP address table on your router to save time or to make it easier to remember which device to ping or connect to.

```
Router(config)#ip host R2 192.168.1.2
Router(config)#ip host R3 192.168.1.3
Router(config)#exit
Router#ping R2
Router#pinging 192.168.1.2
!!!!!
```

Troubleshooting DNS Issues

A default command on the router configuration will be `ip domain-lookup`. If this command has been disabled, then DNS won't work. Sometimes router administrators disable it because when you mistype a command you have to wait several seconds while the router performs a look up. You turn off DNS lookups with the following command:

```
Router(config)#no ip domain-lookup
```

Access lists often block DNS, so this is another possible cause of problems. You can debug DNS on the router with the `debug domain` command.

DAY 10 QUESTIONS

1. DHCP uses UDP ports _____ and _____.

2. What are the six DHCP states for clients?

3. Which command will prevent IP addresses 192.168.1.1 to 10 from being used in the pool?

4. Which command will set a DHCP lease of 7 days, 7 hours, and 7 minutes?

5. Which command will enable the router to forward a DHCP broadcast as a unicast?

6. DNS uses UDP port _____.

7. Which command will set a DNS server address of 192.168.1.1 on your router?

8. If the _____ _____-_____ command has been disabled on your router, then DNS won't work.

9. Which command will debug DNS packets on your router?

DAY 10 LAB—DHCP ON A ROUTER

Topology

10.0.0.1/18

Purpose

Learn how routers can be used as DHCP servers.

Walkthrough

1. If you are using your home PC or laptop, set the network adaptor to obtain the IP address auto-matically. You can also set this in Packet Tracer. Connect the PC to your router Ethernet port with a crossover cable.

> **Internet Protocol (TCP/IP) Properties** ? X
>
> General | Alternate Configuration
>
> You can get IP settings assigned automatically if your network supports this capability. Otherwise, you need to ask your network administrator for the appropriate IP settings.
>
> ⦿ Obtain an IP address automatically
>
> ◯ Use the following IP address:
>
> IP address:
>
> Subnet mask:
>
> Default gateway:

2. Add the IP address 172.16.1.1 255.255.0.0 to your router interface. Please see previous labs if you can't remember how to do this. Make sure you `no shut` it.

3. Configure your DHCP pool. Then, configure a lease of 3 days, 3 hours, and 5 minutes for your address. Lastly, exclude all the addresses from 1 to 10 from being assigned to hosts. Presume that these are already in use for other servers or interfaces.

```
Router#conf t
Router(config)#ip dhcp pool 60days
Router(chcp-config)#network 172.16.0.0 255.255.0.0
Router1(dhcp-config)#lease 3 3 5 ← command won't work on Packet Tracer (PT)
```

```
Router1(dhcp-config)#exit
Router(config)#ip dhcp excluded-address 172.16.1.1 172.16.1.10
Router(config)#
```

4. Issue an `ipconfig /all` command to check whether an IP address has been assigned to your PC. You may need to issue an `ipconfig /renew` command if an old IP address is still in use.

```
PC>ipconfig /all

Physical Address.................: 0001.C7DD.CB19
IP Address.......................: 172.16.0.1
Subnet Mask......................: 255.255.0.0
Default Gateway..................: 0.0.0.0
DNS Servers......................: 0.0.0.0
```

5. If you wish, you can go back into the DHCP pool and add a default gateway and a DNS server address, which will also be set on the host PC.

```
Router(config)#ip dhcp pool 60days
Router(dhcp-config)#default-router 172.16.1.2
Router(dhcp-config)#dns-server 172.16.1.3

PC>ipconfig /renew

IP Address.......................: 172.16.0.1
Subnet Mask......................: 255.255.0.0
Default Gateway..................: 172.16.1.2
DNS Server.......................: 172.16.1.3
```

Variable Length Subnet Masking

DAY 11 TASKS

- Read today's theory notes
- Review yesterday's theory notes
- Complete the lab(s) of your choice
- Read the CCENT cram guide
- Spend 15 minutes on the subnetting.org website

Here's another toughie. Give the information in this section time to sink in over the review sessions. Also, do lots of practise and post your ideas and questions on networking forums.

After you have subnetted your network, Variable Length Subnet Masking (VLSM) permits you to take a subnet and chop it down into more usable chunks. You may want to do this to make managing the network easier, to reduce routing tables, or to make more efficient use of the addresses you have available within the network.

Today you will learn about the following:

- Using VLSM
- Slicing down networks

This lesson maps to the following CCNA syllabus requirements:

- Calculate and apply an addressing scheme, including VLSM IP addressing design, to a network
- Determine the appropriate classless addressing scheme using VLSM and summarisation to satisfy addressing requirements in a LAN/WAN environment

Using VLSM

Look at the following network:

- 192.168.1.0/24 = 1 network—254 hosts
  While this may work fine, what if your network requires more than one subnet? What if your subnets have less than 254 hosts in them? Either situation requires some changes to be made. If you applied a /26 mask to your network instead, you would get this:

- 192.168.1.0/26 = 4 subnets—62 hosts
  If that wasn't suitable, what about a /28 mask?

- 192.168.1.0/28 = 16 subnets—14 hosts
  You can refer back to the Subnetting Secrets cheat sheet design section to help you work out how to apply VLSM to your network or to an exam question. With the /26 mask, you can see how many subnets and hosts you will get.

Bits	128	64	32	16	8	4	2	1
Subnets	✔	✔						
128	✔							
192	✔							
224								
240								
248								
252								
254								
255								
	Subnets	Hosts -2						
2	✔	✔						
4	✔	✔						
8		✔						
16		✔						
32		✔						
64		✔						

You have to take away 2 bits for the hosts, so you get four subnets, each with 62 hosts.

Slicing Down Networks

The point of VLSM is to take your network block and make it work for your particular network needs.

Taking the typical network address of 192.168.1.0/24 you can, with VLSM, use a /26 mask and now do this:

192.168.1.0/26	Subnet	Hosts
192.168.1.0	1	62
192.168.1.64—IN USE	2	62
192.168.1.128—IN USE	3	62
192.168.1.192—IN USE	4	62

This may work fine until you realise that you have two smaller networks on your infrastructure which require 30 hosts each. What if three of your smaller subnets are taken (marked as IN USE above) and you have only one left (192.168.1.0, in fact)? VLSM lets you take any of your chopped down subnets and chop them down further. The only rule is that any IP address can be used only once, no matter which mask it has.

If you use the design section of the Subnetting Secrets cheat sheet, you will see which mask gives you 30 hosts.

	Subnets	Hosts -2						
2	✔	✔						
4	✔	✔						
8	✔	✔						
16		✔						
32		✔						
64								

The upper section of the chart shows that three ticks down on the left column gives you a mask of 224 or /27 (3 stolen bits).

192.168.1.0/27	Subnet	Hosts
192.168.1.0	1	30
192.168.1.32	2	30
192.168.1.64	CAN'T USE	CAN'T USE

You can't use the .64 subnet because this is already in use. You are now free to use either of the other two subnets. If you needed only one, you could chop down the remaining one to give you more subnets, each with fewer hosts.

Please also read Appendix B - VLSM

DAY 11 QUESTIONS

1. Starting with 192.168.1.0/24 you can, with VLSM, use a /26 mask and generate which subnets?

DAY 12

Router Architecture

DAY 12 TASKS

- Read today's theory notes
- Review yesterday's theory notes
- Complete the lab(s) of your choice
- Read the CCENT cram guide
- Spend 15 minutes on the subnetting.org website

By architecture, we are referring to the components which go into making the router and how they are used during the router booting process. This is all fundamental stuff to a Cisco CCNA engineer who needs to know what the various types of memory do and how to backup or manipulate them using IOS commands.

Today you will learn about the following:

- Router memory and files
- Managing the IOS

This lesson maps to the following CCNA syllabus requirements:

- Describe the operation of Cisco routers (including router boot up process, POST, and router components)
- Manage IOS configuration files (including save, edit, upgrade, and restore)
- Manage Cisco IOS

Router Memory and Files

Figure 12.1 below illustrates the main memory components inside the router. Each type of memory performs a different role and contains different files:

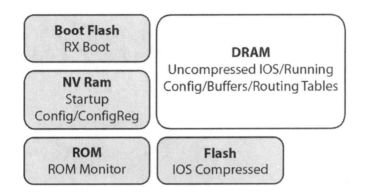

FIG 12.1—Router Memory Components

You can usually see memory banks inside the router when the cover is removed. You can often also see flash memory cards inserted into router slots.

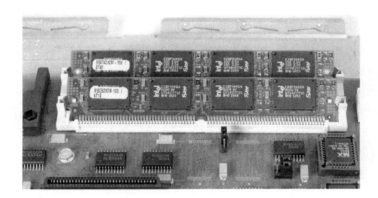

FIG 12.2—DRAM SIMMs on a Router Motherboard

Here is what each memory and file type does:

Boot ROM—EEPROM for startup diagram/Rommon and loads IOS. When the router boots, if no IOS file is present, it will boot into an emergency mode called Rommon, which allows some limited commands to be entered to recover the router and load another IOS. This is known as bootstrap mode and you can recognise it with either of the router prompts below:

```
>
Rommon>
```

NVRAM—Stores router startup configuration and configuration register. The startup configuration is the file used to store the saved router configuration. It is not erased when the router reloads.

Flash/PCMCIA—Contains IOS and some configuration files. Flash memory is also referred to as EEPROM, and Cisco IOS is usually stored here in a compressed form. You can in fact have more than one version of Cisco IOS on flash memory if there is room.

DRAM—Also known as RAM, it stores full IOS, running configuration, and routing tables. This is the working memory, which is erased upon the router being rebooted.

ROM Monitor—System diagnostics and startup. The ROM monitor has a very small code in it to check for attached memory and interfaces.

RxBoot—Mini-IOS, allows for an upload of full IOS. It is also known as the boot loader and can be used to perform some router maintenance activities.

Router Configuration—Although not strictly a router component, it is stored in NVRAM and pulled into DRAM on boot up. You put commands from DRAM into NVRAM with the `copy run start` command, while you put files from NVRAM into DRAM with the `copy start run` command.

The Configuration Register—Sets instructions for booting. It is critical that you understand this because you will need to manipulate the configuration register on routers for use in labs (i.e., boot clean with no configuration) or to perform a password recovery. Some models differ but the two most common settings are as follows:

Boot and ignore startup configuration—0x2142

Boot normally—0x2102

```
Router(config)#config-register 0x2102
```

You can see the current configuration register setting with a `show version` command:

```
Router#show version
Cisco Internetwork Operating System Software
IOS (tm) 2500 Software (C2500-JS-L), Version 12.1(17), RELEASE SOFTWARE (fc1)
Copyright (c) 1986-2002 by Cisco Systems, Inc.
Compiled Wed 04-Sep-02 03:08 by kellythw Image text-base: 0x03073F40, data-base:
0x00001000
```

```
ROM: System Bootstrap, Version 11.0(10c)XB2, PLATFORM SPECIFIC RELEASE SOFTWARE
(fc1)
BOOTLDR: 3000 Bootstrap Software (IGS-BOOT-R), Version 11.0(10c)XB2, PLATFORM
SPECIFIC RELEASE SOFTWARE (fc1)

Router uptime is 12 minutes
System returned to ROM by reload
System image file is "flash:c2500-js-1.121-17.bin"

Cisco 2500 (68030) processor (revision L) with 14336K/2048K bytes of memory.
Processor board ID 01760497, with hardware revision 00000000 Bridging software.
X.25 software, Version 3.0.0.
SuperLAT software (copyright 1990 by Meridian Technology Corp).
TN3270 Emulation software.
2 Ethernet/IEEE 802.3 interface(s)
2 Serial network interface(s)
32K bytes of non-volatile configuration memory.
16384K bytes of processor board System flash (Read ONLY)


Configuration register is 0x2102
```

And the same command will display the various types of memory on the router:

```
Router#show version Cisco Internetwork Operating System Software IOS (tm)
2500 Software (C2500-IS-L), Version 12.2(4)T1, RELEASE SOFTWARE Copyright
(c) 1986-2001 by Cisco Systems, Inc.
ROM: System Bootstrap, Version 11.0(10c), SOFTWARE  ← ROM code
BOOTLDR: 3000 Bootstrap Software (IGS-BOOT-R), Version 11.0(10c)
System image file is "flash:c2500-is-1_122-4_T1.bin"  ← Flash image
Cisco 2522 (68030) processor  CPU  ← CPU
with 14336K/2048K bytes of memory.  ← DRAM Processor board ID 18086064, with
hardware revision 00000003
32K bytes of non-volatile configuration memory.  ← NVRAM
16384K bytes of processor System flash (Read ONLY)  ← EEPROM/FLASH
```

Here is a graphical representation of the router booting process:

ROM Monitor
System diagnostics, check config register, test hardware & interfaces
Boots RX Boot image or goes into *Rommon>*

RX Boot
Sets up interfaces and loads full IOS or goes into *Router(boot)>*

Cisco IOS
Allocates buffers, loads startup config, goes into *Router>*

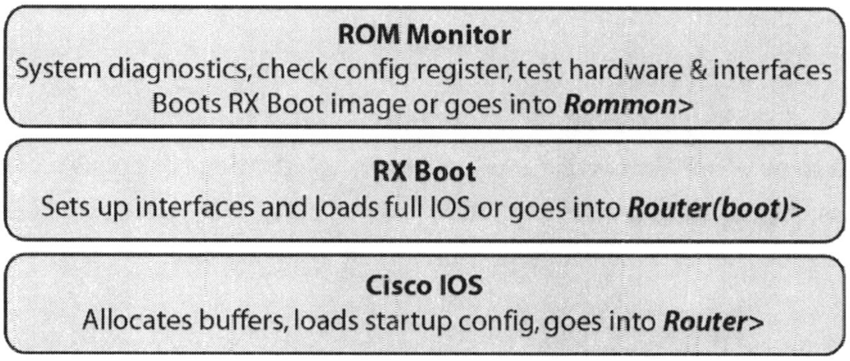

FIG 12.3—Router Booting Process

Managing the IOS

Many a network disaster could have been avoided with simple router and switch housekeeping. If your router configuration file is important to you and your business, then you should back it up.

If you are happy that the current running configuration of the router is going to be your working version, then you can copy this into NVRAM with the `copy run start` command.

In order to save the router configuration, you need to have a PC or server on your network running TFTP server software. You can download this free software from companies such as Solarwinds. The same process is used to upgrade the flash image.

Router configurations can be moved around the router or stored on a PC or server on the network. The running configuration on the router is stored in DRAM. Any changes to the configuration will remain in DRAM and will be lost if the router is reloaded for any reason.

You can copy the configuration onto a PC or server running TFTP server software (see the TFTP lab for more details):

```
Router(config)#copy startup-config tftp:   ← You need to include the colon
```

You can also copy your IOS to a TFTP server. You must always do this if you are updating the router IOS to a newer version just in case of issues with the new version (often, network administrators try to fit a file onto the router which is too big for the installed memory).

```
Router(config)#copy flash tftp:
```

The router will prompt you for the IP address of the TFTP server, which I recommend you have in the same subnet as your router. If you want to reverse the process, then you simply reverse the commands:

```
Router(config)#copy tftp flash:
```

The issue with these commands is that most engineers use them only a couple of times a year or when there has been a network disaster. Usually, you will find that your Internet access has also gone down with your network, so you have to do this all from memory!

I strongly recommend that you do some backup and restoring of your configurations and IOS on your home network. In addition, check out my recovery lab on YouTube: www.youtube.com/user/paulwbrowning

You can view the flash filename with the `show version` command or the `show flash` command, or you can drill down into the flash with the `dir flash:` command and this will show you all the files present in flash memory:

```
RouterA#show flash
System flash directory:
File      Length         Name/status
1         14692012          c2500-js-1.121-17.bin
[14692076 bytes used, 2085140 available, 16777216 total]
16384K bytes of processor board System flash (Read ONLY)
```

I would like to dwell on this subject in more detail, but you should focus on the CCNA exam and your daily tasks. Disaster recovery should be on your list of stuff to research and lab up, though.

Booting Options

There are several options available when the router boots. Usually, there is one IOS image in flash memory so the router will boot using that. You may have more than one image, or the image may be too big for the flash memory to hold, so you might prefer the router to boot from a TFTP server on the network which holds the IOS.

The commands differ slightly, depending upon which boot options you want to configure. Try all of the options on a live router.

```
RouterA(config)#boot system ?
WORD           TFTP filename or URL
flash          Boot from flash memory
mop            Boot from a Decnet MOP server
ftp            Boot from server via ftp
```

```
mop          Boot from a Decnet MOP server
rcp          Boot from server via rcp
tftp         Boot from tftp server
```

For flash:

```
RouterB(config)#boot system flash ? WORD System image filename <cr>
```

For TFTP:

```
Enter configuration commands, one per line. End with CNTL/Z.
RouterB(config)#boot system tftp: c2500-js-1.121-17.bin ? Hostname or
A.B.C.D Address from which to download the file <cr>
RouterB(config)#boot system tftp:
```

DAY 12 QUESTIONS

1. Which files would you usually find in DRAM?
2. Where is the compressed IOS held?
3. You want to boot the router and skip the startup configuration. Which configuration register setting do you require?
4. Which command puts the running configuration into NVRAM?
5. Which command will copy your startup configuration onto a network server?
6. You want to boot your router from a network server holding the IOS. Which command will achieve this?

DAY 13

Routing RIPv2

DAY 13 TASKS

- Read today's theory notes
- Review yesterday's theory notes
- Complete today's lab
- Read the CCENT cram guide
- Spend 15 minutes on the subnetting.org website

The CCENT exam requires you to have an understanding of basic routing and how Routing Information Protocol version 2 (RIPv2) works, as well as how to configure it. RIP is rarely used nowadays, but it does the job well and is a good introduction to routing protocols.

Today you will learn about the following:

- Basic routing
- Classful and classless protocols
- Routing protocol classes
- RIP
- RIPv2
- Configuring RIPv2
- Troubleshooting RIPv2

This lesson maps to the following CCNA syllabus requirements:

- Describe basic routing concepts (including packet forwarding and the router lookup process)
- Configure, verify, and troubleshoot RIPv2

Basic Routing

The role of routing protocols is to learn about other networks dynamically, exchange routing information with other devices, and connect internal and/or external networks.

It is important to note that routing protocols DO NOT send packets across the network. Their role is to determine the best path for routing. Routed protocols actually send the data, and the most common example of a routed protocol is IP.

Different routing protocols use different means of determining the best or most optimal path to a network or network node. Some types of routing protocols work best in static environments or environments with few or no changes, but it might take a long time to converge when changes to those environments are made. Other routing protocols, however, respond very quickly to changes in the network and can converge rapidly.

Network convergence occurs when all routers in the network have the same view and agree on optimal routes. When convergence takes a long time to occur, intermittent packet loss and loss of connectivity may be experienced between remote networks. In addition to these problems, slow convergence can result in network routing loops and outright network outages. Convergence is determined by the routing protocol algorithm used.

Because routing protocols have different characteristics, they differ in their scalability and performance. Some routing protocols are suitable only for small networks, while others may be used in small, medium, and large networks.

Administrative Distance

Administrative distance is used to determine the reliability of one source of routing information from another. Some sources are considered more reliable than others are; therefore, administrative distance can be used to determine the best or preferred path to a destination network or network node when there are two or more different paths to the same destination from two or more different routing protocols.

In Cisco IOS software, all sources of routing information are assigned a default administrative distance value. This default value is an integer between 0 and 255, with a value of 0 assigned to the most reliable source of information and a value of 255 assigned to the least reliable source of information. Any routes that are assigned an administrative distance value of 255 are considered untrusted and will not be placed into the routing table.

The administrative distance is a locally significant value that affects only the local router. This value is not propagated throughout the routing domain. Therefore, manually adjusting the default administrative distance for a routing source or routing sources on a router affects the preference of routing information sources only on that router. Table 13.1 below shows the default administrative values used in Cisco IOS software:

TABLE 13.1—Router Administrative Distances

Route Source	AD
Connected Interfaces	0
Static Routes	1
Enhanced Interior Gateway Routing Protocol (EIGRP) Summary Routes	5
External Border Gateway Protocol (eBGP) Routes	20
Internal Enhanced Interior Gateway Routing Protocol (EIGRP) Routes	90
Open Shortest Path First (OSPF) Internal and External Routes	110
Intermediate System-to-Intermediate System (IS-IS) Internal and External Routes	115
Routing Information Protocol (RIP) Routes	120
Exterior Gateway Protocol (EGP) Routes	140
On-Demand Routing (ODR) Routes	160
External Enhanced Interior Gateway Routing Protocol (EIGRP) Routes	170
Internal Border Gateway Protocol (iBGP) Routes	200
Unreachable or Unknown Routes	255

The default route source administrative distance is displayed in the output of the show ip protocols command. This is illustrated in the following output:

```
R1#show ip protocols
Routing Protocol is "isis"
  Invalid after 0 seconds, hold down 0, flushed after 0
  Outgoing update filter list for all interfaces is not set
  Incoming update filter list for all interfaces is not set
  Redistributing: isis
  Address Summarization:
    None
  Maximum path: 4
  Routing for Networks:
    Serial0/0
  Routing Information Sources:
    Gateway         Distance      Last Update
    10.0.0.2              115      00:06:53
  Distance: (default is 115)
```

Routing protocol algorithms use metrics, which are numerical values that are associated with specific routes. These values are used to prioritise or prefer routes learned by the routing protocol, from the most preferred to the least preferred. In essence, the lower the route metric, the more preferred the route by the routing protocol. The route with the lowest metric is typically the route with the least cost or the best route to the destination network. This route will be placed into the routing table and will be used to forward packets to the destination network.

Different routing algorithms use different variables to compute the route metric. Some routing algorithms use only a single variable, while other advanced routing protocols may use more than one variable to determine the metric for a particular route. In most cases, the metrics that are computed by one routing protocol are incompatible with those used by other routing protocols. The different routing protocol metrics may be based on one or more of the following:

- Bandwidth
- Cost
- Delay
- Load
- Path length
- Reliability

Bandwidth

The term bandwidth refers to the amount of data that can be carried from one point to another in a given period. Routing algorithms may use bandwidth to determine which link type is preferred over another. For example, a routing algorithm might prefer a GigabitEthernet link to a FastEthernet link because of the increased capacity of the GigabitEthernet link over the FastEthernet link.

In Cisco IOS software, the `bandwidth interface` configuration command can be used to adjust the default bandwidth value for an interface, effectively manipulating the selection of one interface against another by a routing algorithm. For example, if the FastEthernet interface was configured with the `bandwidth 1000000 interface` configuration command, both the FastEthernet and the GigabitEthernet links would appear to have the same capacity to the routing algorithm and would be assigned the same metric value. The fact that one of the links is actually a FastEthernet interface while the other is actually a GigabitEthernet link is irrelevant to the routing protocol.

From a network administrator's point of view, it is important to understand that the `bandwidth` command does not affect the physical capability of the interface. In other words, configuring the higher bandwidth on the FastEthernet interface does not mean that it is capable of supporting

GigabitEthernet speeds. Open Shortest Path First (OSPF) and Enhanced Interior Gateway Routing Protocol (EIGRP) use bandwidth in metric calculations.

Cost

The cost, as it pertains to routing algorithms, refers to communication cost. The cost may be used when, for example, a company prefers to route across private links rather than public links that include monetary charges for sending data across them or for the usage time. Intermediate System-to-Intermediate System (IS-IS) supports an optional expense metric that measures the monetary cost of link utilisation.

Delay

There are many types of delay, all of which affect different types of traffic. In general, delay refers to the length of time required to move a packet from source to destination through the internetwork. In Cisco IOS software, the interface delay value is in microseconds (μs).

The interface value is configured using the `delay interface` configuration command. When you configure the interface delay value, it is important to remember that this does not affect traffic. For example, configuring a delay value of 5000 does not mean that traffic sent out of that interface will have an additional delay of 5000. Table 13.2 below shows the default delay values for common interfaces in Cisco IOS software:

Table 13.2—Interface Delay Values

Interface Type	Delay (μs)
10Mbps Ethernet	1000
FastEthernet	100
GigabitEthernet	10
T1 Serial	20000

EIGRP uses the interface delay value as part of its metric calculation. Manually adjusting the interface delay value results in the re-computation of the EIGRP metric.

Load

The term load means different things to different people. For example, in general computing terminology, load refers to the amount of work a resource, such as the CPU, is performing. Load, as it applies in this context, refers to the degree of use for a particular router interface. The load on the interface is a fraction of 255. For example, a load of 255/255 indicates that the interface is completely saturated, while a load of 128/255 indicates that the interface is 50% saturated. By default, the load is calculated as an average over a period of five minutes. The interface load value can be used by EIGRP in its metric calculation.

Path Length

The path length metric is the total length of the path that is traversed from the local router to the destination network. Different routing algorithms represent this in different forms. For example, Routing Information Protocol (RIP) counts all intermediate routers (hops) between the local router and the destination network and uses the hop count as the metric, while Border Gateway Protocol (BGP) counts the number of traversed autonomous systems between the local router and the destination network and uses the autonomous system count to select the best path.

Reliability

Like load, the term reliability means different things depending upon the context in which it is used. Here, unless stated otherwise, it should always be assumed that reliability refers to the dependability of network links or interfaces. In Cisco IOS software, the reliability of a link or interface is represented as a fraction of 255. For example, a reliability value of 255/255 indicates the interface is 100% reliable. Similar to the interface load, by default the reliability of an interface is calculated as an average over a period of five minutes.

Prefix Matching

Cisco routers use the longest prefix match rule when determining which of the routes placed into the routing table should be used to forward traffic to a destination network or node. Longer, or more specific, routing table entries are preferred over less specific entries, such as summary addresses, when determining which entry to use to route traffic to the intended destination network or node.

The longest prefix or the most specific route will be used to route traffic to the destination network or node, regardless of the administrative distance of the route source, or even the routing protocol metric assigned to the prefix if multiple overlapping prefixes are learned via the same routing protocol. Table 13.3 below illustrates the order of route selection on a router sending packets to the address 1.1.1.1. This order is based on the longest prefix match lookup:

Table 13.3—Matching the Longest Prefix

Routing Table Entry	Order Used
1.1.1.1/32	First
1.1.1.0/24	Second
1.1.0.0/16	Third
1.0.0.0/8	Fourth
0.0.0.0/0	Fifth

NOTE: Although the default route is listed last in the route selection order in Table 13.3, keep in mind that a default route is not always present in the routing table. If that is the case, and no other entries to the address 1.1.1.1 exist, packets to that destination are simply discarded by the router. In most cases, the router will send the source host an ICMP message indicting that the destination is unreachable.

Building the IP Routing Table

Without a populated routing table, or Routing Information Base (RIB), that contains entries for remote networks, routers will not be able to forward packets to those remote networks. The routing table may include specific network entries or simply a single default route. The information in the routing table is used by the forwarding process to forward traffic to the destination network or host. The routing table itself does not actually forward traffic.

Cisco routers use the administrative distance, routing protocol metric, and the prefix length to determine which routes will actually be placed into the routing table, which allows the router to build the routing table. The routing table is built via the following general steps:

1. If the route entry does not currently exist in the routing table, add it to the routing table.
2. If the route entry is more specific than an existing route, add it to the routing table. It should also be noted that the less specific entry is still retained in the routing table.
3. If the route entry is the same as an existing one, but it is received from a more preferred route source, replace the old entry with the new entry.
4. If the route entry is the same as an existing one, and it is received from the same protocol, then:
   i. Discard the new route if the metric is higher than the existing route; or
   ii. Replace the existing route if the metric of the new route is lower; or
   iii. Use both routes for load balancing if the metric for both routes is the same.

When building the RIB by default, the routing protocol with the lowest administrative distance value will always be chosen when the router is determining which routes to place into the routing table. For example, if a router receives the 10.0.0.0/8 prefix via external EIGRP, OSPF, and internal BGP, the OSPF route will be placed into the routing table. If that route is removed or is no longer received, the external EIGRP route will be placed into the routing table. Finally, if both the OSPF and the external EIGRP routes are no longer present, the internal BGP route is used.

Once routes have been placed into the routing table, by default the most specific or longest match prefix will always be preferred over less specific routes. This is illustrated in the following example, which shows a routing table that contains entries for the 80.0.0.0/8, 80.1.0.0/16, and 80.1.1.0/24 prefixes. These three route prefixes are received via the EIGRP, OSPF, and RIP routing protocols, respectively.

```
R1#show ip route
Codes: C - connected, S - static, R - RIP, M - mobile, B - BGP
       D - EIGRP, EX - EIGRP external, O - OSPF, IA - OSPF inter area
       N1 - OSPF NSSA external type 1, N2 - OSPF NSSA external type 2
       E1 - OSPF external type 1, E2 - OSPF external type 2
       i - IS-IS, L1 - IS-IS level-1, L2 - IS-IS level-2, ia - IS-IS inter
       area
       * - candidate default, U - per-user static route, o - ODR
       P - periodic downloaded static route

Gateway of last resort is not set
R        80.1.1.0/24 [120/1] via 10.1.1.2, 00:00:04, Ethernet0/0.1
D        80.0.0.0/8 [90/281600] via 10.1.1.2, 00:02:02, Ethernet0/0.1
O E2     80.1.0.0/16 [110/20] via 10.1.1.2, 00:00:14, Ethernet0/0.1
```

Referencing the output shown above, the first route is 80.1.1.0/24. This route is learned via RIP and therefore has a default administrative distance value of 120. The second route is 80.0.0.0/8. This route is learned via internal EIGRP and therefore has a default administrative distance value of 90. The third route is 80.1.0.0/16. This route is learned via OSPF and is an external OSPF route that has an administrative distance of 110.

NOTE: Because the routing protocol metrics are different, they are a non-factor in determining the best route to use when routes from multiple protocols are installed into the routing table. The following section will describe how Cisco IOS routers build the routing table.

Based on the contents of this routing table, if the router received a packet destined to 80.1.1.1, it would use the RIP route because this is the most specific entry, even though both EIGRP and OSPF have better administrative distance values and are therefore more preferred route sources. The show ip route 80.1.1.1 command illustrated below can be used to verify this statement:

```
R1#show ip route 80.1.1.1
Routing entry for 80.1.1.0/24
  Known via "rip", distance 120, metric 1
  Redistributing via rip
  Last update from 10.1.1.2 on Ethernet0/0.1, 00:00:15 ago
  Routing Descriptor Blocks:
  * 10.1.1.2, from 10.1.1.2, 00:00:15 ago, via Ethernet0/0.1
      Route metric is 1, traffic share count is 1
```

Classful and Classless Protocols

Classful protocols can't use VLSM (i.e., RIP and IGRP). This is because they don't recognise anything other than default network masks:

```
Router#debug ip rip
RIP protocol debugging is on
01:26:59: RIP: sending v1 update to 255.255.255.255 via Loopback0
192.168.1.1
```

Classless protocols use VLSM (i.e., RIPv2 and EIGRP):

```
Router#debug ip rip
RIP protocol debugging is on
01:29:15: RIP: received v2 update from 172.16.1.2 on Serial0
01:29:15:192.168.2.0/24 via 0.0.0.0
```

Routing Protocol Classes

There are two major classes of routing protocols—Distance Vector and Link State. Distance Vector routing protocols traditionally use a one-dimensional vector when determining the most optimal path(s) through the network, while Link State routing protocols use the Shortest Path First (SPF) when determining the most optimal path(s) through the network. Before delving into the specifics of these two classes of routing protocols, we will first take a look at vectors, as well as at the elusive SPF algorithm.

Understanding Vectors

A one-dimensional vector is a directed quantity. It is simply a quantity (number) in a particular direction or course. The vector concept is illustrated in Figure 13.1 below:

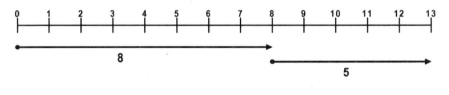

FIG 13.1—Understanding Vectors

Referencing Figure 13.1, the first line starts at 0 and ends at 8, and the second line begins at 8 and ends at 13. The vector for the first line is 8, while the vector for the second line is 5. Using basic math, we know that 8 + 5 = 13. The starting and ending points of the vector are not relevant. Instead, the only thing that actually matters is how long the vector is and how far it travels.

NOTE: Vectors can also travel in the opposite direction (i.e., they represent negative numbers).

The Shortest Path First Algorithm

The SPF algorithm creates a shortest-path tree to all hosts in an area or in the network backbone, with the router that is performing the calculation at the root of that tree. In order for the SPF algorithm to work in the correct manner, all routers in the area should have the same database information. In OSPF, this is performed via the database exchange process.

Distance Vector Routing Protocols

Distance Vector is a routing protocol that uses distance or hop count as its primary metric for determining the best forwarding path. Distance Vector routing protocols are primarily based on the Bellman-Ford algorithm. Distance Vector routing protocols periodically send their neighbour routers copies of their entire routing tables to keep them up to date on the state of the network. While this may be acceptable in a small network, it increases the amount of traffic that is sent across networks as the size of the network grows. All Distance Vector routing protocols share the following characteristics:

- Counting to infinity
- Split horizon
- Poison reverse
- Hold-down timers

Utilising the counting to infinity characteristic, if a destination network is farther than the maximum number of hops allowed for that routing protocol, the network would be considered unreachable. The network entry would therefore not be installed into the IP routing table.

Split horizon mandates that routing information cannot be sent back out of the same interface through which it was received. This prevents the re-advertising of information back to the source from which it was learned. While this characteristic is a great loop prevention mechanism, it is also a significant drawback, especially in hub-and-spoke networks.

Poison reverse (or route poisoning) expands on split horizon. When used in conjunction with split horizon, poison reverse allows the networks to be advertised back out of the same interface on which were received. However, poison reverse causes the router to advertise these networks back to the sending router with a metric of 'unreachable' so that the router that receives those entries will not add them back into its routing table.

Hold-down timers are used to prevent networks that were previously advertised as down from being placed back into the routing table. When a router receives an update that a network is down, it begins its hold-down timer. This timer tells the router to wait for a specific amount of time before accepting any changes to the status of that network.

During the hold-down period, the router suppresses the network and prevents advertising false information. The router also does not route to the unreachable network, even if it receives information from another router (that may not have received the triggered update) that the network is reachable. This mechanism is designed to prevent black-holing traffic.

The two most common Distance Vector routing protocols are RIP and IGRP. EIGRP is an advanced Distance Vector routing protocol, using features from both Distance Vector and Link State.

Link State Routing Protocols

Link State routing protocols are hierarchical routing protocols that use the concept of areas to logically group routers within a network. This allows Link State protocols to scale better and operate in a more efficient manner than Distance Vector routing protocols. Routers running Link State routing protocols create a database that comprises the complete topology of the network. This allows all routers within the same area to have the same view of the network.

Because all routers in the network have the same view of the network, the most optimal paths are used for forwarding packets between networks and the possibility of routing loops is eliminated. Therefore, techniques such as split horizon and route poisoning do not apply to Link State routing protocols as they do to Distance Vector routing protocols.

Link State routing protocols operate by sending Link State Advertisements or Link State Packets to all other routers within the same area. These packets include information on attached interfaces, metrics, and other variables. As the routers accumulate this information, they run the SPF algorithm and calculate the shortest (best) path to each router and destination network.

Using the received Link State information, routers build the Link State Database (LSDB). When the LSDBs of two neighbouring routers are synchronised, the routers are said to be adjacent.

Unlike Distance Vector routing protocols, which send their neighbours their entire routing table, Link State routing protocols send incremental updates when a change in the network topology is detected, which makes them more efficient in larger networks. The use of incremental updates also allows Link State routing protocols to respond much faster to network changes and thus converge in a shorter amount of time than Distance Vector routing protocols. Table 13.4 below lists the different Interior Gateway Protocols (IGPs) and their classification:

Table 13.4 - IGP Classification

Protocol Name	Classful/Classless	Protocol Classification
RIP (version 1)	Classful	Distance Vector
IGRP	Classful	Distance Vector
RIP (version 2)	Classless	Distance Vector
EIGRP	Classless	Advanced Distance Vector
IS-IS	Classless	Link State
OSPF	Classless	Link State

The Objectives of Routing Protocols

Routing algorithms, while different in nature, all have the same basic objectives. While some algorithms are better than others are, all routing protocols have their advantages and disadvantages. Routing algorithms are designed with the following objectives and goals:

- Optimal routing
- Stability
- Ease of use
- Flexibility
- Rapid convergence

Optimal Routing

One of the primary goals of all routing protocols is to select the most optimal path through the network from the source subnet or host to the destination subnet or host. The most optimal route depends upon the metrics used by the routing protocols. A route that may be considered the best by one protocol may not necessarily be the most optimal route from the perspective of another protocol. For example, RIP might consider a path that is only two hops long as the most optimal path to a destination network, even though the links were 64Kbps links, while advanced protocols such as OSPF and EIGRP might determine that the most optimal path to that same destination is the one traversing four routers but using 10Gbps links.

Stability

Network stability, or a lack thereof, is another major objective for routing algorithms. Routing algorithms should be stable enough to accommodate unforeseen network events, such as hardware failures and even incorrect implementations. While this is typically a characteristic of all routing algorithms, the manner and time in which they respond to such events makes some better than others and thus more preferred in modern-day networks.

Ease of Use

Routing algorithms are designed to be as simple as possible. In addition to providing the capability to support complex internetwork deployments, routing protocols should take into consideration the resources required to run the algorithm. Some routing algorithms require more hardware or software resources (e.g., CPU and memory) to run than others do; however, they are capable of providing more functionality than alternative simple algorithms.

Flexibility

In addition to providing routing functionality, routing algorithms should also be feature-rich, allowing them to support the different requirements encountered in different networks. It should be noted that this capability typically comes at the expense of other features, such as convergence, which is described next.

Rapid Convergence

Rapid convergence is another primary objective of all routing algorithms. As stated earlier, convergence occurs when all routers in the network have the same view and agree on optimal routes. When convergence takes a long time to occur, intermittent packet loss and loss of connectivity may be experienced between remote networks. In addition to these problems, slow convergence can result in network routing loops and outright network outages.

Routing Information Protocol (RIP)

RIP was one of the earliest routing protocols developed for use on internetworks. RIP is a Distance Vector protocol and the first version of the protocol (version 1) is classful, so it doesn't recognise VLSM. RIP sends broadcast messages in order to advertise its routing table to neighbour routers. RIP uses hop counts as a metric, and the maximum for version 1 is 15, with the sixteenth hop considered unreachable.

Bear in mind that RIP was developed in 1988, when the size and requirements of today's networks were considered impossible.

RIP uses the following timers:

- Routing table sent—every 30 seconds
- Expires learned routes—after 180 seconds
- Flushes routes—after 240 seconds
- Cisco hold-down timer—begins after 180 seconds

Routing updates are sent using UDP with a destination port of 520.

You should not be asked about the first version of RIP in the CCNA exam, but because RIPv2 is an extension of RIP, you need to have an understanding of it.

RIPv2

Designed to overcome some of the shortfalls of RIP, RIPv2 is classless and supports VLSM. MD5 authentication is built into RIPv2, which, instead of broadcasting routing tables (as RIP does), sends them via multicast over IP address 224.0.0.9. RIPv2 can be used on networks running RIP with some minor additional commands. The hop count limitation of 15 remains.

Configuring RIPv2

To configure RIPv2, follow these three steps:

1. Enable RIP on the router.
2. Add the `version 2` command.
3. Add the networks you want to advertise.

```
Router(config)#router rip
Router(config-router)#version 2
Router(config-router)#network 172.16.1.0
```

RIPv2 will auto-summarise networks at network boundaries, which means that if you have subnetted your network and, for example, the advertising networks are 172.16.1.4/30, 172.16.1.8/30, and 172.16.1.12/30, then your router will summarise this to 172.16.0.0/16, which is the default subnet mask.

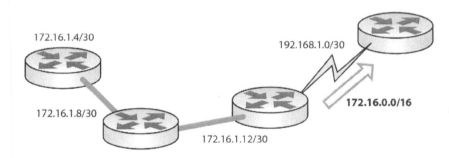

FIG 13.2—RIP Auto-summarises at Major Network Boundaries

In order to change the default behaviour, you need to add the `no auto-summary` command at the `Router(config-router)#` prompt. Just bear in mind that if you have 172.16.x.x networks on the other side of a WAN connection (i.e., discontiguous networks), then auto-summary may cause issues. The flip side of this is if you don't need to send every single subnet address out of your router, then why would you?

If you want all the 172.16 networks to be advertised, then just add the 172.16.0.0 network to the configuration; you don't need to type each subnet individually.

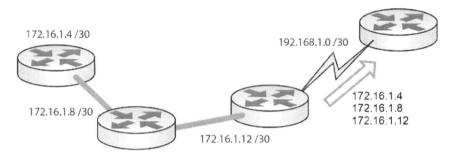

172.16.1.4 /30

192.168.1.0 /30

172.16.1.8 /30

172.16.1.4
172.16.1.8
172.16.1.12

172.16.1.12 /30

FIG 13.3—The No Auto-Summary Command Lets the Router Advertise all Subnets

Here is a sample RIPv2 network configuration. Please try this out on some routers, you will need to add the IP addresses to your interfaces:

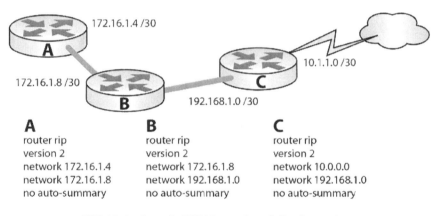

172.16.1.4 /30

A

10.1.1.0 /30

172.16.1.8 /30

B

192.168.1.0 /30

C

A	B	C
router rip	router rip	router rip
version 2	version 2	version 2
network 172.16.1.4	network 172.16.1.8	network 10.0.0.0
network 172.16.1.8	network 192.168.1.0	network 192.168.1.0
no auto-summary	no auto-summary	no auto-summary

FIG 13.4—Sample RIP Network and Configurations

Troubleshooting RIP

Issues with RIP are often due to shut interfaces, incorrectly configured networks or forgetting to advertise the connected network.

The three main RIP troubleshooting commands are as follows:

```
show ip protocols
show ip route
debug ip rip
```

I have underlined some of the important parts of the show/debug outputs in the configuration below:

```
RouterA#show ip protocols
Routing Protocol is "rip"
Sending updates every 30 seconds, next due in 18 seconds
Invalid after 180 seconds, hold down 180, flushed after 240

Default version control: send version 1, receive any version

Interface Send
Loopback0 1
Serial0   1
Automatic network summarization is in effect
Maximum path: 4
Routing for Networks:
172.16.0.0
192.168.1.0
Routing Information Sources:
Gateway   Distance
172.16.1.2      120
Distance: (default is 120)
RouterA#show ip route
Codes: C - connected, S - static, I - IGRP, R - RIP, M - mobile, B - BGP
D - EIGRP, EX - EIGRP external, O - OSPF, IA - OSPF inter area
N1 - OSPF NSSA external type 1, N2 - OSPF NSSA external type 2
E1 - OSPF external type 1, E2 - OSPF external type 2, E - EGP
i - IS-IS, L1 - IS-IS level-1,L2 - IS-IS level-2,ia - IS-IS inter-area
* - candidate default, U - per-user static route, o - ODR
P - periodic downloaded static route

Gateway of last resort is not set

C      172.16.0.0/16 is directly connected, Loopback0
C      172.20.0.0/16 is directly connected, Loopback1
R      172.31.0.0/16 [120/1] is possibly down
C      192.168.1.0 is directly connected, Serial0
Router#debug ip rip
RIP protocol debugging is on
01:29:15: RIP: received v2 update from 172.16.1.2 on Serial0
01:29:15:192.168.2.0/24 via 0.0.0.0 in 1 hops
01:29:40: RIP: sending v2 update to 224.0.0.9 via Loopback0 192.168.1.1
01:29:40: RIP: build update entries
01:29:40: 172.16.0.0/16 via 0.0.0.0, metric 1, tag 0
01:29:40: 192.168.2.0/24 via 0.0.0.0, metric 2, tag 0
```

DAY 13 QUESTIONS

1. Routing protocols send packets across the network. True or false?
2. What is the administrative distance for RIP, OSPF, and internal EIGRP?
3. The lower the route metric, the more preferred the route by the routing protocol. True or false?
4. Name the six most common routing metrics.
5. Cisco routers use the _____ prefix match rule when determining which of the routes placed into the routing table should be used to forward traffic to a destination network or node.
6. Name two classless routing protocols.
7. Explain the split horizon rule.
8. Which commands will enable RIPv2 on your router and advertise network 172.16.1.0?

DAY 13 LAB—RIPV2

Topology

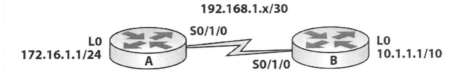

192.168.1.x/30
S0/1/0
LO
172.16.1.1/24   A   S0/1/0   B   LO
10.1.1.1/10

Purpose

Learn how to configure RIPv2 and see how auto-summarisation works.

Walkthrough

1. Apply the IP addresses to the interfaces as per the topology. For the Serial interfaces, you have a /30 mask, giving you .1 to apply to Router A and .2 to apply to Router B. The /24 mask you should know, and the /10 mask you can work out from the Subnetting Secrets cheat sheet.

2. Ping across the Serial interface. If your ping doesn't work, ensure you have applied the clock rate to the DCE and have issued the no shut command on each side.

3. Configure RIPv2 on each router. Advertise the connected network as well as the networks on the Loopbacks; otherwise, your routing won't work!

```
RouterA(config)#
RouterA(config)#router rip
RouterA(config-router)#version 2
RouterA(config-router)#net 172.16.0.0
RouterA(config-router)#net 192.168.1.0
RouterA(config-router)#
RouterA(config-router)#^Z
RouterA#
RouterA#show ip protocols
Routing Protocol is "rip"
Sending updates every 30 seconds, next due in 27 seconds
Invalid after 180 seconds, hold down 180, flushed after 240
Outgoing update filter list for all interfaces is not set
Incoming update filter list for all interfaces is not set
Redistributing: rip
Default version control: send version 2, receive 2
   Interface            Send  Recv  Triggered RIP  Key-chain
   Loopback0            2     2
Automatic network summarization is in effect
Maximum path: 4
```

```
Routing for Networks:
   172.16.0.0
   192.168.1.0
Passive Interface(s):
Routing Information Sources:
   Gateway          Distance      Last Update
Distance: (default is 120)
RouterA#
```

On Router B:

```
RouterB(config)#router rip
RouterB(config-router)#ver 2
RouterB(config-router)#net 10.0.0.0
RouterB(config-router)#net 192.168.1.0
RouterB(config-router)#^Z
RouterB#
```

4. Issue a `show ip route` command on Router A to check whether the RIP route can be seen. Do the same on Router B.

```
RouterA#show ip route
Codes: C - connected, S - static, I - IGRP, R - RIP, M - mobile, B - BGP
       D - EIGRP, EX - EIGRP external, O - OSPF, IA - OSPF inter area
       N1 - OSPF NSSA external type 1, N2 - OSPF NSSA external type 2
       E1 - OSPF external type 1, E2 - OSPF external type 2, E - EGP
       i - IS-IS, L1 - IS-IS level-1, L2 - IS-IS level-2, ia - IS-IS inter
area
       * - candidate default, U - per-user static route, o - ODR
       P - periodic downloaded static route

Gateway of last resort is not set

R    10.0.0.0/8 [120/1] via 192.168.1.2, 00:00:25, Serial0/1/0
     172.16.0.0/24 is subnetted, 1 subnets
C       172.16.1.0 is directly connected, Loopback0
     192.168.1.0/30 is subnetted, 1 subnets
C       192.168.1.0 is directly connected, Serial0/1/0
RouterA#


RouterB#show ip route
Codes: C - connected, S - static, I - IGRP, R - RIP, M - mobile, B - BGP
       D - EIGRP, EX - EIGRP external, O - OSPF, IA - OSPF inter area
       N1 - OSPF NSSA external type 1, N2 - OSPF NSSA external type 2
       E1 - OSPF external type 1, E2 - OSPF external type 2, E - EGP
       i - IS-IS, L1 - IS-IS level-1, L2 - IS-IS level-2, ia - IS-IS inter
area
```

```
        * - candidate default, U - per-user static route, o - ODR
        P - periodic downloaded static route

Gateway of last resort is not set

     10.0.0.0/10 is subnetted, 1 subnets
C       10.0.0.0 is directly connected, Loopback0
R     172.16.0.0/16 [120/1] via 192.168.1.1, 00:00:10, Serial0/1/0
     192.168.1.0/30 is subnetted, 1 subnets
C       192.168.1.0 is directly connected, Serial0/1/0
RouterB#
```

5. You can see the routes are in the tables and the AD is 120, which is RIP. Now, turn off auto-sum-
    mary on Router B and see whether the correct /10 network can be seen. You may need to issue a
    clear ip route * command on Router A to clear the routing table.

```
RouterB(config)#router rip
RouterB(config-router)#no auto-summary

RouterA#show ip route
Codes: C - connected, S - static, I - IGRP, R - RIP, M - mobile, B - BGP
       D - EIGRP, EX - EIGRP external, O - OSPF, IA - OSPF inter area
       N1 - OSPF NSSA external type 1, N2 - OSPF NSSA external type 2
       E1 - OSPF external type 1, E2 - OSPF external type 2, E - EGP
       i - IS-IS, L1 - IS-IS level-1, L2 - IS-IS level-2, ia - IS-IS inter
area
       * - candidate default, U - per-user static route, o - ODR
       P - periodic downloaded static route

Gateway of last resort is not set

R       10.0.0.0/10 [120/1] via 192.168.1.2, 00:00:03,        172.16.0.0/24
is subnetted, 1 subnets
C       172.16.1.0 is directly connected, Loopback0
     192.168.1.0/30 is subnetted, 1 subnets
C       192.168.1.0 is directly connected, Serial0/1/0
RouterA#
```

NOTE: Your output may appear different to mine, but you should see the /10 network advertised.

DAY 14

Static Routing

DAY 14 TASKS

- Read today's theory notes
- Review yesterday's theory notes
- Complete today's lab
- Read the CCENT cram guide
- Spend 15 minutes on the subnetting.org website

Your choices as a network administrator are to use dynamic routing protocols on your network or stick to static routing, which is where you manually add each route for your network onto each router.

I'm often asked which routing protocol is the 'best'. There is no method which will suit every network, as even a particular company's network requirements will change over time. Static routing will take time and effort to configure, but you will save on network bandwidth and CPU cycles. If a new route is added, then you will have to add this manually to every router. In addition, if a route goes down, static routing has no method to deal with this, so it will continue to send traffic to the down network.

Today you will learn about the following:

- Configuring static routes
- Troubleshooting static routes

This lesson maps to the following CCNA syllabus requirement:

- Perform and verify routing configuration tasks for a static or default route given specific routing requirements

If you look back at the administrative distances table in Day 13, you will see that manually configured networks are preferred over routing protocols. The reason for this is as a network administrator, you will be expected to know your network better than any protocol can and to understand what you want to achieve. By now, it should be clear that you can use static routing with dynamic routing if your needs require it.

Configuring Static Routes

The commands to configure a static route include the following:

- Network address/prefix mask
- Address or exit interface
- Distance (optional)

```
RouterA(config)#ip route network prefix mask {address | interface} [distance]
```

FIG 14.1—Sample Network for Static Routes

In order to add a static route for the network above, you would write the following line of configuration:

```
Router(config)#ip route 192.168.1.0 255.255.255.0 172.16.1.2
```

With static routes, you can specify a next hop IP address the router needs to go to on the way to the destination address, or you can specify an exit interface. Often, you won't know your next hop because it is your ISP, or your IP address will change over time. If this is the case, use an exit interface.

FIG 14.2—You Might Not Always Know Your Next Hop Address

```
Router(config)#ip route 192.168.1.0 255.255.255.0 s0/0
```

The command line above tells the router to send traffic destined for the 192.168.1.0 network out of the Serial interface. The next command tells the router to send all traffic for all networks out of the Serial interface:

```
Router(config)#ip route 0.0.0.0 0.0.0.0 s0/0
```

The above is actually a default route. Default routes are used to direct packets addressed to networks not explicitly listed in the routing table.

Troubleshooting Static Routes

Troubleshooting will almost always involve a configuration issue (unless your interface is down). If traffic isn't arriving at the destination, you can test the route with the traceroute command or tracert command for a Windows PC.

DAY 14 LAB—STATIC ROUTES

Topology

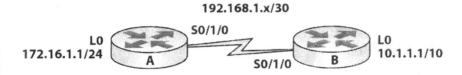

172.16.1.1/24 LO A S0/1/0 192.168.1.x/30 S0/1/0 B LO 10.1.1.1/10

Purpose

Learn how to assign static routes to a router with a next hop address and exit interface.

Walkthrough

1. Assign all the IP addresses according to the above topology. Router A can be 192.168.1.1/30 and Router B .2. Ping across the Serial link to ensure it is working.

2. Assign a static route on Router A, sending all traffic for the 10.1.1.0 /10 network out of the Serial interface. Use your own serial number, of course; don't just copy mine if yours has a different number!

```
RouterA(config)#ip route 10.0.0.0 255.192.0.0 serial 0/1/0
RouterA(config)#exit
RouterA#ping 10.1.1.1

Type escape sequence to abort.
Sending 5, 100-byte ICMP Echos to 10.1.1.1, timeout is 2 seconds:
!!!!!
Success rate is 100 percent (5/5), round-trip min/avg/max = 18/28/32 ms

RouterA#
RouterA#show ip route
Codes: C - connected, S - static, I - IGRP, R - RIP, M - mobile, B - BGP
       D - EIGRP, EX - EIGRP external, O - OSPF, IA - OSPF inter area
       N1 - OSPF NSSA external type 1, N2 - OSPF NSSA external type 2
       E1 - OSPF external type 1, E2 - OSPF external type 2, E - EGP
       i - IS-IS, L1 - IS-IS level-1, L2 - IS-IS level-2, ia - IS-IS inter
area
       * - candidate default, U - per-user static route, o - ODR
       P - periodic downloaded static route

Gateway of last resort is not set

     10.0.0.0/10 is subnetted, 1 subnets
S       10.0.0.0 is directly connected, Serial0/1/0
     172.16.0.0/24 is subnetted, 1 subnets
```

```
C        172.16.1.0 is directly connected, Loopback0
      192.168.1.0/30 is subnetted, 1 subnets
C        192.168.1.0 is directly connected, Serial0/1/0
RouterA#

RouterA#show ip route 10.1.1.1
Routing entry for 10.0.0.0/10
Known via "static", distance 1, metric 0 (connected)
  Routing Descriptor Blocks:
  * directly connected, via Serial0/1/0
      Route metric is 0, traffic share count is 1
RouterA#
```

3. Configure a static route on Router B, sending all traffic for the 172.16.1.0/24 network to next hop address 192.168.1.1.

```
RouterB(config)#ip route 172.16.1.0 255.255.255.0 192.168.1.1
RouterB(config)#exit

RouterB#ping 172.16.1.1
Type escape sequence to abort.
Sending 5, 100-byte ICMP Echos to 172.16.1.1, timeout is 2 seconds:
!!!!!

RouterB#show ip route 172.16.1.1
Routing entry for 172.16.1.0/24
Known via "static", distance 1, metric 0
  Routing Descriptor Blocks:
  * 192.168.1.1
      Route metric is 0, traffic share count is 1
RouterB#
```

Network Security Threats

DAY 15 TASKS

- Read today's theory notes
- Review yesterday's theory notes
- Complete any lab(s) of your choice
- Read the CCENT cram guide
- Spend 15 minutes on the subnetting.org website

Along with voice over IP, network security is one of the hottest areas of internetworking. So much so, in fact, that you can easily specialise as a network security engineer.

Companies want to keep their data secure from hackers who want to access it for any number of reasons. We regularly hear embarrassing stories about big-name companies or government departments who have neglectfully, or due to security holes, had their confidential data exposed.

Network engineers need to protect their networks from threats such as these:

- Viruses
- Hackers
- Industrial espionage
- Disgruntled employees

Today you will learn about the following:

- Network threats
- Countermeasures

This lesson maps to the following CCNA syllabus requirements:

- Describe today's increasing network security threats and explain the need to implement a comprehensive security policy to mitigate these threats
- Explain general methods to mitigate common security threats to network devices, hosts, and applications
- Describe the functions of common security appliances and applications
- Describe security-recommended practises, including initial steps to secure network devices

Network Threats

Denial of Service (DoS)
DoS attacks include the following:

- Data destroyers
- Crashers—designed to detach the host from the network
- Flooders—saturates the network with traffic

Distributed Denial of Service (DDoS)
DDoS attacks use many systems to attack one system. One system starts the attack, which infects others, which, in turn, infects others and attacks the host.

Hackers' Tools
Hackers have a huge arsenal of tools available for them to use. Many of these are freely available on the web and can be used with little or no knowledge of how to hack. Hackers' tools include the following:

- Port scanners—discovers open TCP ports
- Spyware—collects information
- Worm—self-replicating program
- Keystroke logger
- Phishing—bogus websites
- Malware—malicious software

Countermeasures

Firewalls

Firewalls can be hardware or software based. Depending upon the requirement and the OSI layer at which it functions, firewalls can scan ports, protocols, and applications for suspicious behaviour. They can also divide your network into trusted and untrusted zones, in addition to a DMZ, which allows outside hosts to use resources on your network (such as a web server) without giving access to your internal network.

Cisco manufactures a device referred to as an Adaptive Security Appliance (ASA). This is designed to counter phishing attacks, spam, and viruses on your network. It can also perform NAT for your network, give VPN access, and offer intrusion protection.

A virtual private network (VPN) gives access to your network over an insecure medium, such as the Internet. It allows remote workers access by authenticating the connection and then creating a virtual tunnel, giving the data confidentiality and integrity.

Another device Cisco provides to protect your network is the Intrusion Protection system (IPS). The function of an IPS is to:

- Focus on 'prevention'
- Monitor the network/system for malicious activity
- Monitor logs/reports and actively block/prevent
- Constantly upgrade and update system status

Network Hardening

Some basic steps to keep your network secure include the following:

- Update firewall and antivirus software
- Keep router and switch IOS-current
- Do not use dictionary passwords
- Utilise role-specific devices, such as firewalls, IPS, etc.

Practical steps for switch security include the following:

- Add enable passwords
- Add banner messages
- Turn off CDP

- Control Telnet access
- Transport input SSH

We cover how to do this in the switch and router security modules.

DAY 15 QUESTIONS

1. Name the three main types of DoS attacks.
2. Name common tools hackers can employ.
3. Firewalls cannot perform NAT. True or false?
4. Name the main functions of an IPS.

DAY 16

Wireless Networking

DAY 16 TASKS

- Read today's theory notes
- Review yesterday's theory notes
- Complete lab(s) of your choice
- Read the CCENT cram guide
- Spend 15 minutes on the subnetting.org website

Wireless networking has made huge leaps in performance and security over recent years. Most home-based networks now employ wireless technology for laptop and mobile device access. Commercial wireless networking is a good solution for companies that have staff roaming the building or that can't or don't want to run cables.

Today you will learn about the following:

- Wireless networking basics
- Wireless standards
- Wireless security
- Troubleshooting wireless networks

This lesson maps to the following CCNA syllabus requirements:

- Describe standards associated with wireless media (including IEEE Wi-Fi Alliance and ITU/FCC)
- Identify and describe the purpose of the components in a small wireless network (including SSID, BSS, and ESS)

- Identify the basic parameters to configure on a wireless network to ensure that devices connect to the correct access point
- Compare and contrast wireless security features and capabilities of WPA security (including open, WEP, WPA, and WPA2)
- Identify common issues with implementing wireless networks

Wireless Networking Basics

A standard wireless connection consists of a wireless device connected to an access point, which is connected to a network switch.

Wireless client   Access point   Access switch

FIG 16.1—A Typical Wireless Setup

In wireless networking, a radio transmits a signal on a specified frequency (e.g., a 2.4 Ghz or 5 Ghz band, depending upon the standard) and this is received by a receiver (antenna). Looking at Figure 16.1 above, the wireless client radio sends a signal to the receiver of the access point. The access point converts the wireless signal in order to send it on to the wired network. This way the client can access the resources on the LAN.

The strength of the radio (i.e., its transmitting power) is defined in the US by the Federal Communications Commission (FCC). These limitations are called Equivalent Isotropically Radiated Power (EIRP). EIRP represents the total effective transmitting power of the radio, including the gain that the antenna provides and the loss of the antenna cable.

The gain of the antenna represents how well it increases the effective power signal in decibels (dB). The two types of antennas are directional and omnidirectional.

The omnidirectional signal travels in all directions. This results in signal loss that can be caused by the following:

- Reflection—signal bounces off surface
- Scattering—signal bounces off uneven surface
- Absorption—signal hits people or objects
- Attenuation—signal loses amplitude

These should all be remembered for the CCNA exam.

The two types of wireless modes available are referred to as ad-hoc and infrastructure. Ad-hoc is where you connect two wireless devices together with no access point. With infrastructure, you use an access point.

Client A   Client B

FIG 16.2—An Ad-hoc Network

It is important to note that in ad-hoc mode, client A and client B use the same channel/frequency and Service Set Identifier (SSID). The SSID, or network name, is a 32-bit alphanumeric (letters and numbers) character, case-sensitive variable. Clients who want to communicate with each other must have the same SSID.

Benefits of ad-hoc mode are that it is easy and quick to set up and there is no need to buy access points. But it also has drawbacks: access points offer better performance, network management (e.g., monitoring) is much harder, and there is limited network access.

Access point

Client A   Client B

FIG 16.3—Infrastructure Mode

Infrastructure mode employs two connection methods, a Basic Service Set (BSS) and an Extended Service Set (ESS). A BSS consists of an access point, which is wired to local resources (not shown) and multiple clients. An ESS consists of two or more BSSs from the same subnetwork.

Access point

Client A   Client B

FIG 16.4—Basic Service Set

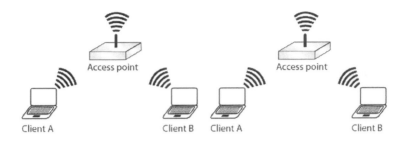

FIG 16.5—Extended Service Set

In infrastructure mode, the clients need to be configured with the same SSID to be able to communicate with each other. Benefits of infrastructure mode are centralised security management, scalability, and increased reach. The extra cost of the access points is the only drawback of this type of wireless network.

Wireless configuration changes from device to device because each one usually comes with its own web-based configuration tool. Some Cisco access points have command line configuration available.

CISCO SYSTEMS	Close Window

Cisco 1200 Access Point

HOME	Hostname ap
EXPRESS SET-UP	
NETWORK MAP +	**Express Set-Up**
ASSOCIATION	
NETWORK INTERFACES +	**System Name:** ap
SECURITY +	**MAC Address:** 000f.245d.bc4d
SERVICES +	
WIRELESS SERVICES +	**Configuration Server Protocol:** ⊙ DHCP ○ Static IP
SYSTEM SOFTWARE +	**IP Address:** 192.168.2.14
EVENT LOG +	**IP Subnet Mask:** 255.255.255.0
	Default Gateway: 192.168.2.1
	SNMP Community: defaultCommunity
	⊙ Read-Only ○ Read-Write
	Radio1-802.11A
	SSID: tsunami
	Broadcast SSID in Beacon: ⊙ Yes ○ No
	Role in Radio Network: ⊙ Access Point Root ○ Repeater Non-Root

FIG 16.6—A Typical Cisco Web-based Wireless Configuration Tool

Wireless Standards

In 1997, the 802.11 standard (or Wi-Fi standard) was created by the Institute of Electrical and Electronic Engineers (IEEE), and it had a maximum bandwidth of 2Mbps. This bandwidth was used in the 2.4 to 2.5 Ghz frequency spectrum. In that standard, the speeds and frequency were defined. In addition, carrier sense, multiple access with collision avoidance (CSMA/CA) was used as a protocol because on a wireless LAN, a node cannot listen while it is sending data, and therefore collision detection was not possible. In CSMA/CA, a node will send a signal to the other nodes not to transmit, and then it will wait a little while longer before checking to see whether the channel is still free. If it is free, it will transmit the data and wait for an acknowledgment that the data has been received.

Modulation is carried out using either frequency hopping or Direct-Sequence Spread Spectrum (DSSS). The range is approximately 20 metres indoors and 100 metres outdoors (i.e., in good conditions and line of sight, number of walls, etc.).

802.11b became a standard in 1999, and the bandwidth increased to 11Mbps (the actual throughput was 7.1Mbps UDP and 5.9Mbps TCP because of the CSMA/CA overhead). Another change was the modulation used by 802.11b. It still used DSSS, but, technically, it used Complementary Code Keying (CCK). As the signal degrades, the speed can drop to 5.5Mbps, 2Mbps, and 1Mbps. This is called adaptive-rate selection; the range for 802.11b indoors is 38 metres at 11Mbps and 90 metres at 1Mbps, and outdoors it is about 140 metres.

Because 802.11b operates in the 2.4 GHz band, interference arises from microwave ovens, cordless phones, and baby monitors. Another interference source is the channel overlap that exists in the 2.4 GHz band. There are 14 available channels among the range of frequencies, but channels 1, 6, and 11 are the only ones that do not overlap. Each of these channels has a width of 22 MHz.

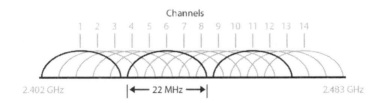

FIG 16.7 - Channel Width of 22 MHz

Also in 1999, 802.11a was ratified, and it used the 5 GHz frequency spectrum. Using Orthogonal Frequency-Division Multiplexing (OFDM) on 52 subcarriers, it achieved a maximum bandwidth of 54Mbps and data rates of 54, 48, 36, 24, 18, 12, 9, and 6Mbps. This OFDM-type modulation was later used in 802.11g, which will be described later.

802.11a has twelve non-overlapping channels, as you can see in Figure 16.8 below. The first eight channels are intended for indoor use, while the last four are intended for outdoor use (point-to-point links). The benefit of 802.11a is that it does not have the interference issues of 802.11b/g, so it is more reliable, but the range of 802.11a, which is 35 metres indoors and 120 metres outdoors, is not as great as the ranges of 802.11b/g.

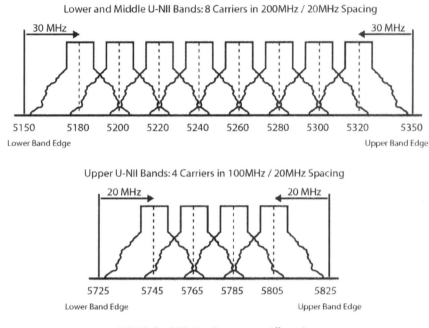

FIG 16.8—802.11a Frequency Allocation

In June 2003, 802.11g was ratified, and it has a maximum bandwidth of 54Mbps, using the 2.4 Ghz band. This means that 802.11g has the same interference issues as 802.11b. The increase in speed is achieved using OFDM, with data rates of 54, 48, 36, 24, 18, 12, 9, and 6Mbps. CCK is used for data rates of 5.5Mbps and 11Mbps, and Differential Binary Phase Key Shifting/Differential Quaternary Phase Key Shifting (DBPKS/DQPKS+DSSS) is used for data rates of 2Mbps and 1Mbps. The range of 802.11g is 38 metres indoors and 140 metres outdoors—just like 802.11b.

The Future...802.11n

802.11n has recently been approved. 802.11n adds Multiple-Input Multiple-Output (MIMO) to improve system performance-increased bandwidth and range. This is done by using multiple transmitters (radios) and receivers (antennas). Features of 802.11n include an operating frequency of 5 Ghz or 2.4 Ghz, 144Mbps, an indoor range of around 300 feet (91 metres), and an outdoor range of around 600 feet (182 metres).

The standards described above were all defined by the IEEE, an international non-profit professional organisation for the advancement of technology related to electricity. Besides IEEE, there is also the FCC in the US, and its European counterpart, the European Telecommunications Standards Institute (ETSI). Both organisations are responsible for the use of the frequency spectrum (i.e., 2.4 GHz and 5 GHz, the unlicensed frequencies used for WLAN).

The main role of the Wi-Fi Alliance is to improve the interoperability between vendors' products based on the 802.11 standard. Its members include Cisco, Nokia, Apple, Microsoft, and Pioneer, among others. When products have been tested and verified by the Wi-Fi Alliance, it will receive the following logo:

FIG 16.9—Wi-Fi Logo

Wireless Security

In this section, you will learn how to secure your wireless network. We'll start by delving deeper into how a station/node connects to an access point. You already know that the SSID has to be the same for the client and the access point. But how is a connection built?

Before a station can send data, it must authenticate and associate with an access point. The two methods for authentication include the following:

1. Open-system authentication
2. Shared-key authentication

Open-system Authentication

With this method, the client sends an association request to the access point. The latter will respond with a success or failure message. A failure can occur when the client's MAC address is denied in the configuration of the access point.

Shared-key Authentication

Here, a shared key or passphrase is configured for both the client and the access point. The client sends an association request, then the access point sends a challenge based on the shared key to which the clients sends a response, and if this response is correct, then the authentication is a success.

The three types of shared-key authentication are WEP, WPA, and WPA2. Once authentication is a success, then the client will associate with the access point. Next, we will take a closer look at the three types of shared-key authentication.

WEP

Wired Equivalent Privacy (WEP) is an encryption algorithm built into the 802.11 standard. It uses RC4 40-bit or 104-bit keys and a 24-bit initialisation vector. It is also a symmetrical algorithm because the encryption and the decryption use the same key.

WPA

Wi-Fi Protected Access (WPA), an improvement over weak WEP security, was created by the Wi-Fi Alliance to make wireless networks more secure. This method uses dynamic-key management, adds a stronger encryption cipher, and is built on the EAP/802.1X mechanism. One of the enhancements of WPA is the use of Temporal Key Integrity Protocol (TKIP). Another enhancement is the Initialization Vector is increased to 48 bits, which can create more than 500 trillion key combinations.

WPA is mainly used in the enterprise environment in combination with a RADIUS server. A WPA Pre-shared Key (WPA-PSK) is what you would find in SoHo, as well as for home users who wanted improved security compared to WEP.

WPA2

Wi-Fi Protected Access 2 (WPA2) is the next generation in wireless security, the Wi-Fi Alliance interoperable implementation of the IEEE 802.11n ratified standard. Even stronger encryption than WPA is achieved by using the Advanced Encryption Standard (AES). In addition, WPA2 creates a new key for every new association. This has a benefit over WPA in that the client's keys are unique and specific to that client. As with WPA, WPA2 has both a personal mode and an enterprise mode.

Troubleshooting Wireless Networks

Wireless troubleshooting can prove quite frustrating because, often, the problems are intermittent. The four main issues you will find as the root cause are as follows:

- Typos in passwords or pass phrases
- Overlapping channels (microwave, baby monitor, etc.)
- Signal bounces off walls
- Signal degradation via walls and distance

DAY 16 QUESTIONS

1. Explain the four main causes of wireless signal loss.

2. The SSID, or network name, is a _____-bit alphanumeric (letters and numbers) character, case-sensitive variable.

3. 802.11_____ became a standard in 1999, and the bandwidth increased to 11Mbps.

4. Name the two methods for authentication.

5. Which method of authentication uses TKIP (Temporal Key Integrity Protocol)?

6. Name the four main troubleshooting issues for wireless networks.

DAY 17

Wide Area Networking

DAY 17 TASKS

- Read today's theory notes
- Review yesterday's theory notes
- Complete lab(s) of your choice
- Read the CCENT cram guide
- Spend 15 minutes on the subnetting.org website

Cisco split WAN concepts between the CCENT and ICND2 exams, with the latter focusing on Frame Relay and PPP protocols. For this reason, we will look at basic WAN concepts and HDLC.

Today you will learn about the following:

- WAN components
- WAN protocols
- Basic serial line configuration
- Troubleshooting WAN connections

This lesson maps to the following CCNA syllabus requirements:

- Describe different methods for connecting to a WAN
- Configure and verify a basic WAN serial connection

WAN Components

Wide area networking (WAN) will require a number of physical components to enable a connection. These will differ depending upon the type of connection you are using (e.g., ISDN, ADSL, Frame Relay, leased line, etc.) and other factors, such as back-up connections and the number of incoming networks.

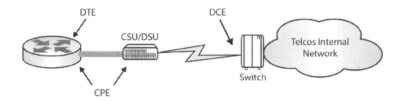

FIG 17.1—Basic WAN Components

The figure above shows a basic serial connection going out to an ISP. As the customer, you are responsible for the Data Terminal Equipment (DTE). This will be your router interface accepting the incoming link. You will also be responsible for the cable going to your Channel Service Unit/ Data Service Unit (CSU/DSU), which converts your data into a format that your ISP can transport. The CSU/DSU is usually built into your router WAN interface card (WIC). CPE is the Customer Premise Equipment and is your responsibility.

From this point on, your ISP or Telco is usually responsible for the connection. They lay the cables and provide switching stations, which transport the data across their network. The ISP will own the Data Communication Equipment (DCE), which is the end that provides the clocking, meaning the rate at which the data can pass on the line.

Common types of WAN connections include the following:

- Leased line—a dedicated connection available 24/7
- Circuit switching—set up when required
- Packet switching—shared link/virtual circuit

The type of link you buy depends on your requirements and budget. If you can afford a dedicated line, you will have exclusive use of the bandwidth and security is less of an issue. A shared connection can mean a slower connection during peak times.

WAN Protocols

Common WAN protocols include PPP, HDLC, and Frame Relay. There are others, of course; however, they are not in the current CCNA syllabus.

Point-to-Point Protocol (PPP) can be used when you have a Cisco device connecting to a non-Cisco device. PPP also has the advantage of including authentication. It can be used over a number of connection types, including DSL, circuit switched, and asynchronous and synchronous connections.

Cisco's High-Level Data Link Control (cHDLC) is its implementation of the open standard version of HDLC. HDLC requires DTE and DCE and is the default encapsulation type on Cisco routers. Keepalives are sent from the DCE in order to check link status.

Frame Relay is a packet switching technology which has become less popular in recent years, as DSL has become both more affordable and more readily available. It works at speeds, from 56k to 2Mbps, and builds virtual circuits every time a connection is required. There is no security built into Frame Relay (but see Farai's comment below). Frame Relay will be covered in more detail later.

> **FARAI SAYS:** 'Frame Relay commonly uses permanent virtual circuits (PVCs), which are always present, although it can use switched virtual circuits (SVCs), which are created on demand. A PVC is a type of virtual private network (VPN). However, some people run PPP over Frame Relay (PPPoFR) to allow for PPP security for Frame Relay connections.'

Basic Serial Line Configuration

If you don't want to change the default HDLC encapsulation, then, in order to set up your WAN connection, you need only to do the following:

1. Add an IP address to your interface
2. Bring the interface up (with the no shut command)
3. Ensure there is a clock rate on the DCE side

Here is the configuration if you have the DCE cable attached:

```
Router#config t
Router(config)#interface serial 0
Router(config-if)#ip address 192.168.1.1 255.255.255.0
Router(config-if)#clock rate 64000
Router(config-if)#no shutdown
Router(config-if)#^Z
Router#
```

Troubleshooting WAN Connections

When trying to bring up a WAN connection (forgetting PPP and Frame Relay for the moment), you could use the OSI model:

Layer 1—Check the cable to ensure it is attached correctly. Has the no shut command been applied? Is there a clock rate applied to the DCE side?

```
RouterA#show controllers serial 0
HD unit 0, idb = 0x1AE828, driver structure at 0x1B4BA0
buffer size 1524 HD unit 0, V.35 DTE cable
RouterA#show ip interface brief
Interface     IP-Address     OK? Method Status               Protocol
Serial0       11.0.0.1       YES unset  administratively down down
Ethernet0     10.0.0.1       YES unset  up                   up
```

Layer 2—Check to ensure the correct encapsulation is applied to the interface. Ensure that the other side of the link has the same encapsulation type.

```
RouterB#show interface serial 0
Serial1 is down, line protocol is down
 Hardware is HD64570
 Internet address is 12.0.0.1/24
 MTU 1500 bytes, BW 1544 Kbit, DLY 1000 usec, rely 255/255, load 1/255
 Encapsulation HDLC, loopback not set, keepalive set (10 sec)
```

Layer 3—Is the IP address and subnet mask correct? Does the subnet mask match the other side?

```
RouterB#show interface serial 0
Serial1 is down, line protocol is down
 Hardware is HD64570
 Internet address is 12.0.0.1/24
 MTU 1500 bytes, BW 1544 Kbit, DLY 1000 usec, rely 255/255, load 1/255
 Encapsulation HDLC, loopback not set, keepalive set (10 sec)
```

DAY 17 QUESTIONS

1. What function does the CSU/DSU perform?
2. You can connect a Cisco device to a non-Cisco device using HDLC. True or false?
3. Which command reveals the type of serial cable attached to your interface?
4. Which command will show you the encapsulation type on your Serial interface?

DAY 17 LAB

Topology

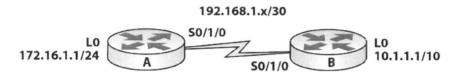

Purpose

Try your hand at WAN troubleshooting.

Walkthrough

No walkthrough for this lab. Configure the network above. Your WAN will work using HDLC automatically. Ping across the Serial link to ensure it is working. Then, break the network in the following ways.

1. Change the encapsulation type on Router B to PPP. Do this with the following configuration:

    ```
    RouterB(config)#int ser 0/1/0
    RouterB(config-if)#encapsulation ppp

    %LINEPROTO-5-UPDOWN: Line protocol on Interface Serial0/1/0, changed state
    to down
    RouterB(config-if)#
    ```

2. Issue a `shut` command on the Serial interface on Router A. Then issue a `show ip interface brief` command. You should see your interface up/down.

3. Take the clock rate off your DCE interface side. Then issue the `show controllers serial x` command. It should tell you there is no clock rate configured.

4. Change the subnet mask on the Router B side to 255.255.255.0. You can see the subnet mask with a `show interface serial x` command. If that command isn't permitted in the exam, then issue a `show run` command.

5. Now fix all of the issues above. This is what you will have to do in the exam, and these are the most common issues.

Review 1

Welcome to your first review day. I told you that you'd have plenty of time for going over previous lessons! We have covered pretty much everything you need to know to get through the CCENT exam. If you are doing the full CCNA exam, then you still need to review everything you have learned so far. I don't want to dwell on the more ambiguous areas, such as the OSI model or CSMA/CD, because they are less likely to come up in the exam, and because the few facts you need to know should be easily remembered AND you can review them in the cram guide.

DAY 18 TASKS

- Take the OSI exam below
- Complete the switching and switch security challenge labs
- Read the CCENT cram guide
- Spend 15 minutes on the subnetting.org website

DAY 18 EXAM

1. Data take the form of segments at which OSI layer?
2. Which OSI layer deals with compression?
3. Which OSI layer sets up, manages, and terminates dialogues across the network?
4. Logical addressing takes place at which OSI layer?
5. Flow control, windowing, and acknowledgements take place at which OSI layer?
6. What are the typical types of Layer 1 network issues?
7. Name the four layers of the TCP (DoD) model.
8. Which TCP layer maps to the Transport Layer of the OSI model?
9. Check the OSI theory notes for the answers.

DAY 18 LAB 1—SWITCH CONFIGURATION

Topology

Instructions

Follow Day 5 Lab.

DAY 18 LAB 2—SWITCH SECURITY

Topology

Instructions

Connect to the switch using a console connection. Connect a PC to the switch or connect the switch to the FastEthernet port on a router:

1. Add port security to an interface on the switch
2. Hard-set the MAC address of the PC/router interface as the permitted address
3. Ensure the switch interface is up (and an IP address is on the PC)
4. Set the port security violation action to restrict
5. Change the MAC address of the PC, or plug in another machine
6. Issue a `show port-security interface x` command on the switch

In this review session, we will be going over the earlier lessons in order and cementing in hands-on knowledge. I know you have been choosing which labs to follow, but I'm going to suggest which ones to do here. Whatever you do, don't keep repeating the same labs once you have mastered them. Mix up the IP addresses and the router interfaces and do it all from memory.

If you have to look up commands to remember them, you won't get through the exam, so, as fast as possible, commit the configuration commands to memory.

DAY 19

Review 2

DAY 19 TASKS

- Take the cables exam below
- Review all switching theory
- Review the switching lab in Day 5
- Complete today's switching challenge lab
- Read the CCENT cram guide
- Spend 15 minutes on the subnetting.org website

DAY 19 EXAM

1. You are trying to find a crossover cable. When you look at the pin colors, what are you looking for?
2. What is the minimum category of cable which can support 100Mbps?
3. You want to configure an Ethernet interface to enable traffic to pass in both directions at the same time. In `Switch(config-if)#` mode, what do you type?
4. At the `Switch(config-if)#` prompt, you want to change the speed from auto to 100. What do you type?
5. What could you connect to using a crossover cable?
6. You can easily use a straight-through Ethernet cable to connect to a router console port if a rollover/console cable is not available. True or false?

DAY 20

Review 3

DAY 20 TASKS

- Read IP addressing theory notes
- Take the subnetting exam below
- Complete today's three NAT challenge labs
- Read the CCENT cram guide
- Spend 15 minutes on the subnetting.org website
- Watch the network design videos on www.in60days.net/book-updates

DAY 20 EXAM

1. Which subnet is host 200.200.100.103/27 in?
2. Which subnet is host 190.100.23.45/28 in?
3. Which subnet is host 19.200.12.120/13 in?
4. Which subnet is host 100.123.45.12/15 in?
5. Which subnet is host 130.23.34.3/18 in?
6. Network 192.168.1.0 needs subnetting to create three subnets, each with at least 20 hosts. Which subnet mask needs to be applied? (you need to watch the design videos first)
7. Network 200.100.1.0 needs subnetting to create five subnets, each with at least 30 hosts. Which subnet mask needs to be applied?
8. Network 30.0.0.0 needs subnetting to create 200 subnets, with as many hosts as possible. Which subnet mask needs to be applied?
9. Network 192.168.1.0 needs subnetting to create subnets that will contain only two hosts. Which subnet mask needs to be applied?
10. Network 170.24.0.0 needs subnetting to create 100 subnets, each with at least 500 hosts. Which subnet mask needs to be applied?

DAY 20 EXAM ANSWERS

1. 200.200.100.96
2. 190.100.23.32
3. 19.200.0.0
4. 100.122.0.0
5. 130.23.0.0
6. 255.255.255.192
7. 255.255.255.224
8. 255.255.0.0
9. 255.255.255.252
10. 255.255.254.0

DAY 20 LAB 1—STATIC NAT

Topology

192.168.1.0/30

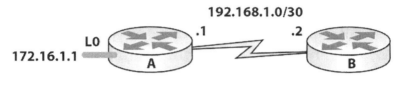

NAT 10.1.1.1

Instructions

Connect two routers together with a serial or crossover cable:

1. Add IP addresses to the routers and a Loopback interface on Router A, according to the diagram. The 172 network can use the default subnet mask.
2. Designate NAT inside and outside interfaces
3. Add a static route on Router B to send all traffic back to Router A
4. Ping between Router A and Router B to test the Serial line (remember clock rates)
5. Create a static NAT for 172.16.1.1 to 10.1.1.1 and turn on NAT debugging
6. Do an extended ping source from Loopback 0
7. Check the NAT translation table

DAY 20 LAB 2—NAT POOL

Topology

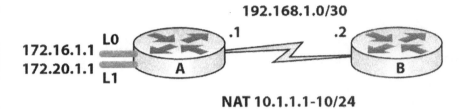

192.168.1.0/30

LO
172.16.1.1
172.20.1.1
L1

.1   .2

A   B

NAT 10.1.1.1-10/24

Instructions

Connect two routers together with a serial or crossover cable:

1. Add IP addresses to the routers and a Loopback interface on Router A, according to the diagram
2. Designate NAT inside and outside interfaces
3. Add a static route on Router B to send all traffic back to Router A
4. Ping between Router A and Router B to test the Serial line (remember clock rates)
5. Create a NAT pool of 10.1.1.1 to 10, inclusive
6. Create two access list lines to permit the Loopback networks (/16)
7. Turn on NAT debugging
8. Source two extended pings, one each from L0 and L1
9. Check the NAT translation table

DAY 20 LAB 3—NAT OVERLOAD

Topology

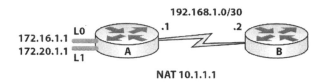

192.168.1.0/30

172.16.1.1 L0
172.20.1.1 L1
A   .1   .2   B

NAT 10.1.1.1

Instructions

Connect two routers together with a serial or crossover cable:

1. Add IP addresses to the routers and a Loopback interface on Router A, according to the diagram
2. Designate NAT inside and outside interfaces
3. Add a static route on Router B to send all traffic back to Router A
4. Ping between Router A and Router B to test the Serial line (remember clock rates)
5. Create a NAT pool of address 10.1.1.1 only and overload this pool (address)
6. Create two access list lines to permit the Loopback networks (/16)
7. Turn on NAT debugging
8. Source two extended pings, one each from L0 and L1
9. Check the NAT translation table

Hint: `Router(config)#ip nat pool ad_team 10.1.1.1 10.1.1.1 prefix-length 24`

DAY 21

Review 4

DAY 21 TASKS

- Review switch security
- Take the subnetting exam below
- Follow the DHCP lab in Day 10
- Complete the DHCP challenge lab
- Read the CCENT cram guide
- Spend 15 minutes on the subnetting.org website

DAY 21 EXAM

1. Which subnet is host 200.200.100.103/29 in?
2. Which subnet is host 190.100.23.45/25 in?
3. Which subnet is host 19.200.12.120/15 in?
4. Which subnet is host 100.12.45.12/15 in?
5. Which subnet is host 130.23.34.3/27 in?
6. Network 192.168.1.0 needs subnetting to create five subnets, each with at least 20 hosts. Which subnet mask needs to be applied?
7. Network 200.100.1.0 needs subnetting to create eight subnets, each with at least 15 hosts. Which subnet mask needs to be applied?
8. Network 30.0.0.0 needs subnetting to create 260 subnets, each with at least 1000 hosts. Which subnet mask needs to be applied?
9. Network 200.168.1.0 needs subnetting to create subnets that will contain only two hosts. Which subnet mask needs to be applied?
10. Network 170.24.0.0 needs subnetting to create 10 subnets, each with at least 500 hosts. Which subnet mask needs to be applied?

DAY 21 EXAM ANSWERS

1. 200.200.100.96
2. 190.100.23.0
3. 19.200.0.0
4. 100.12.0.0
5. 130.23.34.0
6. 255.255.255.224
7. 255.255.255.224
8. 255.255.128.0
9. 255.255.255.252
10. 255.255.240.0

DAY 21 LAB—DHCP

Topology

10.0.0.1/18

Instructions

Connect a PC to a router Ethernet interface:

1. Configure IP address 10.0.0.1/8 onto the router
2. Create a DHCP pool for the 10.0.0.0/8 network
3. Add an excluded address of the router interface
4. Add a default router address of 192.168.1.1
5. Configure the PC to obtain the IP address via DHCP
6. Check the IP configuration of the PC for the IP address assignment

DAY 22

Review 5

We are a few short days away from completing the CCENT part of the course. I hope you have the exam booked if you are doing the two-exam route. There are lots of free challenge labs on www. howtonetwork.net, by the way; check under the CCNA section and in the back of this guide.

DAY 22 TASKS

- Take the router exam below
- Review router architecture theory (if required)
- Complete the static routes challenge lab
- Read the CCENT cram guide
- Spend 15 minutes on the subnetting.org website

DAY 22 EXAM

1. Router running configuration is held in which type of memory?
2. Router startup configuration is held in which type of memory?
3. Your router loses its IOS. Which prompt will it boot into?
4. Which configuration register setting will you use to boot and ignore startup configuration?
5. The router file which checks interfaces when the router first boots is held where?
6. Router IOS is compressed and held in which memory?
7. Router IOS is uncompressed into which memory?

DAY 22 EXAM ANSWERS

1. DRAM
2. NVRAM
3. Rommon>
4. 0x2142
5. ROM
6. Flash/PCMCIA Card
7. DRAM

DAY 22 LAB—STATIC ROUTES

Topology

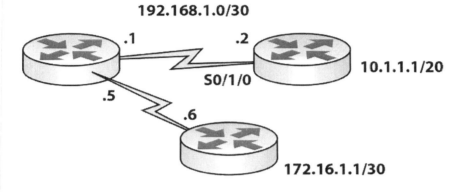

192.168.1.0/30

.1   .2

S0/1/0

10.1.1.1/20

.5

.6

172.16.1.1/30

Instructions

Connect three routers together with Serial or Ethernet connections:

1. Configure the connections between the routers and ping
2. Add Loopback addresses to the two spoke routers, as per the diagram
3. Add a static route exit interface on the hub router for the 10.1.1.0/20 subnet
4. Add a next hop address for network 172.16.1.0/30
5. Ping both networks
6. Issue a `show ip route 172.16.1.1` and the same for 10.1.1.1
7. Confirm that you have exit interface and next hop listed

DAY 23

Review 6

DAY 23 TASKS

- Take the VLSM exam below
- Review VLSM (if required)
- Complete the RIPv2 challenge lab
- Read the CCENT cram guide
- Spend 15 minutes on the subnetting.org website

DAY 23 EXAM

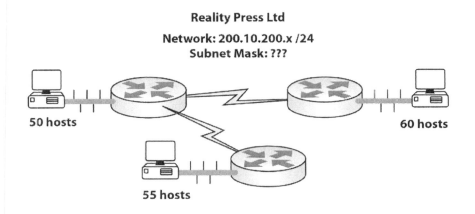

Reality Press Ltd

Network: 200.10.200.x /24
Subnet Mask: ???

50 hosts

60 hosts

55 hosts

You are the network administrator for the network 200.10.220.0/24. You are asked to redesign the network to cater for a change in the company. Now they require the network to be broken into three smaller networks. One requires 55 hosts, one requires 50, and another 60. There will also be two WAN connections required.

DAY 23 LAB—RIPV2

Topology

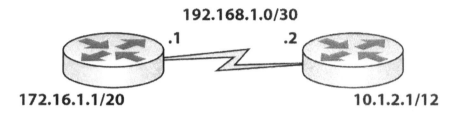

192.168.1.0/30

.1   .2

172.16.1.1/20   **10.1.2.1/12**

Instructions

Connect two routers together with Serial or Ethernet connections:

1. Configure the connections between the routers and ping
2. Add Loopback addresses to the two routers, as per the diagram
3. Configure RIPv2 on both routers
4. Issue a `show ip route` command and check all networks on both routers
5. Now configure `no auto-summary` on both routers and check for the /12 and /20 routes

Review 7

DAY 24 TASKS

- Take the exam below
- Review any theory (if required)
- Complete any challenge lab
- Read the CCENT cram guide
- Spend 15 minutes on the subnetting.org website

DAY 24 EXAM

1. What is the administrative distance (AD) for RIP?
2. What protocol has the AD of 90?
3. What protocol has the AD of 110?
4. What is the AD for a next hop address?
5. Is RIPv2 classful or classless?
6. Which TCP service uses port 22?
7. Name TCP port 53.
8. UDP port 69 is used by _____.
9. SMTP uses which port?
10. How many hops will a RIPv2 packet traverse before expiry?

Check the theory notes from Day 13 for the answers.

DAY 25

Review 8

DAY 25 TASKS

- Take the exam below
- Review any theory (if required) or NAT
- Complete the challenge lab
- Read the CCENT cram guide
- Spend 15 minutes on the subnetting.org website

DAY 25 EXAM

1. Write down the commands to configure a DHCP pool on a router for network addresses 172.16.1.0 to 10. Exclude one of the addresses. Add a lease of two days and a DNS IP address.
2. Which commands will turn off CDP for the entire router? Which commands will turn off CDP for the interface only?
3. Name the WLAN network standards and the security available for WLANs. What are the four common problems with the signal?

DAY 25 LAB—MULTI-TECHNOLOGY

Topology

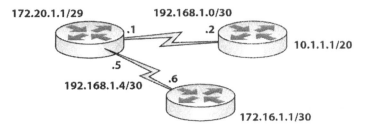

172.20.1.1/29   192.168.1.0/30

.1   .2

10.1.1.1/20

.5

192.168.1.4/30   .6

172.16.1.1/30

Instructions

Connect three routers together with Serial or Ethernet connections:

1. Configure the connections between the routers and ping
2. Add Loopback addresses to the three routers, as per the diagram
3. Put 172.16.1.0/30 and 10.1.1.0/20 and both 192 networks into RIPv2
4. Add a static route on the two spoke routers for network 192.168.20.0/24 to go to the hub
5. Configure a NAT pool on the hub router for network 172.20.1.0/29 to perform NAT to pool 192.168.20.0/24
6. Check to ensure all RIP routes are in the routing table with their correct networks
7. Source a ping from 172.20.1.1 to the Loopback addresses on the spoke routers. Turn on a NAT debug first and check the NAT table afterwards

DAY 26

Review 9

DAY 26 TASKS

- Take the exam below
- Review any theory (if required) or NAT
- Complete a CCENT lab from the appendix
- Read the CCENT cram guide
- Spend 15 minutes on the subnetting.org website

DAY 26 EXAM

1. How do you turn off CDP on a router? How about on a router interface?
2. Write down a NAT pool and then the command to overload the pool.
3. Write down all the administrative distances and TCP ports you remember.

Is there anything else you need to cover from the CCENT syllabus? You should have nailed all your weak areas by now.

You should be able to do the following:

- Recite the entire cram guide
- Configure RIPv2, static routes, NAT, and IP addressing
- Configure basic switch security and VLANs
- Configure DHCP
- Answer VLSM and subnetting questions very quickly
- Understand TCP, OSI, cables, specifications, and WLANs
- Understand router architecture (and the booting process)

DAY 27

Review 10

DAY 27 TASKS
- Take the exam below
- Review any theory (if required)
- Complete any lab you wish
- Write the CCENT cram guide from memory
- Spend 15 minutes on the subnetting.org website

DAY 27 EXAM
1. Which command turns switch-port security on?
2. What type of switch port can security be applied to?
3. What is the command to hard-set one permitted MAC address on a switch port?
4. Which command will permit only SSH traffic into the VTY lines on a switch?
5. Name the common types of network threats and attacks.

Review 11

DAY 28 TASKS

- Take the exam below
- Review any theory (if required)
- Complete any lab you wish
- Write the CCENT cram guide from memory
- Spend 15 minutes on the subnetting.org website

DAY 28 EXAM

1. You have networks 172.16.1.0 and 172.16.2.0 on either side of a 10 network. Which command would you add to RIP to prevent routing issues?
2. What is the range of IP addresses you are free to use on your internal networks, so long as you don't try to route them on the Internet?
3. Which subnet mask will always generate two hosts and no more?
4. Which cable pins go where on a crossover cable?
5. Describe the role of each layer of the OSI model; what is the data representation?

Review 12

DAY 29 TASKS

- Take the exam below
- Review any theory (if required)
- Complete any lab you wish
- Write the CCENT cram guide from memory
- Spend 15 minutes on the subnetting.org website

DAY 29 EXAM

Can you do the following?

- Secure a switch with Telnet passwords/SSH and switch ports
- Put switch ports into VLANs
- Troubleshoot simple switch and VLAN issues
- Configure static routes and RIPv2
- Configure static NAT, dynamic NAT, and PAT
- Name WLAN standards and problems
- Carve a network down using VLSM
- Find the correct subnet for a host
- Configure a DHCP pool

Exam Day

Today you should be taking the CCENT exam. If you are doing the full CCNA route, then take a day off. You have earned it.

DAY 31

Access Control Lists

DAY 31 TASKS

- Read today's theory notes
- Complete today's lab
- Read the ICND2 cram guide
- Spend 15 minutes on the subnetting.org website

We are starting out on phase two of your journey to the CCNA exam. This part focuses on the ICND2 subjects. If you are doing the one-exam route, then please make sure you regularly review the earlier lessons so the information stays fresh in your memory, because you are still 30 days away from the CCNA exam.

Along with subnetting and VLSM, Access Control Lists (ACLs) are one of the bugbear subjects for new Cisco students. Among the problems are learning the IOS configuration commands, understanding ACL rules (including the 'implicit deny' rule), and learning the port numbers and protocol types.

Like any subject, you should take the learning process one step at a time, apply every command you see here to a router, and do lots and lots of labs. Because Cisco does not seem to be testing SDM in the CCNA exam (and never has), we will not delve into this.

Today you will learn about the following:

- ACL basics
- ACL rules
- Wildcard masks

- ACL configuration
- Troubleshooting ACLs

This lesson maps to the following CCNA syllabus requirements:

- Describe the purpose for and types of ACLs
- Configure and apply ACLs based upon network filtering requirements
- Configure and apply an ACL to limit Telnet and SSH access to the router using CLI
- Verify and monitor ACLs in a network environment
- Troubleshoot ACL issues

ACL Basics

The point of access lists is to filter the traffic which passes through your router. I don't know of any network which should permit any traffic type to enter or leave it.

As well as filtering traffic, ACLs can be used to reference NAT pools, to filter your debugging commands, and with route maps (this is outside of the CCNA syllabus). Depending upon the type of access list you configure, you can filter traffic based upon source network or IP address, destination network or IP address, protocol, or port number. You can apply access lists to any router interface, including your Telnet ports.

The three main types of access lists are as follows:

- Standard numbered
- Extended numbered
- Standard or extended named

Standard numbered access lists are the most basic form of ACL you can apply to the router. While they are the easiest to configure, they have the most limited range of filters available. They can only filter based upon the source IP address or network. The way to recognise a standard ACL is by the number which precedes the configuration lines; these numbers will be from 1 to 99.

Extended numbered access lists allow far more granularity but can be trickier to configure and troubleshoot. They can filter a destination or source IP address or network, a protocol type, and a port number. The numbers you can use to configure extended ACLs are 100 to 199, inclusive.

Named access lists allow you to associate a list of filters with a name rather than a number. This makes them easier to identify in router configurations. Named access lists can actually be either extended or standard; you choose which at the initial configuration line of the access list.

For success in the CCNA exam, and to make it as a new Cisco engineer, you need to understand the following:

- Port numbers
- Command syntax for ACLs
- ACL rules

Port Numbers

You simply must know the common port numbers by heart if you want to pass the CCNA exam and to work on live networks. Looking up common port numbers isn't an option when you have customers watching what you are doing.

Here are the most common port numbers you will encounter and will need to know:

TABLE 31.1—Common CCNA Port Numbers

Port	Service	Port	Service
20	FTP Data	80	HTTP
21	FTP Control	110	POP3
22	SSH	119	NNTP
23	Telnet	123	NTP
25	SMTP	161/162	SNMP
53	DNS	443	HTTPS (HTTP with SSL)
69	TFTP		

Access List Rules

This is one of the hardest parts to understand. I've never seen a complete list of rules written down in one Cisco manual. Some refer to them generally or explain some of them, but then miss others completely. The difficulty the rules always apply but (until now) you only found them by trial and error.

Here are the rules you need to know:

ACL Rule 1—Use only one ACL per interface per direction.

This makes good sense. You wouldn't have several access lists doing different things on the same interface. Simply configure one ACL which does everything you need it to, rather than spreading out filters over two or more lists. I could have added 'per protocol' to the above rule because you could have an IPX access list, but IP is really the only protocol in use in modern networks.

FIG 31.1—One ACL per Interface per Direction

ACL Rule 2—The lines are processed top-down.

Some engineers become confused when their ACL doesn't perform as expected. The router will look at the top line of the ACL, and if it sees a match, it will stop there and will not examine the other lines. For this reason, you need to put the most specific entries at the top of the ACL.

For example, take the ACL blocking host 172.16.1.1:

Permit 10.0.0.0		No match
Permit 192.168.1.1		No match
Permit 172.16.0.0	✔	Match—Permit
Permit 172.16.1.0		Not processed
Deny 172.16.1.1		Not processed

In the example above, you should have put the Deny 172.16.1.1 line at the top, or at least above the Permit 172.16.0.0 statement.

ACL Rule 3—There is an implicit 'deny all' at the bottom of every ACL

This catches many engineers out. There is an invisible command at the bottom of every access list. This command is set to deny all traffic which hasn't been matched yet. The only way to stop this command coming into effect is to configure a 'permit all' at the bottom manually.

For example, take an incoming packet from IP address 172.20.1.1:

Permit 10.0.0.0	No match
Permit 192.168.1.1	No match
Permit 172.16.0.0	No match
Permit 172.16.1.0	No match
[Deny all]	Match—DROP PACKET

You actually wanted the packet to be permitted by the router, but instead it denies it. The reason is the implicit 'deny all', which is a security measure.

ACL Rule 4—The router can't filter self-generated traffic.

This can cause confusion when doing testing before implementing your ACL on a live network. A router won't filter traffic it generated itself. This is demonstrated in Figure 31.2 below:

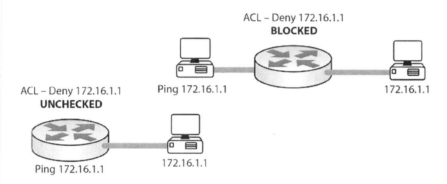

FIG 31.2—ACL Testing with Self-generated Traffic

ACL Rule 5—You can't edit a live ACL.

In fact, you should be able to edit a named access list but not standard or extended access lists. This is a limitation of ACL architecture. If you want to edit a standard or extended access list, you should follow these steps:

1. Stop ACL traffic on the interface with the `no ip access-group 99 in` command.
2. Copy and paste the ACL into notepad and edit it there.
3. Go into ACL mode and paste in the new ACL.
4. Apply ACL to the interface again.

Here are the steps on a live router:

Access list created and applied to interface:

```
Router>er
Router#conf t
```

```
Enter configuration commands, one per line.  End with CNTL/Z.
Router(config)#access-list 1 permit 172.16.1.1
Router(config)#access-list 1 permit 172.16.2.1
Router(config)#interface fast 0/0
Router(config-if)#ip access-group 1 in
```

Take off the active interface:

```
Router(config)#int fast 0/0
Router(config-if)#no ip access-group 1 in
Router(config-if)#^Z
```

Show the access lists. Copy and paste into notepad and make the changes:

```
Router#show run ← or show ip access lists

access-list 1 permit host 172.16.1.1
access-list 1 permit host 172.16.2.1
```

You actually need to add an exclamation mark in-between each line of configuration (if you are pasting it in) to tell the router to do a carriage return:

```
access-list 1 permit host 172.16.1.1
!
access-list 1 permit host 172.16.2.2
```

The lines being pasted into the router configuration are shown below. Delete the previous ACL and then paste in the new version:

```
Router#conf t
Enter configuration commands, one per line.  End with CNTL/Z.
Router(config)#no access-list 1
Router(config)#access-list 1 permit host 172.16.1.1
Router(config)#!
Router(config)#access-list 1 permit host 172.16.2.2
Router(config)#exit
Router#
%SYS-5-CONFIG_I: Configured from console by console
show ip access
Router#show ip access-lists
Standard IP access list 1
    permit host 172.16.1.1
    permit host 172.16.2.2
Router#
Router(config)#int fast 0/0
Router(config-if)#no ip access-group 1 in ← reapply to the interface
```

ACL Rule 6—Disable the ACL on the interface.

Many engineers, when they want to test or deactivate the ACL for a while, will actually delete it altogether. This isn't necessary. If you want to stop the ACL from working, simply remove it from the active interface it is applied to:

```
Router(config)#int fast 0/0
Router(config-if)#no ip access-group 1 in
Router(config-if)#^Z
```

ACL Rule 7—You can reuse the same ACL.

I've seen this often on live networks. You will usually have the same ACL policy throughout your network. Rather than configuring several ACLs, simply refer to the same ACL and apply it to as many interfaces as you require.

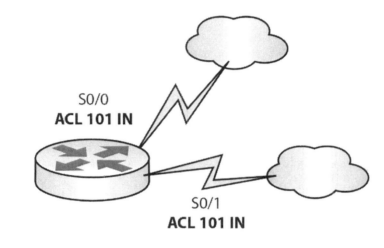

S0/0
ACL 101 IN

S0/1
ACL 101 IN

FIG 31.3—You Can Reuse an ACL

ACL Rule 8—Keep them short!

The rule with ACLs is to keep them short and focused. Many novice Cisco engineers stretch their ACL over many lines when, with some thought, it could be tightened to just a few lines of configuration. I've mentioned previously that you want your most specific lines of configuration on top. This is good practise and saves CPU cycles on the router.

Good ACL configuration skills come with knowledge and practise.

ACL Rule 9—Put your ACL as close to the source as possible.

Cisco and other Cisco manuals may teach otherwise but consider this: Would you want your router to receive an incoming packet, do a routing table lookup, and send the traffic to the exit interface, only to have the ACL on that interface drop the packet? I'm thinking no.

FIG 31.4—Put Your ACL Close to the Source

FARAI SAYS: 'The official Cisco advice is EXTENDED as close to the SOURCE as possible and STANDARD as close to the DESTINATION as possible.'

Wildcard Masks

Wildcard masks are essential to learn because they are used as part of command line configuration in access lists and some routing protocols. They exist because there has to be a way to tell the router which parts of an IP address or network address you want to match.

The matching is done at the binary level, but you can easily configure wildcard masks using the same notation you use for subnet masks. A binary 1 tells the router to ignore the digit and a 0 means match the digit.

The easy way to perform wildcard masking for the CCNA exam is simply to ensure that you add a number to the subnet mask which will give you a total of 255. So, if your subnet mask in one octet was 192, you would add 63 to it to make 255. If it was 255, you would add 0. Take a look at the examples below:

Subnet	255	255	255	192
Wildcard	0	0	0	63
Equals	255	255	255	255

Subnet	255	255	224	0
Wildcard	0	0	31	255
Equals	255	255	255	255

Subnet	255	128	0	0
Wildcard	0	127	255	255
Equals	255	255	255	255

You need to enter a wildcard mask if you want your access list to match a subnet or an entire network. For example, if you wanted to match 172.20.1.0 255.255.224.0, you would enter the following:

```
Router(config)#access-list 1 permit 172.20.1.0 0.0.31.255
```

Matching subnet 192.200.1.0 255.255.255.192 would require the following:

```
Router(config)#access-list 1 permit 192.200.1.0 0.0.0.63
```

Be careful when applying network statements with OSPF, which also requires a wildcard mask. The mask must match the network you wish to advertise.

The same principle applies when you have a network with two host bits, as you will need to enter an ACL to match these. For example, matching subnet 192.168.1.0 255.255.255.252 or /30, you will need to enter the following:

```
Router(config)#access-list 1 permit 192.168.1.0 0.0.0.3
```

I have left off some configuration, as I just want to show the relevant part. This will match hosts 1 and 2 on the 192.168.1.0 network. If you wanted to match hosts 5 and 6 on the 192.168.1.4/30 network, you would enter the following:

```
Router(config)#access-list 1 permit 192.168.1.4 0.0.0.3
```

Read through the subnetting and VLSM notes to understand this concept further. It is important.

Configuring Access Lists

As with any skill, repetition makes mastery. As I've said before, you must type on a router every example I give, do as many labs as possible, and then make up your own examples. You need to be fast and you need to be accurate, both in the exam and in the real world.

Standard ACLs

Standard ACLs are the easiest to configure, so this is the best place to start. Standard ACLs can only filter based upon a source network or IP address.

Source: 172.16.1.1
Destination: 192.168.1.1 Port 80

FIG 31.5—Incoming Packet with Source and Destination

In the figure above, the incoming packet has a source and destination address, but your standard access list will only look at the source. Your access list would permit or deny this source address:

```
Router(config)#access-list 1 permit host 172.16.1.1
```

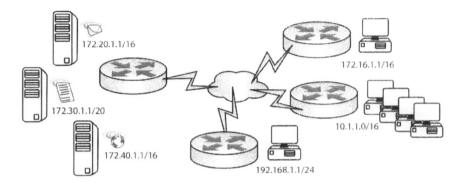

FIG 31.6—Network with Multiple Hosts/Networks

```
Router(config)#access-list 1 permit host 172.16.1.1
Router(config)#access-list 1 permit host 192.168.1.1
Router(config)#access-list 1 permit 10.1.0.0 0.0.255.255
```

This would be applied to the server side router. Remember that there will be an implicit 'deny all' at the end of this list, so all other traffic will be blocked.

Extended ACLs

Far more granularity is built into extended access lists; however, this makes them trickier to configure. You can filter source or destination networks, ports, protocols, and services.

Generally, you can look at the configuration syntax for extended access lists, as follows:

```
access list# permit/deny {service/protocol} {source network/IP} {destina-
tion network/IP} {port#}
```

For example:

```
access-list 101 deny tcp 10.1.0.0 0.0.255.255 host 172.30.1.1 eq telnet
access-list 100 permit tcp 10.1.0.0 0.0.255.255 host 172.30.1.1 eq ftp
access-list 100 permit icmp any any
```

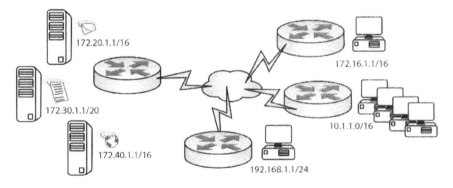

FIG 31.7 - Blocking Server Access Example

An access list you could configure for the network above, featuring e-mail, web, and file servers, would be as follows (applied on the server side):

```
access-list 100 permit tcp host 172.16.1.1 host 172.20.1.1 eq smtp
access-list 100 permit tcp 10.1.0.0 0.0.255.255 host 172.30.1.1 eq ftp
access-list 100 permit tcp host 192.168.1.1 host 172.40.1.1 eq www
```

Or, it could be the next ACL, if you had different requirements:

```
access-list 101 deny icmp any 172.20.0.0 0.0.255.255
access-list 101 deny tcp 10.1.0.0 0.0.255.255 host 172.30.1.1 eq telnet
```

Or, it could be as follows:

```
access-list 102 permit tcp any host 172.30.1.1 eq ftp established
```

The [established] keyword tells the router only to permit the traffic if it was originated by hosts on the inside. The three-way handshake flags (ACK or RST bit) will indicate this.

Named ACLs

Named access lists have a slightly different syntax than the other types of ACLs do. You can also edit live named access lists, which is a useful feature. You simply need to tell the router that you want to configure a named access list, and whether you want it to be standard or extended.

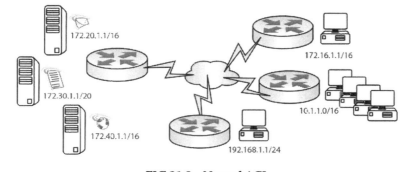

FIG 31.8—Named ACL

```
Router(config)#ip access-list extended BlockWEB
Router(config-ext-nacl)#deny tcp any any eq 80
```

Applying ACLs

In order to come into effect, you must apply your ACL to an interface or router port. I say this because I've seen many novice Cisco engineers type the ACL and then wonder why it isn't working! Or they configure it but apply the wrong ACL number or name to the interface.

If you are applying an ACL to a port, you have to specify with the `access-class` command, and to an interface, it is `ip access-group`. Why Cisco has you do this, I will never know!

Here are three examples of access lists being applied to a port or interface.

Interface:
```
Router(config)#int fast 0/0
Router(config-if)#ip access-group 101 in
```

Port:
```
Router(config)#line vty 0 15
Router(config-line)#access-class 101 in
```

Interface:
```
Router(config)#int fast 0/0
Router(config-if)#ip access-group BlockWEB in
```

Troubleshooting ACLs

I think with an understanding of the configuration commands and rules you should be fine with access lists. If Your ACL isn't working then first check that there is basic IP connectivity by pinging. Check you have applied your access list, there are no typos and if you need to allow any IP traffic to pass (remember the implicit deny).

DAY 31 QUESTIONS

1. FTP uses which port number(s)?
2. NNTP uses which port number?
3. Port number 53 is used by which service?
4. SSL uses which port number?
5. You can have a named, extended, and standard ACL on one incoming interface. True or false?
6. You want to test why your ping is blocked on your Serial interface. You ping out from the router but it is permitted. What went wrong? (Hint: See ACL Rule 4.)
7. Write a wildcard mask to match subnet mask 255.255.224.0.
8. The _____ keyword tells the router only to permit the traffic if it instigated the connection.
9. What do you type to apply an IP access list to the Telnet lines on a router?

DAY 31 LAB—STANDARD ACL

Topology

10.0.0.0/30

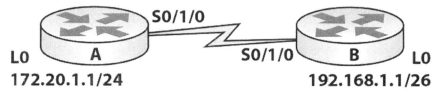

LO **A** S0/1/0
172.20.1.1/24

S0/1/0 **B** LO
192.168.1.1/26

Purpose

Learn how to configure a standard ACL.

Walkthrough

1. Configure the network above. Add a static route on each router so any traffic for any network leaves the Serial interface. You are doing this because, though not a routing lab, you still need the traffic to route. Add the .1 to RouterA serial interface and .2 to RouterB.

```
RouterA(config)#ip route 0.0.0.0 0.0.0.0 s0/1/0
RouterB(config)#ip route 0.0.0.0 0.0.0.0 s0/1/0
```

2. Configure a standard ACL on Router A permitting the 192.168.1.0/10 network. By default, all other networks will be blocked.

```
RouterA(config)#access-list 1 permit 192.168.1.0 0.0.0.63
RouterA(config)#int ser 0/1/0
RouterA(config-if)#ip access-group 1 in
RouterA(config-if)#exit
RouterA(config)#exit
RouterA#
```

3. Test the ACL by pinging from Router B, which by default will use the 10.0.0.1 address.

```
RouterB#ping 10.0.0.1
Type escape sequence to abort.
Sending 5, 100-byte ICMP Echos to 10.0.0.1, timeout is 2 seconds:
UUUUU
Success rate is 0 percent (0/5)
```

4. Test another ping, but source it from 192.168.1.1 and this should work.

```
RouterB#ping
Protocol [ip]:
Target IP address: 10.0.0.1
```

```
Repeat count [5]:
Datagram size [100]:
Timeout in seconds [2]:
Extended commands [n]: y
Source address or interface: 192.168.1.1
Type of service [0]:
Set DF bit in IP header? [no]:
Validate reply data? [no]:
Data pattern [0xABCD]:
Loose, Strict, Record, Timestamp, Verbose[none]:
Sweep range of sizes [n]:
Type escape sequence to abort.
Sending 5, 100-byte ICMP Echos to 10.0.0.1, timeout is 2 seconds:
Packet sent with a source address of 192.168.1.1
!!!!!
Success rate is 100 percent (5/5), round-trip min/avg/max = 31/31/32 ms
```

DAY 32

Extended ACL

DAY 32 TASKS

- Read yesterday's theory notes
- Complete today's lab
- Read the ICND2 cram guide
- Spend 15 minutes on the subnetting.org website

DAY 32 LAB

Topology

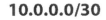

10.0.0.0/30

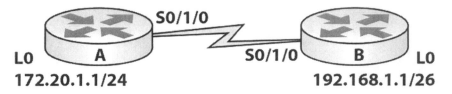

LO   A   S0/1/0   B   LO
172.20.1.1/24   192.168.1.1/26

Purpose

Learn how to configure an extended ACL.

Walkthrough

1. Configure the network above. Add a static route on Router B so any traffic for any network leaves the Serial interface. You are doing this because, though not a routing lab, you still need the traffic to route.

   ```
   RouterB(config)#ip route 0.0.0.0 0.0.0.0 s0/1/0
   ```

2. Add an extended ACL to Router A. Permit Telnet traffic to your Loopback interface only. Remember to permit Telnet also.

   ```
   RouterA(config)#access-list 100 permit tcp any host 172.20.1.1 eq 23
   RouterA(config)#int s0/1/0
   RouterA(config-if)#ip access-group 100 in
   RouterA(config-if)#line vty 0 15
   RouterA(config-line)#password cisco
   RouterA(config-line)#login
   RouterA(config-line)#^Z
   RouterA#
   ```

   The ACL line above is number 100, which tells the router it is extended. What you want to block uses TCP. It is blocking TCP from any network destined for host 172.20.1.1 on the Telnet port, which is 23. When you issue a show run command, the router actually replaces the port number with the name, as illustrated below:

   ```
   access-list 100 permit tcp any host 172.20.1.1 eq telnet
   ```

3. Now test a Telnet from Router B. First, telnet to the Serial interface on Router A, which should be blocked. Then test the Loopback interface.

```
RouterB#telnet 10.0.0.1
Trying 10.0.0.1 ...
% Connection timed out; remote host not responding

RouterB#telnet 172.20.1.1
Trying 172.20.1.1 ...Open

User Access Verification
Password:    ← password won't show when you type it
RouterA>  ←  Hit control+shift+6 together and then let go and press the X key to quit.
```

NOTE: We will be covering ACLs in other labs, but you really need to know these cold. For this reason, try other TCP ports, such as 80, 25, etc. In addition, try UDP ports, such as 53. You won't be able to test them easily without a PC attached to Router B.

Going further, mix up the IP addresses, permitting Telnet (in this example) to the Serial interface but not the Loopback interface. Then put an ACL on Router B instead. I can't over-emphasise how important this is. If you need to wipe the ACL, you can simply type the following:

```
RouterA(config)#no access-list 100
```

Named ACL

DAY 33 TASKS

- Read the ACL theory notes
- Complete today's lab
- Read the ICND2 cram guide
- Spend 15 minutes on the subnetting.org website

DAY 33 LAB

Topology

10.0.0.0/30

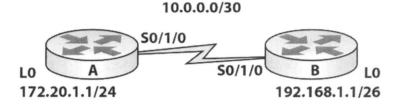

LO — A — S0/1/0 ⟋ S0/1/0 — B — LO
172.20.1.1/24   192.168.1.1/26

Purpose

Learn how to configure a named ACL.

Walkthrough

1. Configure the network above. Add a static route on each router so any traffic for any network leaves the Serial interface. You are doing this because, though not a routing lab, you still need the traffic to route.

    ```
    RouterA(config)#ip route 0.0.0.0 0.0.0.0 s0/1/0
    RouterB(config)#ip route 0.0.0.0 0.0.0.0 s0/1/0
    ```

2. Add an extended named ACL on Router B. Permit pings from host 172.20.1.1 but no other hosts or networks.

    ```
    RouterB(config)#ip access-list extended blockping
    RouterB(config-ext-nacl)#permit icmp host 172.20.1.1 any RouterB(config-
    ext-nacl)#exit
    RouterB(config)#int s0/1/0
    RouterB(config-if)#ip access-group blockping in
    RouterB(config-if)#
    ```

3. Now test the ACL with pings from the Serial interface on Router A and the Loopback interface (which should work).

    ```
    RouterA#ping 192.168.1.1

    Type escape sequence to abort.
    Sending 5, 100-byte ICMP Echos to 192.168.1.1, timeout is 2 seconds:
    UUUUU
    Success rate is 0 percent (0/5)

    RouterA#ping
    Protocol [ip]:
    Target IP address: 192.168.1.1
    Repeat count [5]:
    ```

```
Datagram size [100]:
Timeout in seconds [2]:
Extended commands [n]: y
Source address or interface: 172.20.1.1
Type of service [0]:
Set DF bit in IP header? [no]:
Validate reply data? [no]:
Data pattern [0xABCD]:
Loose, Strict, Record, Timestamp, Verbose[none]:
Sweep range of sizes [n]:
Type escape sequence to abort.
Sending 5, 100-byte ICMP Echos to 192.168.1.1, timeout is 2 seconds:
Packet sent with a source address of 172.20.1.1
!!!!!
Success rate is 100 percent (5/5), round-trip min/avg/max = 31/34/47 ms
```

NOTE: You need to understand which service is which, as well as which port numbers various services use. Otherwise, you will really struggle to configure an ACL. This ACL is pretty straightforward and can be achieved with one line. If you had routing protocols running, then they would need to be permitted.

To permit RIP, specify the following:

```
access-list 101 permit udp any any eq rip
```

To permit OSPF, specify the following:

```
access-list 101 permit ospf any any
```

To permit EIGRP, specify the following:

```
access-list 101 permit eigrp any any
```

DAY 34

Trunking and VLANs

DAY 34 TASKS

- Read today's theory notes
- Review the ACL theory notes
- Complete today's lab
- Read the ICND2 cram guide
- Spend 15 minutes on the subnetting.org website

The bread-and-butter work of any Cisco engineer is installing, configuring, and troubleshooting switches. Strangely enough, this is the weakest area for many of them. Perhaps some people rely on the switches' plug-and-play capabilities, or they try to work through issues as they crop up. This 'fly by the seat of your pants' mentality backfires for many engineers when there is a switching-related issue.

I suggest you give every subject just a cursory read-over to start with, and then reread them a few times over, each time making notes or highlighting the main learning points.

Today you will learn about the following:

- VLANs
- Trunking
- Configuring VLANs
- Inter-VLAN routing
- Troubleshooting VLANs
- VTP
- Troubleshooting trunking and VTP

This lesson maps to the following CCNA syllabus requirements:

- Describe enhanced switching technologies (including VTP, RSTP, VLAN, PVSTP, and 802.1q)
- Describe how VLANs create logically separate networks and the need for routing between them
- Configure, verify, and troubleshoot VLANs
- Configure, verify, and troubleshoot trunking on Cisco switches
- Configure, verify, and troubleshoot inter-VLAN routing
- Configure, verify, and troubleshoot VTP
- Interpret the output of various show and debug commands to verify the operational status of a Cisco switched network

Virtual Local Area Networks (VLANs)

A switch breaks the collision domain and a router breaks a broadcast domain, which means a network would look something like the following figure:

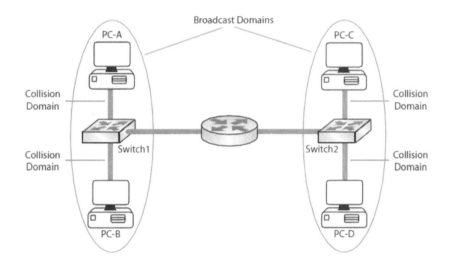

FIG 34.1—Routers Separate Broadcast Domains

Before we continue, let's discuss what a LAN really is. A LAN is essentially a broadcast domain. In the network shown in the figure above, if PC-A sends a broadcast, it will be received by PC-B but not PC-C or PC-D. This is because the router breaks the broadcast domain. Now we can use virtual LANs (VLANs) to put switch ports into different broadcast domains, as illustrated in the figure below:

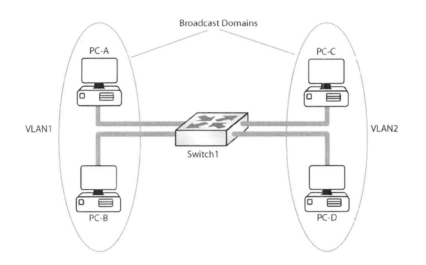

FIG 34.2—Broadcast Domains with VLAN

In the figure above, the Layer 2 network has been divided into two broadcast domains using VLANs. Now a broadcast sent by PC-A will be received by PC-B but not PC-C and PC-D. Without VLANs PC-C and PC-D would have received the broadcasts sent by PC-A.

The following are some advantages of VLANs:

- Containing broadcasts within a smaller group of devices will make the network faster.
- Saves resources on devices because they process less broadcasts.
- Added security by keeping devices in a certain group (or function) in a separate broadcast domain. A group, as implied here, can mean department, security level, etc. For example, devices belonging to a development or testing lab should be kept separate from the production devices.
- Flexibility in expanding a network across a geographical location of any size. For example, it does not matter where in the building a PC is. It thinks it is on the same segment of the network as any other PC configured to be in the same VLAN. In Figure 34.3 below, all hosts in VLAN 1 can talk to each other, even though they are on different floors. The VLAN is transparent or invisible to them.

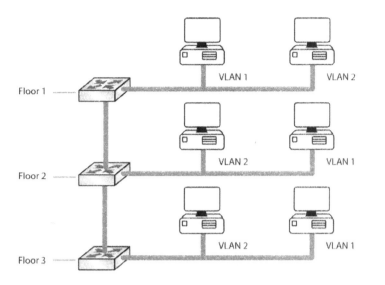

FIG 34.3—VLANs Remove the Physical Boundaries from a LAN

VLAN Membership

There are two common ways to associate ports with VLANs—statically or dynamically.

With static VLAN assignment or configuration, the ports on the switch are configured by the network administrator to be in different VLANs, and the relevant device is then connected to the port. If the user needs to move to another part of the building, this will require the administrator to change the configuration on the switch. All switch ports belong to VLAN 1 by default.

Dynamic VLAN assignment allows devices to join a specific VLAN based upon the MAC address of the device. This gives the administrator the flexibility to allow users to connect to any switch or move around the building without having to change the configuration on the switch. This is achieved using a VLAN Management Policy Server (VMPS).

> **FARAI SAYS:** 'Ports are assigned to VLANs and devices are connected to ports.'

Please note that since each VLAN is a different broadcast domain, this means:

- Hosts in one VLAN cannot reach hosts in another VLAN, by default;
- A Layer 3 device is needed for inter-VLAN communication (covered later);
- Each VLAN needs its own subnets, for example, VLAN 1—192.168.1.0/24, VLAN 2—192.168.2.0/24; and
- All hosts in a VLAN should belong to the same subnet.

VLAN Links

We know that one switch can have hosts connected to multiple VLANs. What happens when traffic goes from one host to another? For example, in Figure 34.3 above, when the host in VLAN 1 on Floor 1 tries to reach the host in VLAN 1 on Floor 2, how will the switch on Floor 2 know which VLAN the traffic belongs to?

Switches use a mechanism called 'frame tagging' to keep traffic on different VLANs separate. The switch adds a header on the frame, which contains the VLAN ID. In Figure 34.3, the switch on Floor 1 will tag the traffic originating from VLAN 1 and pass it to Switch 2, which will see the tag and know that the traffic needs to be kept within that VLAN. Such tagged traffic can only flow across special links called trunk links.

Switch ports can be divided into the following:

- Access links or ports
- Trunk links or ports

Access Links

A switch port, which is defined as an access link, can be a member of only one VLAN. The device connected to the access link is not aware of the existence of any other VLANs. The switch will add a tag to a frame as it enters a trunk link from the host and remove the tag when a frame exits the switch trunk link towards the host. Access links are used to connect to hosts, but they can also be used to connect to a router. Trunk links are covered in the following section.

Trunking

A switch port usually will connect either to a host on the network or to another network switch or router or server. If this is the case, then the link may need to carry traffic from several VLANs. In order to do this, each frame needs to identify which VLAN it is from. This identification method is known as frame tagging. The tag in the frame contains the VLAN ID.

When the frame reaches the switch where the destination host resides, the tag is removed.

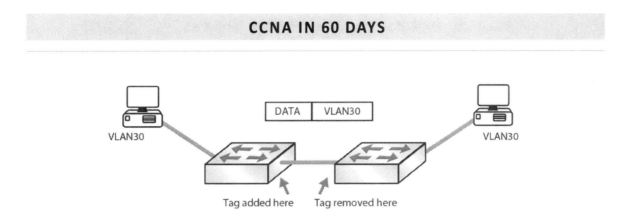

FIG 34.4—VLAN Tagging

VLAN trunks are used to carry data from multiple VLANs. In order to differentiate one VLAN frame from another, all frames sent across a trunk link are specially tagged so that the destination switch knows which VLAN the frame belongs to. ISL and 802.1Q are the two primary encapsulation methods which can be used to ensure that VLANs that traverse a switch trunk link can be uniquely identified.

ISL is Cisco proprietary; however, the model tested in the CCNA exam is the 2950 switch, which only recognises 802.1Q.

FARAI SAYS: 'All new switches now default to 802.1Q. ISL is being deprecated.'

All frames are tagged before passing over the trunk link, apart from the native VLAN.

802.1Q differs from ISL in several ways. The first significant difference is that 802.1Q supports up to 4096 VLANs, whereas ISL supports up to 1000. Another significant difference is that of the native VLAN concept used in 802.1Q. By default, all frames from all VLANs are tagged when using 802.1Q. The only exception to this rule is frames that belong to the native VLAN, which are not tagged.

However, keep in mind that it is possible to specify which VLAN will not have frames tagged by specifying that VLAN as the native VLAN on a particular trunk link. For example, to prevent tagging of frames in VLAN 400 when using 802.1Q, you would configure that VLAN as the native VLAN on a particular trunk. IEEE 802.1Q native VLAN configuration will be illustrated in detail later.

The following summarises some 802.1Q features:

- It can support up to 4096 VLANs.
- It uses an internal tagging mechanism, modifying the original frame.
- It is an open standard protocol developed by the IEEE.
- It does not tag frames on the native VLAN; however, all other frames are tagged.

Following is a short sample configuration of a switch. I have included the `switchport` command, which tells the switch to act as a switch port for Layer 2 as opposed to Layer 3. You can't actually use this command on a Cisco 2950 switch because it only operates at Layer 2.

```
Sw(config)#interface fastethernet 0/1
Sw(config-if)#switchport
Sw(config-if)#switchport mode trunk
Sw(config-if)#switchport trunk encapsulation dot1q
Sw(config-if)#exit
```

And, of course, on a 2950 switch, the encapsulation command won't be recognised because there is only one type available. You will need to set the interface as a trunking interface when connecting to another switch to allow VLANs to be tagged.

A trunk link on a switch can be in one of five possible modes:

1. On—forces the port into permanent trunking mode. The port becomes a trunk even if the connected device does not agree to convert the link into a trunk link.
2. Off—link is not used as a trunk link, even if the connected device is set to trunk.
3. Auto—port is willing to become a trunk link. If the other device is set to on or desirable, then the link becomes a trunk link. If both sides are left as auto, then the link will never become a trunk, as neither side will attempt to convert.
4. Desirable—the port actively tries to convert to a trunk link. If the other device is set to on, auto, or desirable, then the link will become a trunk link.
5. No-negotiate—prevents the port from negotiating a trunk connection. It will be forced into an access or trunk mode as per the configuration.

Configuring VLANs

Now that you understand VLANs and trunk links, let's configure the network as shown in Figure 34.5 below. You need to configure the switches such that the hosts on fa0/1 are in VLAN 5 and the link on port fa0/15 is a trunk link.

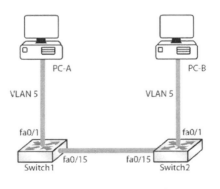

FIG 34.5—Test Network

Before assigning ports to VLANs, the VLAN itself must be created using the `vlan <vlan#>` global configuration command. This will put you into VLAN Configuration mode, where a descriptive name can be given to the VLANs. Here is an example:

```
Switch1(config)#vlan 5
Switch1(config-vlan)#name RnD
Switch2(config)vlan 5
Switch2(config-vlan)#name RnD
```

To see which VLANs exist on a switch, use the `show vlan` command. The output will be similar to the one below:

```
Switch1#show vlan
VLAN    Name      Status       Ports
----    --------  -------      --------------------------------
                               Fa0/1, Fa0/2, Fa0/3, Fa0/4 Fa0/5, Fa0/6,
                               Fa0/7, Fa0/8 Fa0/9, Fa0/10, Fa0/11, Fa0/12,
1       default   active       Fa0/13 Fa0/14, Fa/15, Fa0/16, Fa0/17,
                               Fa0/18

--output truncated--

5       RnD       active

--output truncated
```

Let's assign port fa0/1 to VLAN 5 using the switchport access vlan (vlan#)

```
interface command:
Switch1(config)#int fa0/1
Switch1(config-if)#switchport access vlan 5

Switch2(config)#int fa0/1
Switch2(config-if)#switchport access vlan 5
```

Let's look at the output of show vlan now:

```
Switch1#show vlan

VLAN    Name      Status    Ports
----    ----      -----     --------------------------------
                            Fa0/2, Fa0/3, Fa0/4, Fa0/5 Fa0/6, Fa0/7, Fa0/8,
1       default   active    Fa0/9 Fa0/10, Fa0/11, Fa0/12, Fa0/13 Fa0/14,
                            Fa/15,Fa0/16, Fa0/17, Fa0/18
--output truncated--
5       RnD       active    Fa0/1
--output truncated
```

Note that fa0/1 is now assigned to VLAN 5. Let's configure interface fa0/15 on both switches as trunk links. It should be noted here that the default mode on switch ports is desirable. Hence, DTP will cause fa0/15 on both switches to become ISL trunk links. This can be verified using the show interface trunk command:

```
Switch1#show interface trunk

Port    Mode        Encapsulation  Status      Native vlan
Fa0/15  desirable   n-isl          trunking    1
```

Note that the mode is desirable and the encapsulation is ISL (n stands for negotiated).

The following output shows how to configure the trunk to use ISL trunking:
```
Switch1(config)#interface fa0/15
Switch1(config-if)#switchport trunk encapsulation isl
Switch1(config-if)#switchport mode trunk

Switch2(config)#interface fa0/15
Switch2(config-if)#switchport trunk encapsulation isl
Switch2(config-if)#switchport mode trunk
```

The switchport trunk encapsulation command sets the trunking protocol on the port, and the switchport mode trunk command sets the port to trunking. The output of show interface trunk will now look like this:

```
Switch2#show interface trunk

Port    Mode   Encapsulation  Status      Native vlan
Fa0/15  on     isl            trunking    1
```

Note that the encapsulation is now ISL instead of N-ISL. This is because this time the protocol was not negotiated but configured on the interface.

IMPORTANT NOTE: Trunk encapsulation needs to be configured on the switch port before setting it to trunk mode. Please note that this does not apply to switch model 2950 (currently used for the CCNA syllabus), which can only use dot1q (another name for 802.1Q) encapsulation. For this reason, the switchport trunk encapsulation command will not work on the 2950 switch.

Similarly, we can configure the switch port to use 802.1q instead of ISL, as illustrated in the output below:

```
Switch1(config)#interface fa0/15
Switch1(config-if)#switchport trunk encapsulation dot1q
Switch1(config-if)#switchport mode trunk

Switch2(config)#interface fa0/15
Switch2(config-if)#switchport trunk encapsulation dot1q
Switch2(config-if)#switchport mode trunk
```

The show interface trunk output now looks like this:

```
Switch2#show interface trunk

Port    Mode   Encapsulation       Status       Native vlan
Fa0/15  on     802.1q              trunking     1
```

Note that the native VLAN is 1. That is, the default native VLAN on an 802.1q trunk can be changed using the `switchport trunk native vlan <vlan#>` command. This command is part of the CCNA syllabus and is considered a security measure.

> **IMPORTANT NOTE:** Switches remember all VLAN info, even when reloaded. If you want your switch to boot with a blank configuration, then you need to issue the `delete vlan.dat` command on your switch. This applies to live switches only, not switch emulators such as Packet Tracer.

```
SwitchA#dir flash:
Directory of flash:/

1  -rw-     3058048        <no date>  c2950-i6q412-mz.121-22.EA4.bin
2  -rw-     676            <no date>  vlan.dat

64016384 bytes total (60957660 bytes free)
SwitchA#
SwitchA#
SwitchA#delete vlan.dat
Delete filename [vlan.dat]?
Delete flash:/vlan.dat? [confirm]

SwitchA#dir flash:
Directory of flash:/

  1  -rw-     3058048        <no date>  c2950-i6q412-mz.121-22.EA4.bin

64016384 bytes total (60958336 bytes free)
SwitchA#
```

Inter-VLAN Routing

Earlier, we learned that hosts in one VLAN cannot communicate with hosts in another VLAN. To facilitate this, we need a Layer 3 device, such as a router. The link between the router and the switch will be a trunk link. An interface on a router can be divided into logical interfaces called subinterfaces. Each subinterface supports a specific VLAN. The network shown in Figure 34.6 below is known as a router-on-a-stick.

The concept behind router-on-a-stick is that in order to route between different subnets, it would require a router. The minimum number of routers required would be one, and if it had only one available interface, then it would require subinterfaces (one per VLAN):

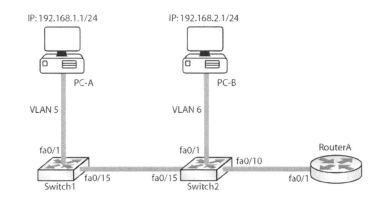

FIG 34.6—Router-on-a-Stick

In such a network, Router A's interface (fa0/1, in our case) is configured with subinterfaces—one for each VLAN. Each subinterface is assigned an IP address from the respective VLAN subnet. Let's configure the network and then look at how the traffic will flow from one VLAN to another:

```
Switch1(config)#interface fa0/1
Switch1(config-if)#switchport mode access
Switch1(config-if)#switchport access vlan 5
Switch1(config-if)#exit
Switch1(config)#interface fa0/15
Switch1(config-if)#switchport trunk encapsulation dot1q
Switch1(config-if)#switchport mode trunk

Switch2(config)#interface fa0/1
Switch2(config-if)#switchport mode access
Switch2(config-if)#switchport access vlan 6
Switch2(config-if)#exit
Switch2(config)#interface fa0/15
Switch2(config-if)#switchport trunk encapsulation dot1q
Switch2(config-if)#switchport mode trunk
Switch2(config-if)#exit
```

```
Switch2(config)#interface fa0/10
Switch2(config-if)#switchport trunk encapsulation dot1q
Switch2(config-if)#switchport mode trunk

RouterA(config)#interface fa0/1.5
RouterA(config-if)#encapsulation dot1q
RouterA(config-if)#ip address 192.168.1.10 255.255.255.0
RouterA(config-if)#exit
RouterA(config)#interface fa0/1.6
RouterA(config-if)#encapsulation dot1q
RouterA(config-if)#ip address 192.168.2.10 255.255.255.0
```

For the router subinterfaces, it is common practise to number them to match the VLAN they are a member of (e.g., FastEthernet 0/1.5 for VLAN 5).

For hosts in VLAN 5, the gateway will be 192.168.1.10, and for hosts in VLAN 6, the gateway will be 192.168.2.10. Both of these IP addresses belong to subinterfaces on Router A. When PC-A needs to communicate with PC-B, the traffic will go from Switch 1 to Switch 2 through the trunk link on fa0/15. From there it will go to interface fa0/1.5 on Router A and will then be routed out off fa0/1.6, finally reaching PC-B on VLAN 6. Lab this up if you can.

Troubleshooting VLANs

VLANs are a fairly straightforward feature which rarely requires troubleshooting. A few of the problems that you will see are mostly configuration errors. Common ones include the following:

1. **Inter-VLAN routing not working:** Check to ensure the link between the switches and the routers is set up correctly, and the relevant VLANs are allowed and not pruned (see VTP pruning). The `show interface trunk` command will provide the required information. Also check to ensure the router's subinterfaces are configured with correct encapsulation and VLAN, and the subinterface's IP address is the default gateway for the hosts.

2. **VLANs cannot be created:** Check whether the VTP mode on the switch is set to client. VLANs cannot be created if the VTP mode is client. Another important factor is the number of VLANs allowed on the switch. The `show vtp status` command will provide the information required. (See VTP below.)

3. **Hosts within the same VLAN cannot reach each other:** It is important that hosts in a VLAN have an IP address belonging to the same subnet. If the subnet is different, then they will not be able to reach each other. Another factor to consider is whether the hosts are connected to the same switch. If they are not connected to the same switch, then ensure that

the trunk link(s) between the switches is/are working correctly and that the VLAN is not excluded/not pruned from the allowed list. The `show interface trunk` command will show needed information regarding the trunk link.

VTP

VLAN Trunking Protocol (VTP) is a Cisco proprietary Layer 2 messaging protocol that manages the addition, deletion, and renaming of VLANs on switches in the same VTP domain. VTP allows VLAN information to propagate through the switched network, which reduces administration overhead in a switched network, whilst enabling switches to exchange and maintain consistent VLAN information.

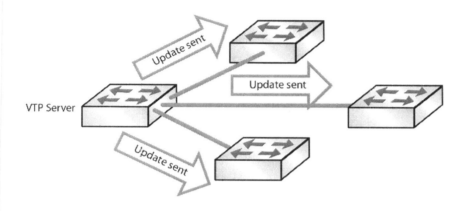

FIG 34.7—VTP Updates

Some benefits to using VTP include the following:

- Accurate monitoring and reporting of VLANs
- VLAN consistency across the network
- Ease of adding and removing VLANs

Configuring VTP

All switches must be configured with the same VTP domain name if they are to exchange VLAN information.

```
Switch(config)#vtp mode server ← this is on by default
Switch(config)#vtp domain in60days
Changing VTP domain name from NULL to in60days

show vtp status
VTP Version                      : 2
Configuration Revision           : 0
Maximum VLANs Supported Locally  : 255
```

```
Number of Existing VLANs        : 5
VTP Operating Mode              : Server
VTP Domain Name                 : in60days
```

If you want to secure your VTP updates, you can add a password, but it must match on each switch in the VTP domain:

```
Switch(config)#vtp password Cisco321
Setting device VLAN database password to Cisco321
```

VTP Modes

VTP runs in the following three modes:

- Server (default)
- Client
- Transparent

You can see the server mode in the configuration and output above.

Server Mode

In server mode, the switch is authorised to create, modify, and delete VLAN information for the entire VTP domain. Any changes you make to a server are propagated to the whole domain.

Client Mode

In client mode, the switch will receive VTP information and apply any changes, but it does not allow adding, removing, or changing VLAN information on the switch. The client will also send the VTP packet received out of its trunk ports. Remember that you cannot add a switch port on a VTP client switch to a VLAN that does not exist on the VTP server.

Transparent Mode

In transparent mode, the switch will forward the VTP information received out of its trunk ports but will not apply the changes. A VTP transparent-mode switch can create, modify, and delete VLANs, but the changes are not propagated to other switches. VTP transparent mode also requires configuration of domain information. A VTP transparent switch is needed when a switch separating a VTP server and client needs to have a different VLAN database.

VTP Pruning

There will often be situations where you have VLANs 20 to 50, for example, on one side of your network and 60 to 80 on the other. It doesn't make sense for VLAN information from the switches on one side to be passed to every switch on the other. For this reason, switches can prune unnecessary VLAN information on the switches.

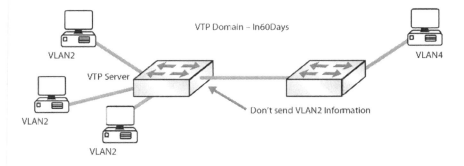

FIG 34.8—VTP Pruning in Operation

The following line of configuration will add VTP pruning to your switch:

```
Switch(config)#vtp pruning
```

It is worth noting that if you have a switch sent to transparent mode in-between two other switches, then pruning will not work.

Troubleshooting Trunking and VTP

Following are examples of problems and possible solutions:

Trunk down?

- Interface must be up/up
- Encapsulation must match both sides

```
SwitchA#show interface fa1/1 switchport
Name: Fa1/1
Switchport: Enabled
Administrative Mode: trunk
Operational Mode: trunk
Administrative Trunking Encapsulation: dot1q
Operational Trunking Encapsulation: dot1q
Negotiation of Trunking: Disabled
Access Mode VLAN: 0 ((Inactive))
```

VLAN information not passing?

- Is the VLAN blocked on the trunk?

```
Switch#show interface trunk
```

VTP information not reaching the client?

- Correct domain and VTP password?

```
show vtp status / show vtp password
```

Added a new switch and all VTP information has changed?
- Always add a new switch in client mode
- Server mode will propagate new information

VTP pruning not working?
- Is there a transparent switch in the middle?
- Is the VLAN allowed across the trunk?

DAY 34 QUESTIONS

1. Name three advantages of using VLANS (there are four in this module).
2. Hosts in the same VLAN can be in different subnets. True or false?
3. An access link is part of more than one VLAN. True or false?
4. Name the two trunk link encapsulation types.
5. Which commands will configure and name a VLAN?
6. A trunk link on a switch can be in which five possible modes?
7. Which command would put your interface into VLAN 5?
8. Which command will change the native VLAN?
9. VTP client mode allows you to configure VLANs. True or false?
10. Name three benefits of using VTP.
11. Which command configures VTP pruning on your switch?

DAY 34 LAB—VLAN AND TRUNKING

Topology

Purpose

Learn how to configure VLANs and trunk links.

Walkthrough

1. You will need to add IP addresses on each PC. Feel free to choose your own, so long as they are in the same subnet!

2. On Switch A, set the hostname, create VLAN 2, and put the interface to which your PC is connected into VLAN 2. You can also give the VLAN a name if you wish.

```
Switch>en
Switch#conf t
Enter configuration commands, one per line.  End with CNTL/Z.
Switch(config)#hostname SwitchA
SwitchA(config)#vlan 2
SwitchA(config-vlan)#name 60days
SwitchA(config-vlan)#interface fast 0/1
SwitchA(config-if)#switchport mode access
SwitchA(config-if)#switchport access vlan 2
SwitchA(config-if)#^Z

SwitchA#show vlan brief

VLAN Name                            Status    Ports
---- ---------- ------------------------------
1    default    active     Fa0/2, Fa0/3, Fa0/4, Fa0/5
Fa0/6, Fa0/7, Fa0/8, Fa0/9
Fa0/10, Fa0/11, Fa0/12, Fa0/13
                        Fa0/14, Fa0/15, Fa0/16, Fa0/17
                        Fa0/18, Fa0/19, Fa0/20, Fa0/21
                        Fa0/22, Fa0/23, Fa0/24
2    60days                          active     Fa0/1
1002 fddi-default                    active
1003 token-ring-default              active
1004 fddinet-default                 active
1005 trnet-default                   active
SwitchA#
```

3. Set your trunk link to trunk mode.

```
SwitchA#conf t
Enter configuration commands, one per line.  End with CNTL/Z.
SwitchA(config)#int fast 0/2
SwitchA(config-if)#switchport mode trunk

SwitchA#show interface trunk
Port         Mode         Encapsulation  Status        Native vlan
Fa0/2        on           802.1q         trunking      1

Port         Vlans allowed on trunk
Fa0/2        1-1005
```

4. If you wish, permit only VLAN 2 on the trunk link.

```
SwitchA(config)#int fast 0/2
SwitchA(config-if)#switchport trunk allowed vlan 2
SwitchA(config-if)#^Z
SwitchA#
%SYS-5-CONFIG_I: Configured from console by console

SwitchA#show int trunk
Port         Mode         Encapsulation  Status        Native vlan
Fa0/2        on           802.1q         trunking      1

Port         Vlans allowed on trunk
Fa0/2        2
```

5. At this point, if you ping from one PC to another, it should fail. This is because one side is in VLAN 1 and the other is in VLAN 2.

```
PC>ping 192.168.1.1

Pinging 192.168.1.1 with 32 bytes of data:

Request timed out.

Ping statistics for 192.168.1.1:
    Packets: Sent = 2, Received = 0, Lost = 2 (100% loss)
```

6. I want you to configure the same commands on Switch B now. For VLAN creation, put the PC port into VLAN 2, and set the interface to access and the trunk link to trunk.

7. Now you should be able to ping across the trunk link from PC to PC.

```
PC>ping 192.168.1.1

Pinging 192.168.1.1 with 32 bytes of data:

Reply from 192.168.1.1: bytes=32 time=188ms TTL=128
Reply from 192.168.1.1: bytes=32 time=78ms TTL=128
Reply from 192.168.1.1: bytes=32 time=94ms TTL=128
Reply from 192.168.1.1: bytes=32 time=79ms TTL=128

Ping statistics for 192.168.1.1:
    Packets: Sent = 4, Received = 4, Lost = 0 (0% loss),
Approximate round trip times in milli-seconds:
    Minimum = 78ms, Maximum = 188ms, Average = 109ms
```

DAY 35

Spanning Tree Protocol

DAY 35 TASKS

- Read today's theory notes
- Review yesterday's theory notes
- Complete today's lab
- Read the ICND2 cram guide
- Spend 15 minutes on the subnetting.org website

The role of Spanning Tree Protocol (STP) is to prevent loops from occurring on your network. With the huge growth in the use of switches on networks, and the main goal of propagating VLAN information, the problem of frames looping endlessly around the network began to occur.

Today you will learn about the following:

- The need for STP
- STP Bridge ID
- STP Root Bridge election
- STP cost and priority
- STP root and designated ports
- STP enhancements
- Troubleshooting STP

This lesson maps to the following CCNA syllabus requirement:

- Describe enhanced switching technologies (including VTP, RSTP, VLAN, PVSTP, and 802.1q)

The Need for STP

STP is defined in the IEEE 802.1D standard. In order to maintain a loop-free topology, every two seconds, switches pass Bridge Protocol Data Units (BPDUs). BPDUs are data messages used within a spanning tree topology to pass information about ports, addresses, priorities, and costs. The BPDUs are tagged with the VLAN ID.

Figure 35.1 below shows how loops can be created in a network. Because each switch learns about VLAN 20, it also advertises to other switches that it can reach VLAN 20. Soon enough, each switch thinks it is the source for VLAN 20 traffic and a loop is caused, so any frame destined for VLAN 20 is passed from switch to switch.

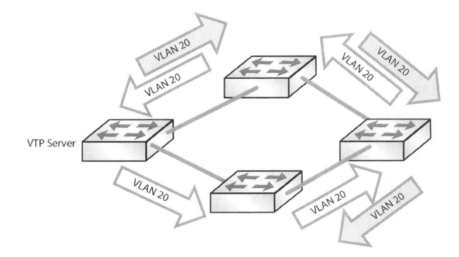

FIG 35.1—How Loops Are Created

STP runs an algorithm to decide which switch ports stay open, or active, as far as a particular VLAN is concerned, and which ones need to be shut for that particular VLAN.

All switches that reside in the Spanning Tree domain communicate and exchange messages using BPDUs. The exchange of BPDUs is used by STP to determine the network topology. The topology of an active switched network is determined by the following three variables:

1. The unique MAC address (switch identifier) that is associated with each switch
2. The path cost to the Root Bridge associated with each switch port
3. The port identifier (MAC address of the port) associated with each switch port

BPDUs are sent every two seconds, which allows for rapid network loop detection and topology information exchanges. The two types of BPDUs are Configuration BPDUs and Topology Change Notification BPDUs; only Configuration BPDUs will be covered here.

IEEE 802.1D Configuration BPDUs

Configuration BPDUs are sent by LAN switches and are used to communicate and compute the Spanning Tree topology. After the switch port initialises, the port is placed into the Blocking state and a BPDU is sent to each port in the switch. By default, all switches initially assume that they are the Root of the Spanning Tree, until they exchange Configuration BPDUs with other switches. As long as a port continues to see its Configuration BPDU as the most attractive, it will continue sending Configuration BPDUs. Switches determine the best Configuration BPDU based on the following four factors (in the order listed):

1. Lowest Root Bridge ID
2. Lowest Root path cost to Root Bridge
3. Lowest sender Bridge ID
4. Lowest sender Port ID

The completion of the Configuration BPDU exchange results in the following actions:

- A Root Switch is elected for the entire Spanning Tree domain
- A Root Port is elected on every Non-Root Switch in the Spanning Tree domain
- A Designated Switch is elected for every LAN segment
- A Designated Port is elected on the Designated Switch for every segment
- Loops in the network are eliminated by blocking redundant paths

NOTE: These characteristics will be described in detail as you progress through this lesson.

Once the Spanning Tree network has converged, which happens when all switch ports are in a Forwarding or Blocking state, Configuration BPDUs are sent by the Root Bridge every Hello Time interval, which defaults to two seconds. This is referred to as the origination of Configuration BPDUs. The Configuration BPDUs are forwarded to downstream neighbouring switches via the Designated Port on the Root Bridge.

When a Non-Root Bridge receives a Configuration BPDU on its Root Port, which is the port that provides the best path to the Root Bridge, it sends an updated version of the BPDU via its Designated Port(s). This is referred to as the propagation of BPDUs.

The Designated Port is a port on the Designated Switch that has the lowest path cost when forwarding packets from that LAN to the Root Bridge.

Once the Spanning Tree network has converged, a Configuration BPDU is always transmitted away from the Root Bridge to the rest of the switches within the STP domain. The simplest way to remember the flow of Configuration BPDUs after the Spanning Tree network has converged is to memorise the following four rules:

1. A Configuration BPDU originates on the Root Bridge and is sent via the Designated Port.
2. A Configuration BPDU is received by a Non-Root Bridge on a Root Port.
3. A Configuration BPDU is transmitted by a Non-Root Bridge on a Designated Port.
4. There is only one Designated Port (on a Designated Switch) on any single LAN segment.

Figure 35.2 below illustrates the flow of the Configuration BPDU in the STP domain, demonstrating the four simple rules listed above:

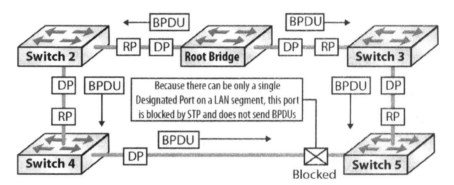

FIG 35.2—Configuration BPDU Flows throughout the STP Domain

5. Referencing Figure 35.2, the Configuration BPDU is originated by the Root Bridge and sent out via the Designated Ports on the Root Bridge towards the Non-Root Bridge switches, Switch 2 and Switch 3.

6. Non-Root Bridge switches, Switch 2 and Switch 3, receive the Configuration BPDU on their Root Ports, which provide the best path to the Root Bridge.

7. Switch 2 and Switch 3 modify (update) the received Configuration BPDU and forward it out of their Designated Ports. Switch 2 is the Designated Switch on the LAN segment for itself and Switch 4, while Switch 3 is the Designated Switch on the LAN segment for itself and Switch 5. The Designated Port resides on the Designated Switch and is the port that has the lowest path cost when forwarding packets from that LAN segment to the Root Bridge.

8. On the LAN Segment between Switch 4 and Switch 5, Switch 4 is elected Designated Switch and the Designated Port resides on that switch. Because there can be only a single Designated

Switch on a segment, the port on Switch 5 for that LAN segment is blocked. This port will not forward any BPDUs.

Spanning Tree Port States

The Spanning Tree Algorithm (STA) defines a number of states that a port under STP control will progress through before being in an active Forwarding state. These port states are as follows:

- Blocking
- Listening
- Learning
- Forwarding
- Disabled

A port moves through these states in the following manner:

1. From initialisation to Blocking
2. From Blocking to either Listening or Disabled
3. From Listening to either Learning or Disabled
4. From Learning to either Forwarding or Disabled
5. From Forwarding to Disabled

Spanning Tree Blocking State

A switch port that is in the Blocking state performs the following actions:

- Discards frames received on the port from the attached segment
- Discards frames switched from another port
- Does not incorporate station location into its address database
- Receives BPDUs and directs them to the system module
- Does not transmit BPDUs received from the system module
- Receives and responds to network management messages

Spanning Tree Listening State

The Listening state is the first transitional state that the port enters following the Blocking state. The port enters this state when STP determines that the port should participate in frame forwarding. A switch port that is in the Listening state performs the following actions:

- Discards frames received on the port from the attached segment
- Discards frames switched from another port

- Does not incorporate station location into its address database
- Receives BPDUs and directs them to the system module
- Receives, processes, and transmits BPDUs received from the system module
- Receives and responds to network management messages

Spanning Tree Learning State

The Learning state is the second transitional state the port enters. This state comes after the Listening state and before the port enters the Forwarding state. In this state, the port learns and installs MAC addresses into its forwarding table. A switch port that is in the Learning state performs the following actions:

- Discards frames received from the attached segment
- Discards frames switched from another port
- Incorporates (installs) station location into its address database
- Receives BPDUs and directs them to the system module
- Receives, processes, and transmits BPDUs received from the system module
- Receives and responds to network management messages

Spanning Tree Forwarding State

The Forwarding state is the final transitional state the port enters after the Learning state. A port in the Forwarding state forwards frames. A switch port that is in the Forwarding state performs the following actions:

- Forwards frames received from the attached segment
- Forwards frames switched from another port
- Incorporates (installs) station location information into its address database
- Receives BPDUs and directs them to the system module
- Processes BPDUs received from the system module
- Receives and responds to network management messages

Spanning Tree Disabled State

The Disabled state is not part of the normal STP progression for a port. Instead, a port that is administratively shut down by the network administrator, or by the system because of a fault condition, is considered to be in the Disabled state. A disabled port performs the following actions:

- Discards frames received from the attached segment
- Discards frames switched from another port
- Does not incorporate station location into its address database

- Receives BPDUs but does not direct them to the system module
- Does not receive BPDUs from the system module
- Receives and responds to network management messages

Spanning Tree Bridge ID

Switches in a Spanning Tree domain have a Bridge ID (BID), which is used to identify uniquely the switch within the STP domain. The BID is also used to assist in the election of an STP Root Bridge, which will be described later. The BID is an 8-byte field that is composed from a 6-byte MAC address and a 2-byte Bridge Priority. The BID is illustrated in Figure 35.3 below:

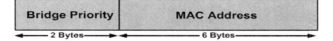

FIG 35.3—Bridge ID Format

The Bridge Priority is the priority of the switch in relation to all other switches. The Bridge Priority values range from 0 to 65,535. The default value for Cisco Catalyst switches is 32,768.

```
Switch2#show spanning-tree vlan 2

VLAN0002
  Spanning tree enabled protocol ieee
  Root ID    Priority    32768
             Address     0009.7c87.9081
             Cost        19
             Port        1 (FastEthernet0/1)
             Hello Time 2 sec Max Age 20 sec Forward Delay 15 sec
  Bridge ID  Priority    32770 (priority 32768 sys-id-ext 2)
             Address     0008.21a9.4f80
             Hello Time 2 sec Max Age 20 sec Forward Delay 15 sec
             Aging Time 300

Interface   Port ID              Designated            Port ID
Name        Prio.Nbr  Cost  Sts Cost        Bridge ID   Prio.Nbr
----------  --------  ----  --- ------ ----- -------------- --------
Fa0/1       128.1       19  FWD      0 32768 0009.7c87.9081 128.13
Fa0/2       128.2       19  FWD     19 32770 0008.21a9.4f80 128.2
```

The MAC address is the hardware address derived from the switch backplane or supervisor engine. In the 802.1D standard, each VLAN requires a unique BID.

Most Cisco Catalyst switches have a pool of 1024 MAC addresses that can be used as BIDs for VLANs. These MAC addresses are allocated sequentially, with the first MAC address in the range assigned to VLAN 1, the second to VLAN 2, the third to VLAN 3, and so forth. This provides the capability to support the standard range of VLANs, but more MAC addresses would be needed to support the extended range of VLANs. This issue was resolved in the 802.1t standard.

Spanning Tree Root Bridge Election

By default, following initialisation, all switches initially assume that they are the Root of the Spanning Tree, until they exchange BPDUs with other switches. When switches exchange BPDUs, an election is held and the switch with the highest Bridge Priority is elected the STP Root Bridge. If two or more switches have the same priority, the switch with the lowest order MAC address is chosen. This concept is illustrated in Figure 35.4 below:

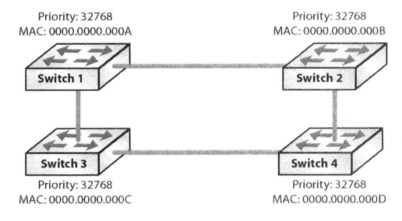

FIG 35.4—Electing the STP Root Bridge

In Figure 35.4, four switches—Switch 1, Switch 2, Switch 3, and Switch 4--are all part of the same STP domain. By default, all of the switches have a Bridge Priority of 32,768. In order to determine which switch will become the Root Bridge, and thus break the tie, STP will select the switch based on the lowest order MAC address. Based on this criterion, and referencing the information printed in Figure 35.4, Switch 1 will be elected the Root Bridge.

Once elected, the Root Bridge becomes the logical centre of the Spanning Tree network. This is not to say that the Root Bridge is physically at the centre of the network. Ensure that you do not make that false assumption.

NOTE: It is important to remember that during STP Root Bridge election, no traffic is forwarded over any switch in the same STP domain.

Cisco IOS software allows administrators to influence the election of the Root Bridge. In addition, administrators can also configure a backup Root Bridge. The backup Root Bridge is a switch that administrators would prefer to become the Root Bridge in the event that the current Root Bridge failed or was removed from the network.

It is always good practise to configure a backup Root Bridge for the Spanning Tree domain. This allows the network to be deterministic in the event that the Root Bridge fails. The most common practise is to configure the highest priority (i.e. the lowest numerical value) on the Root Bridge and then the second-highest priority on the switch that should assume Root Bridge functionality in the event that the current Root Bridge fails. This is illustrated in Figure 35.5 below:

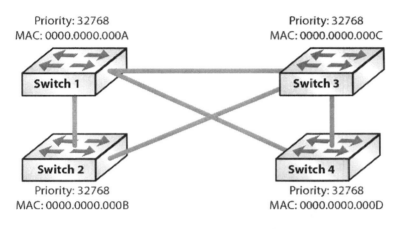

FIG 35.5—Electing the STP Root Bridge (Continued)

Based on the configuration in Figure 35.5, the most likely switch to be elected as the Root Bridge in this network is Switch 1. This is because, although all priority values are the same, this switch has the lowest order MAC address. In the event that Switch 1 failed, STP would elect Switch 2 as the Root Bridge, because it has the second-lowest MAC address. However, this would result in a suboptimal network topology.

To address this, administrators can manually configure the priority on Switch 1 to the lowest possible value (0) and that of Switch 2 to the second-lowest possible value (4096). This will ensure that in the event that the Root Bridge (Switch 1) fails, Switch 2 will be elected the Root Bridge. Because administrators are aware of the topology and know which switch would assume Root Bridge functionality, they created a deterministic network that is easier to troubleshoot. The Root ID is carried in BPDUs and includes the Bridge Priority and MAC address of the Root Bridge.

EXAM TIP: If you want to force a switch to become the Root Bridge, you can perform the following:

- You can manually set the priority

```
Switch(config)#spanning-tree vlan 2 priority ?
  <0-61440>  bridge priority in increments of 4096
```

- Or set as Root Bridge primary or secondary

```
Switch(config)#spanning-tree vlan 2 root ?
  primary    Configure this switch as primary root for this spanning tree
  secondary  Configure switch as secondary root
```

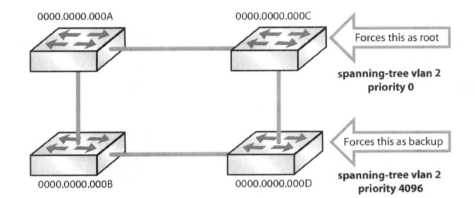

0000.0000.000A   0000.0000.000C
                                              ◁ Forces this as root

                                              **spanning-tree vlan 2
                                              priority 0**

                                              ◁ Forces this as backup

0000.0000.000B   0000.0000.000D
                                              **spanning-tree vlan 2
                                              priority 4096**

FIG 35.6—Forcing a Switch to Become the Root Bridge

```
SwitchC#show spanning-tree vlan 5
VLAN0005
Spanning tree enabled protocol ieee
Root ID   Priority      0
Address   0000.0000.000c
This bridge is the root
Bridge ID       Priority      0 (priority 0 sys-id-ext 5)
SwitchD#show spanning-tree vlan 5
VLAN0005
Spanning tree enabled protocol ieee
Root ID   Priority      4096
Address   0000.0000.000d
Bridge ID       Priority      4096 (priority 8192 sys-id-ext 5)

SwitchD#show spanning-tree vlan 5
VLAN0005
Spanning tree enabled protocol ieee
Root ID   Priority      4096
Address   0000.0000.000d
Bridge ID       Priority      4096 (priority 8192 sys-id-ext 5)
Note that the VLAN number is often added to the priority number:
SwitchA#show spanning-tree vlan 5
Bridge ID       Priority 32773 (priority 32768 sys-id-ext 5)
Address 0013.c3e8.2500
Hello Time     2 sec Max Age 20 sec Forward Delay 15 sec
Aging Time 300
Interface Role  Sts   Cost  Prio.Nbr     Type
------------- ------------- ------------- -------------
------------- -------------
Fa0/15   Desg  FWD   19    128.15       P2p
Fa0/18   Desg  FWD   19    128.18 P2
```

Spanning Tree Cost and Priority

STP uses cost and priority values to determine the best path to the Root Bridge. These values are then used in the election of the Root Port, which will be described in the following section. It is important to understand the calculation of the cost and priority values in order to understand how Spanning Tree selects one port over another, for example.

One of the key functions of the STA is to attempt to provide the shortest path to each switch in the network from the Root Bridge. Once selected, this path is then used to forward data, whilst redundant links are placed into a Blocking state. STA uses two values to determine which port will be placed into a Forwarding state (i.e., is the best path to the Root Bridge) and which port(s) will be placed into a Blocking state. These values are the port cost and the port priority. Both are described in the sections that follow.

Spanning Tree Port Cost

The 802.1D specification assigns 16-bit (short) default port cost values to each port that is based upon the port's bandwidth. Because administrators also have the capability to assign manually port cost values (between 1 and 65,535), the 16-bit values are used only for ports that have not been specifically configured for port cost. Table 35.1 below lists the default values for each type of port when using the short method to calculate the port cost:

Table 35.1—Default STP Port Cost Values

Bandwidth	Default Port Cost
4Mbps	250
10Mbps	100
16Mbps	62
100Mbps	19
1Gbps	4
10Gbps	2

In Cisco IOS Catalyst switches, default port cost values can be verified by issuing the show spanning-tree interface [name] command, as illustrated in the following output, which shows the default short port cost for a FastEthernet interface:

```
VTP-Server#show spanning-tree interface fastethernet 0/2
Vlan            Role Sts Cost      Prio.Nbr Type
---------------- ---- --- --------- -------- ------------------------
----
VLAN0050         Desg FWD 19        128.2    P2p
```

The following output shows the same for long port cost assignment:

```
VTP-Server#show spanning-tree interface fastethernet 0/2
Vlan            Role Sts Cost      Prio.Nbr Type
---------------- ---- --- --------- -------- -----------------------------
VLAN0050        Desg FWD 200000    128.2    P2p
```

It is important to remember that ports with lower (numerical) costs are more preferred; the lower the port cost, the higher the probability of that particular port being elected the Root Port. The port cost value is globally significant and affects the entire Spanning Tree network. This value is configured on all Non-Root Switches in the Spanning Tree domain.

Spanning Tree Root and Designated Ports

STP elects two types of ports that are used to forward BPDUs: the Root Port, which points towards the Root Bridge, and the Designated Port, which points away from the Root Bridge. It is important to understand the functionality of these two port types and how they are elected by STP.

Spanning Tree Root Port Election

STA defines three types of ports: the Root Port, the Designated Port, and the Non-Designated Port. These port types are elected by the STA and placed into the appropriate state (e.g., Forwarding or Blocking). During the Spanning Tree election process, in the event of a tie, the following values will be used (in the order listed) as tiebreakers:

1. Lowest Root Bridge ID
2. Lowest Root path cost to Root Bridge
3. Lowest sender Bridge ID
4. Lowest sender Port ID

NOTE: It is important to remember these tiebreaking criteria in order to understand how Spanning Tree elects and designates different port types in any given situation. Not only is this something that you will most likely be tested on, but also it is very important to have a solid understanding of this in order to design, implement, and support internetworks in the real world.

The Spanning Tree Root Port is the port that provides the best path, or lowest cost, when the device forwards packets to the Root Bridge. In other words, the Root Port is the port that receives the best BPDU for the switch, which indicates that it is the shortest path to the Root Bridge in terms of path cost. The Root Port is elected based on the Root Bridge path cost.

The Root Bridge path cost is calculated based on the cumulative cost (path cost) of all the links leading up to the Root Bridge. The path cost is the value that each port contributes to the Root Bridge path cost. Because this concept is often quite confusing, it is illustrated in Figure 35.6 below:

NOTE: All links illustrated in Figure 35.7 are GigabitEthernet links. It should be assumed that the traditional 802.1D method is used for port cost calculation. Therefore, the default port cost of GigabitEthernet is 4, whilst that of FastEthernet is 19.

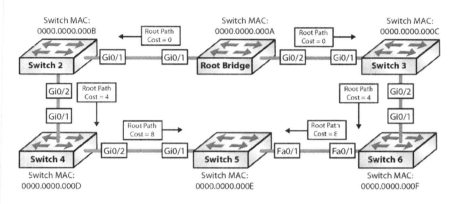

FIG 35.7—Spanning Tree Root Port Election

NOTE: The following explanation illustrates the flow of BPDUs between the switches in the network. Along with other information, these BPDUs contain the Root Bridge path cost information, which is incremented by the ingress port on the receiving switch.

1. The Root Bridge sends out a BPDU with a Root Bridge path cost value of 0 because its ports reside directly on the Root Bridge. This BPDU is sent to Switch 2 and Switch 3.

2. When Switch 2 and Switch 3 receive the BPDU from the Root Bridge, they add their own path cost based on the ingress interface. Because Switch 2 and Switch 3 are both connected to the Root Bridge via GigabitEthernet connections, they add the path cost value received from the Root Bridge (0) to their GigabitEthernet path cost values (4). The Root Bridge path cost from Switch 2 and Switch 3 via GigabitEthernet0/1 to the Root Bridge is 0 + 4 = 4.

3. Switch 2 and Switch 3 send out new BPDUs to their respective neighbours, which are Switch 4 and Switch 6, respectively. These BPDUs contain the new cumulative value (4) as the Root Bridge path cost.

4. When Switch 4 and Switch 6 receive the BPDUs from Switch 2 and Switch 3, they increment the received Root Bridge path cost value based on the ingress interface. Since GigabitEthernet connections are being used, the value received from Switch 2 and Switch 3 is incremented by 4. The Root Bridge path cost to the Root Bridge on Switch 4 and Switch 6 via their respective GigabitEthernet0/1 interfaces is therefore 0 + 4 + 4 = 8.

5. Switch 5 receives two BPDUs: one from Switch 4 and the other from Switch 6. The BPDU received from Switch 4 has a Root Bridge path cost of 0 + 4 + 4 + 4 = 12. The BPDU received from Switch 6 has a Root Bridge path cost of 0 + 4 + 4 + 19 = 27. Because the Root Bridge path cost value contained in the BPDU received from Switch 4 is better than that received from Switch 6, Switch 5 elects GigabitEthernet0/1 as the Root Port.

NOTE: Switches 2, 3, 4, and 6 will all elect their GigabitEthernet0/1 ports as Root Ports.

FURTHER EXPLANATION:

To explain further and to help you understand the election of the Root Port, let's assume that all ports in the diagram used in the example above are GigabitEthernet ports. This would mean that in Step 5 above, Switch 5 would receive two BPDUs with the same Root Bridge ID, both with a Root path cost value of 0 + 4 + 4 + 4 = 12. In order for the Root Port to be elected, STP will progress to the next option in the tiebreaker criteria listed below (the first two options, which have already been used, have been removed):

1. Lowest sender Bridge ID
2. Lowest sender Port ID

Based on the third selection criteria, Switch 5 will prefer the BPDU received from Switch 4 because its BID (0000.0000.000D) is lower than that of Switch 6 (0000.0000.000F). Switch 5 elects port GigabitEthernet0/1 as the Root Port.

Spanning Tree Designated Port Election

Unlike the Root Port, the Designated Port is a port that points away from the STP Root. This port is the port via which the designated device is attached to the LAN. It is also the port that has the lowest path cost when forwarding packets from that LAN to the Root Bridge.

NOTE: Some people refer to the Designated Port as the Designated Switch. The terms are interchangeable and refer to the same thing; that is, this is the switch, or port, that is used to forward frames from a particular LAN segment to the Root Bridge.

The primary purpose of the Designated Port is to prevent loops. When more than one switch is connected to the same LAN segment, all switches will attempt to forward a frame received on that segment. This default behaviour can result in multiple copies of the same frame being forwarded by multiple switches—resulting in a network loop. To avoid this default behaviour, a Designated Port is elected on all LAN segments. By default, all ports on the Root Bridge are Designated Ports. This is because the Root Bridge path cost will always be 0. The STA election of the Designated Port is illustrated in Figure 35.8 below:

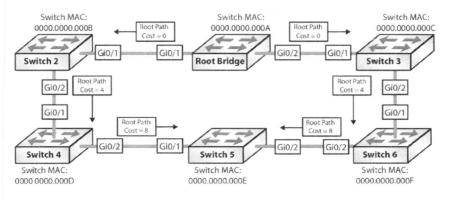

FIG 35.8—Spanning Tree Designated Port Election

1. On the segment between the Root Bridge and Switch 2, the Root Bridge GigabitEthernet0/1 is elected as the Designated Port because it has the lower Root Bridge path cost, which is 0.

2. On the segment between the Root Bridge and Switch 3, the Root Bridge GigabitEthernet0/2 is elected as the Designated Port because it has the lower Root Bridge path cost, which is 0.

3. On the segment between Switch 2 and Switch 4, the GigabitEthernet0/2 port on Switch 2 is elected as the Designated Port because Switch 2 has the lowest Root Bridge path cost, which is 4.

4. On the segment between Switch 3 and Switch 6, the GigabitEthernet0/2 port on Switch 3 is elected as the Designated Port because Switch 3 has the lowest Root Bridge path cost, which is 4.

5. On the segment between Switch 4 and Switch 5, the GigabitEthernet0/2 port on Switch 4 is elected as the Designated Port because Switch 4 has the lowest Root Bridge path cost, which is 8.

6. On the segment between Switch 5 and Switch 6, the GigabitEthernet0/2 port on Switch 6 is elected as the Designated Port because Switch 6 has the lowest Root Bridge path cost, which is 8.

The Non-Designated Port is not really a Spanning Tree Port type. Instead, it is a term that simply means a port that is not the Designated Port on a LAN segment. This port will always be placed into a Blocking state by STP. Based on the calculation of Root and Designated Ports, the resultant Spanning Tree topology for the switched network that was used in the Root Port and Designated Port election examples is shown in Figure 35.9 below:

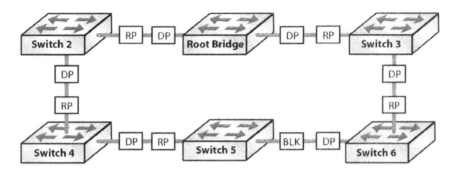

FIG 35.9—Converged Spanning Tree Network

Cisco Spanning Tree Enhancements

As stated earlier, the STP makes two assumptions about the environment in which it has been enabled, as follows:

- All links are bidirectional and can both send and receive Bridge Protocol Data Units
- All switches can regularly receive, process, and send Bridge Protocol Data Units

In real-world networks, these two assumptions are not always correct. In situations where that is the case, STP may not be able to prevent loops from being formed within the network. Because of this possibility, and to improve the performance of the basic IEEE 802.1D STA, Cisco has introduced a number of enhancements to the IEEE 802.1D standard, which are described below.

Port Fast

Port Fast is a feature that is typically enabled only for a port or interface that connects to a host. When the link comes up on this port, the switch skips the first stages of the STA and directly transitions to the Forwarding state. Contrary to popular belief, the Port Fast feature does not disable Spanning Tree on the selected port. This is because even with the Port Fast feature, the port can still send and receive BPDUs.

This is not a problem when the port is connected to a network device that does not send or respond to BPDUs, such as the NIC on a workstation, for example. However, this may result in a switching loop if the port is connected to a device that does send BPDUs, such as another switch. This is because the port skips the Listening and Learning states and proceeds immediately to the Forwarding state. Port Fast simply allows the port to begin forwarding frames much sooner than a port going through all normal STA steps.

BPDU Guard

The BPDU Guard feature is used to protect the Spanning Tree domain from external influence. BPDU Guard is disabled by default but is recommended for all ports on which the Port Fast feature has been enabled. When a port that is configured with the BPDU Guard feature receives a BPDU, it immediately transitions to the errdisable state.

This prevents false information from being injected into the Spanning Tree domain on ports that have Spanning Tree disabled. The operation of BPDU Guard, in conjunction with Port Fast, is illustrated in Figures 35.10, 35.11, and 35.12 below and following:

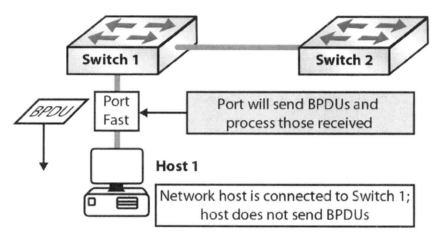

FIG 35.10—Understanding BPDU Guard

In Figure 35.10, Port Fast is enabled on Switch 1 on its connection to Host 1. Following initialisation, the port transitions to a Forwarding state, which eliminates 30 seconds of delay that would have been encountered if STA was not bypassed and the port went through the Listening and Learning states. Because the network host is a workstation, it sends no BPDUs, so disabling Spanning Tree on that port is not an issue.

Either by accident or due to some other malicious intent, Host 1 is disconnected from Switch 1. Using the same port, Switch 3 is connected to Switch 1. Switch 3 is also connected to Switch 2. Because Port Fast is enabled on the port connecting Switch 1 to Switch 3, this port moves from initialisation to the Forwarding state, bypassing normal STP initialisation. This port will also receive and process any BPDUs that are sent by Switch 3, as illustrated in Figure 35.11 below:

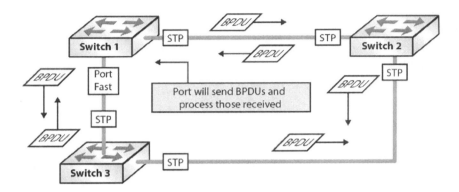

FIG 35.11—Understanding BPDU Guard (Continued)

Based on the port states illustrated above, you can quickly see how a loop would be created in this network. To prevent this from occurring, BPDU Guard should be enabled on all ports with Port Fast enabled. This is illustrated in Figure 35.12 below:

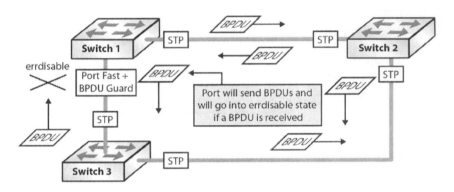

FIG 35.12—Understanding BPDU Guard (Continued)

With BPDU Guard enabled on the Port Fast port, when Switch 1 receives a BPDU from Switch 3, it immediately transitions the port into an errdisabled state. The result is that the STP calculation is not affected by this redundant link and the network will not have any loops.

BPDU Filter

The BPDU Guard and the BPDU Filter features are often confused or even thought to be the same. They are, however, different, and it is important to understand the differences between them. When Port Fast is enabled on a port, the port will send out BPDUs and will accept and process received BPDUs. The BPDU Guard feature prevents the port from receiving any BPDUs but does not prevent it from sending them. If any BPDUs are received, the port will be errdisabled.

The BPDU Filter feature effectively disables STP on the selected ports by preventing them from sending or receiving any BPDUs. This is illustrated in Figure 35.13 below:

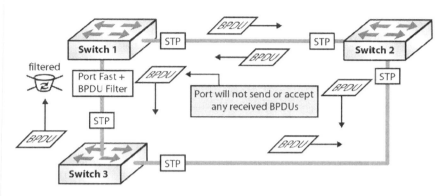

FIG 35.13—Understanding BPDU Filter

Loop Guard

The Loop Guard feature is used to prevent the formation of loops within the Spanning Tree network. Loop Guard detects Root Ports and blocked ports and ensures they continue to receive BPDUs. When switches receive BPDUs on blocked ports, the information is ignored because the best BPDU is still being received from the Root Bridge via the Root Port.

If the switch link is up and no BPDUs are received (due to a unidirectional link), the switch assumes that it is safe to bring this link up, and the port transitions to the Forwarding state and begins relaying received BPUDs. If a switch is connected to the other end of the link, this effectively creates a Spanning Tree loop. This concept is illustrated in Figure 35.14 below:

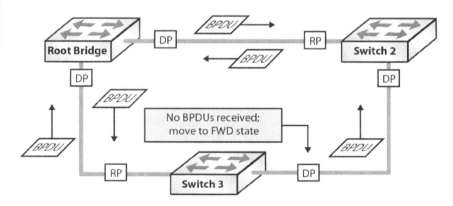

FIG 35.14—Understanding Loop Guard

In Figure 35.13, the Spanning Tree network has converged and all ports are in a Blocking or Forwarding state. However, the Blocking port on Switch 3 stops receiving BPDUs from the Designated Port on Switch 2 due to a unidirectional link. Switch 3 assumes that the port can be transitioned into a Forwarding state and so begins this move. The switch then relays received BPDUs out of that port, resulting in a network loop.

When Loop Guard is enabled, the switch keeps track of all Non-Designated Ports. As long as the port continues to receive BPDUs, it is fine; however, if the port stops receiving BPDUs, it is moved into a loop-inconsistent state. In other words, when Loop Guard is enabled, the STP port state machine is modified to prevent the port from transitioning from the Non-Designated Port role to the Designated Port role in absence of BPDUs. When implementing Loop Guard, you should be aware of the following implementation guidelines:

- Loop Guard cannot be enabled on a switch that also has Root Guard enabled
- Loop Guard does not affect Uplink Fast or Backbone Fast operation
- Loop Guard must be enabled on point-to-point links only
- Loop Guard operation is not affected by the Spanning Tree timers
- Loop Guard cannot actually detect a unidirectional link
- Loop Guard cannot be enabled on Port Fast or Dynamic VLAN ports

Root Guard

The Root Guard feature prevents a Designated Port from becoming a Root Port. If a port on which the Root Guard feature is enabled receives a superior BPDU, it moves the port into a root-inconsistent state, thus maintaining the current Root Bridge status quo. This concept is illustrated in Figure 35.15 below:

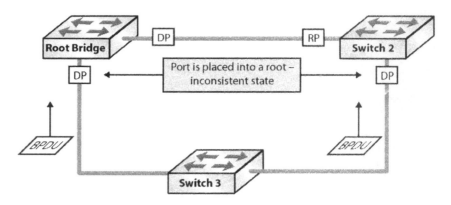

FIG 35.15—Understanding Root Guard

In Figure 35.14, Switch 3 is added to the current STP network and sends out BPDUs that are superior to those of the current Root Bridge. Under ordinary circumstances, STP would recalculate the entire topology and Switch 3 would be elected the Root Bridge. However, because the Root Guard feature is enabled on the Designated Ports on the current Root Bridge, as well as on Switch 2, both switches will place these ports into a root-inconsistent state when they receive the superior BPDUs from Switch 3. This preserves the Spanning Tree topology.

The Root Guard feature prevents a port from becoming a Root Port, thus ensuring that the port is always a Designated Port. Unlike other STP enhancements, which can also be enabled on a global basis, Root Guard must be manually enabled on all ports where the Root Bridge should not appear. Because of this, it is important to ensure a deterministic topology when designing and implementing STP in the LAN.

Uplink Fast

The Uplink Fast feature provides faster failover to a redundant link when the primary link fails. The primary purpose of this feature is to improve the convergence time of STP in the event of a failure of an uplink. This feature is of most use on Access layer switches with redundant uplinks to the Distribution layer; hence, the name.

When Access layer switches are dual-homed to the Distribution layer, one of the links is placed into a Blocking state by STP to prevent loops. When the primary link to the Distribution layer fails, the port in the Blocking state must transition through the Listening and Learning states before it begins forwarding traffic. This results in a 30-second delay before the switch is able to forward frames destined to other network segments. Uplink Fast operation is illustrated in Figure 35.16 below:

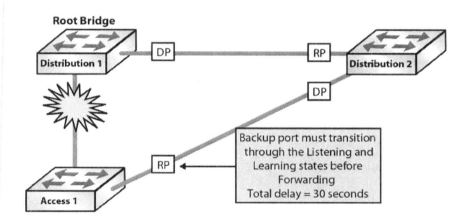

FIG 35.16—Understanding Uplink Fast

In Figure 35.15, a failure on the link between Access 1 and Distribution 1, which is also the STP Root Bridge, would mean that STP would move the link between Access 1 and Distribution 1 into a Forwarding state (i.e., Blocking > Listening > Learning > Forwarding). The Listening and Learning states take 15 seconds each, so the port would begin to forward frames only after a total of 30 seconds had elapsed. When the Uplink Fast feature is enabled, the backup port to the Distribution layer is immediately placed into a Forwarding state, resulting in no network downtime. This concept is illustrated in Figure 35.17 below:

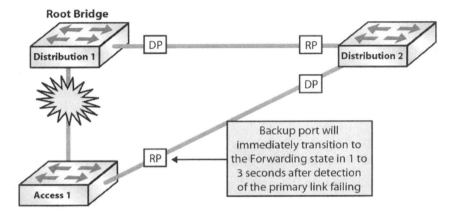

FIG 35.17—Understanding Uplink Fast (Continued)

Backbone Fast

The Backbone Fast feature provides fast failover when an indirect link failure occurs. Failover occurs when the switch receives an inferior BPDU from its designated bridge. An inferior BPDU indicates that the designated bridge has lost its connection to the Root Bridge. This is illustrated in Figure 35.18 below:

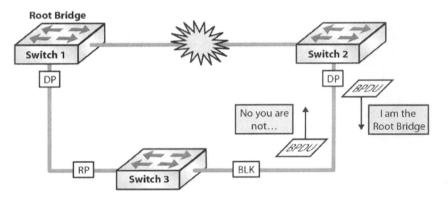

FIG 35.18—Understanding Backbone Fast

In Figure 35.18, the link between Switch 1 and Switch 2 fails. Switch 2 detects this and sends out BPDUs indicating that it is the Root Bridge. The inferior BPDUs are received on Switch 3, which still has the BPDU information received from Switch 1 saved.

Switch 3 will ignore the inferior BPDUs until the Max Age value expires. During this time, Switch 2 continues to send BPDUs to Switch 3. When the Max Age expires, Switch 3 will age out the stored BPDU information from the Root Bridge and transition into a Listening state, and will then send out the received BPDU from the Root Bridge out to Switch 2.

Because this BPDU is better than its own, Switch 2 stops sending BPDUs, and the port between Switch 2 and Switch 3 transitions through the Listening and Learning states, and, finally, into the Forwarding state. This default method of operation by the STP process will mean that Switch 2 will be unable to forward frames for at least 50 seconds.

The Backbone Fast feature includes a mechanism that allows an immediate check to see whether the BPDU information stored on a port is still valid if an inferior BPDU is received. This is implemented with a new PDU and the Root Link Query (RLQ), which is referred to as the RLQ PDU.

Upon receipt of an inferior BPDU, the switch will send out an RLQ PDU on all Non-Designated Ports, except for the port on which the inferior BPDU was received. If the switch is the Root Bridge or it has lost its connection to the Root Bridge, it will respond to the RLQ. Otherwise, the RLQ will be propagated upstream. If the switch receives an RLQ response on its Root Port, connectivity to the Root Bridge is still intact. If the response is received on a Non-Root Port, it means connectivity to the Root Bridge is lost, and the local switch Spanning Tree must be recalculated on the switch and the Max Age timer expired so that a new Root Port can be found. This concept is illustrated in Figure 35.19 below:

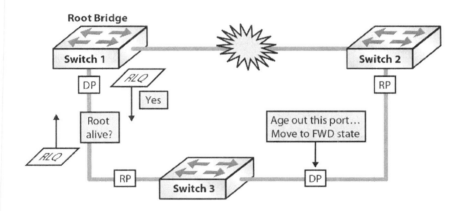

FIG 35.19—Understanding Backbone Fast (Continued)

Referencing Figure 35.19, upon receipt of the inferior BPDU, Switch 3 sends out an RLQ request on all Non-Designated Ports, except for the port on which the BPDU was received. The Root Bridge responds via an RLQ response sent out of its Designated Port. Because the response is received on the Root Port of Switch 3, it is considered a positive response. However, if the response was received on a Non-Root Port, the response would be considered negative and the switch would need to go through the whole Spanning Tree calculation again.

Based on the positive response received on Switch 3, it can age out the port connected to Switch 2 without waiting for the Max Age timer to expire. The port, however, must still go through the

Listening and Learning states. By immediately aging out the Max Age timer, Backbone Fast reduces the convergence time from 50 seconds (20 seconds Max Age + 30 seconds Listening and Learning) to 30 seconds (the time for the Listening and Learning states).

There are two types of RLQs: RLQ requests and RLQ responses. RLQ requests are typically sent out on the Root Port to check for connectivity to the Root Bridge. All RLQ responses are sent out on Designated Ports. Because the RLQ request contains the BID of the Root Bridge that sent it, if another switch in the path to the Root Bridge can still reach the Root Bridge specified in the RLQ response, it will respond back to the sending switch. If this is not the case, the switch simply forwards the query towards the Root Bridge through its Root Port.

> **NOTE:** The RLQ PDU has the same packet format as a normal BPDU, with the only difference being that the RLQ contains two Cisco SNAP addresses that are used for requests and replies.

Troubleshooting STP

STP issues usually fall within the following three categories:

- Incorrect Root Bridge
- Incorrect Root Port
- Incorrect Designated Port

Incorrect Root Bridge

Priority and base MAC address decides this. Issue the `show spanning-tree vlan <vlan#>` command. Note the MAC address and switch priority. Fix with:

```
spanning-tree vlan <vlan#> priority <priority>
```

Incorrect Root Port

Fastest path from switch to Root Bridge. The cost is cumulative across the entire path:

```
show spanning-tree vlan (vlan #)
```

Fix with:

```
spanning-tree cost <cost>
```

Incorrect Designated Port

The lowest cost port connecting a network segment to the rest of the network:

```
show spanning-tree vlan <vlan#>
spanning-tree cost <cost>
```

DAY 35 QUESTIONS

1. How often do switches send Bridge Protocol Data Units (BPDUs)?
2. Where is the BPDU information contained?
3. Name the STP port states in the correct order.
4. What is the default Cisco Bridge ID?
5. Which command will show you the Root Bridge and priority for a VLAN?
6. What is the STP port cost for a 100Mbps link?
7. When a port that is configured with the _____ _____ feature receives a BPDU, it immediately transitions to the errdisable state.
8. The _____ _____ feature effectively disables STP on the selected ports by preventing them from sending or receiving any BPDUs.
9. Which two commands will force the switch to become the Root Bridge for a VLAN?

DAY 35 LAB—SPANNING TREE ROOT SELECTION

Topology

Purpose

Learn how to influence which switch becomes the Spanning Tree Root Bridge.

Walkthrough

1. Set the hostname of each switch and connect them with a crossover cable. You can then check whether the interface between them is set to trunk.

    ```
    SwitchA#show interface trunk
    SwitchA#
    ```

2. You may not see the trunk link become active until you set one side as a trunk link.

    ```
    SwitchB#conf t
    Enter configuration commands, one per line.  End with CNTL/Z.
    SwitchB(config)#int fast 0/1
    SwitchB(config-if)#switchport mode trunk
    SwitchB(config-if)#^Z
    SwitchB#sh int trunk
    Port        Mode            Encapsulation   Status          Native vlan
    Fa0/1       on              802.1q          trunking        1

    Port        Vlans allowed on trunk
    Fa0/1       1-1005

    Port        Vlans allowed and active in management domain
    Fa0/1       1
    ```

3. You will see the other switch is left on auto mode.

    ```
    SwitchA#show int trunk
    Port        Mode            Encapsulation   Status          Native vlan
    Fa0/1       auto            n-802.1q        trunking        1

    Port        Vlans allowed on trunk
    Fa0/1       1-1005

    Port        Vlans allowed and active in management domain
    Fa0/1       1
    ```

4. Create two VLANs on each switch.

```
SwitchA#conf t
Enter configuration commands, one per line.  End with CNTL/Z.
SwitchA(config)#vlan 2
SwitchA(config-vlan)#vlan 3
SwitchA(config-vlan)#^Z
SwitchA#
%SYS-5-CONFIG_I: Configured from console by console

SwitchA#show vlan brief

VLAN Name                             Status    Ports
---- -------------------------------- --------- -------------------------------
--
1    default                          active    Fa0/2, Fa0/3, Fa0/4, Fa0/5
                                                 Fa0/6, Fa0/7, Fa0/8, Fa0/9
                                                 Fa0/10, Fa0/11, Fa0/12, Fa0/13
                                                 Fa0/14, Fa0/15, Fa0/16, Fa0/17
                                                 Fa0/18, Fa0/19, Fa0/20, Fa0/21
                                                 Fa0/22, Fa0/23, Fa0/24
2    VLAN0002                         active
3    VLAN0003                         active
1002 fddi-default                     active
1003 token-ring-default               active
```

Create the VLANs on Switch B as well (copy the commands above).

5. Determine which switch is the Root Bridge for VLANs 2 and 3.

```
SwitchB#show spanning-tree vlan 2
VLAN0002
  Spanning tree enabled protocol ieee
  Root ID    Priority    32770
             Address     0001.972A.7A23
             This bridge is the root
             Hello Time  2 sec  Max Age 20 sec  Forward Delay 15 sec

  Bridge ID  Priority    32770  (priority 32768 sys-id-ext 2)
             Address     0001.972A.7A23
             Hello Time  2 sec  Max Age 20 sec  Forward Delay 15 sec
             Aging Time  20

Interface        Role Sts Cost      Prio.Nbr Type
---------------- ---- --- --------- -------- ---------------------------
Fa0/1            Desg FWD 19        128.1    P2p
```

You can see that Switch B is the root. Do the same command on Switch A and check for VLAN 3. The priority is 32,768 plus the VLAN number, which is 2 in this case. The lowest MAC address will then determine the Root Bridge.

```
SwitchB#show spanning-tree vlan 3
VLAN0003
  Spanning tree enabled protocol ieee
  Root ID     Priority     32771
              Address      0001.972A.7A23
              This bridge is the root
              Hello Time   2 sec   Max Age 20 sec   Forward Delay 15 sec

  Bridge ID   Priority     32771  (priority 32768 sys-id-ext 3)
              Address      0001.972A.7A23
              Hello Time   2 sec   Max Age 20 sec   Forward Delay 15 sec
              Aging Time   20

Interface           Role Sts Cost      Prio.Nbr Type
---------------- ---- --- --------- -------- ---------------------------
----
Fa0/1               Desg FWD 19        128.1    P2p
```

The MAC address I have for Switch A is higher, which is why it didn't become the Root Bridge:

```
0010.1123.D245
```

6. Set the other switch to be the Root Bridge for VLANs 2 and 3. Use the `spanning-tree vlan 2 priority 4096` command for VLAN 2 and the `spanning-tree`

```
Vlan 3 root primary for VLAN 3.
SwitchA(config)#spanning-tree vlan 2 priority 4096
SwitchA(config)#spanning-tree vlan 3 root primary

SwitchA#show spanning-tree vlan 2
VLAN0002
  Spanning tree enabled protocol ieee
  Root ID     Priority     4098
              Address      0010.1123.D245
              This bridge is the root
              Hello Time   2 sec   Max Age 20 sec   Forward Delay 15 sec

  Bridge ID   Priority     4098  (priority 4096 sys-id-ext 2)
              Address      0010.1123.D245
              Hello Time   2 sec   Max Age 20 sec   Forward Delay 15 sec
              Aging Time   20

Interface           Role Sts Cost      Prio.Nbr Type
```

```
- - - - - - - - - - - - - - - -   - - - -   - - -   - - - - - - - - -   - - - - - - - -   - - - - - - - - - - - - - - - - - - - - - - - - - - -
FaO/1            Desg FWD 19          128.1    P2p

SwitchA#show spanning-tree vlan 3
VLAN0003
  Spanning tree enabled protocol ieee
  Root ID    Priority    24579
             Address     0010.1123.D245
             This bridge is the root
             Hello Time   2 sec   Max Age 20 sec   Forward Delay 15 sec

  Bridge ID  Priority    24579  (priority 24576 sys-id-ext 3)
             Address     0010.1123.D245
             Hello Time   2 sec   Max Age 20 sec   Forward Delay 15 sec
             Aging Time   20

Interface        Role Sts Cost        Prio.Nbr Type
- - - - - - - - - - - - - - - -   - - - -   - - -   - - - - - - - - -   - - - - - - - -   - - - - - - - - - - - - - - - - - - - - - - - - - - -
- - - -
FaO/1            Desg FWD 19          128.1    P2p

SwitchA#
```

NOTE: Despite Switch B having the lower Bridge ID, Switch A was forced to be the Root Bridge.

DAY 36

Rapid Spanning Tree Protocol

DAY 36 TASKS

- Read today's theory notes
- Review yesterday's theory notes
- Review ACLs (if necessary)
- Complete today's lab
- Read the ICND2 cram guide
- Spend 15 minutes on the subnetting.org website

The IEEE 802.1D standard was designed at a time when the recovery of connectivity after an outage was within a minute or so, which was considered adequate performance. With the IEEE 802.1D STP, recovery takes around 50 seconds, which includes 20 seconds for the Max Age timer to expire and then an additional 30 seconds for the port to transition from the Blocking state to the Forwarding state.

As computer technology evolved, and networks became more critical, it became apparent that more rapid network convergence was required. Cisco addressed this requirement by developing some proprietary enhancements to STP that included Backbone Fast and Uplink Fast.

Today you will learn about the following:

- The need for RSTP
- RSTP configuration

This lesson maps to the following CCNA syllabus requirement:

- Configure, verify, and troubleshoot RSTP operation

The Need for RSTP

With the continued evolution of technology, and the amalgamation of routing and switching capabilities on the same physical platform, it soon became apparent that switched network convergence lagged behind that of routing protocols such as OSPF and EIGRP, which are able to provide an alternate path in less time. The 802.1w standard was designed to address this.

The IEEE 802.1w standard, or Rapid Spanning Tree Protocol (RSTP), significantly reduces the time taken for STP to converge when a link failure occurs. With RSTP, network failover to an alternate path or link can occur in a subsecond timeframe. RSTP is an extension of 802.1D that performs functions similar to Uplink Fast and Backbone Fast. RSTP performs better than traditional STP, with no additional configuration. Additionally, RSTP is backward compatible with the original IEEE 802.1D STP standard. It does this by using a modified BPDU.

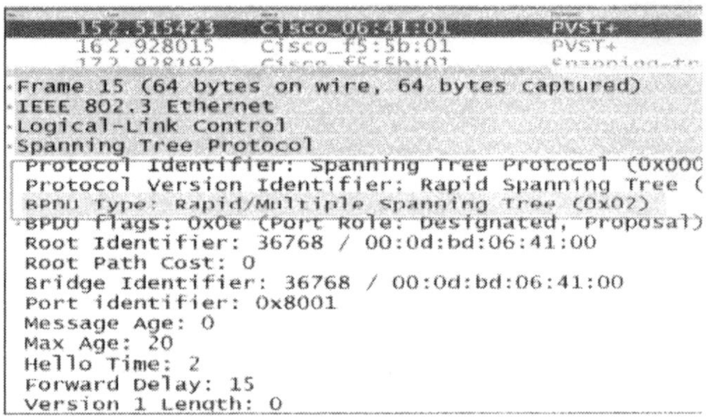

FIG 36.1—Modified BPDU

RSTP port states can be mapped against STP port states as follows:

- Disabled—Discarding
- Blocking—Discarding
- Listening—Discarding
- Learning—Learning
- Forwarding—Forwarding

RSTP port roles include the following:

- Root (Forwarding state)
- Designated (Forwarding state)
- Alternate (Blocking state)
- Backup (Blocking state)

Alternate Ports:

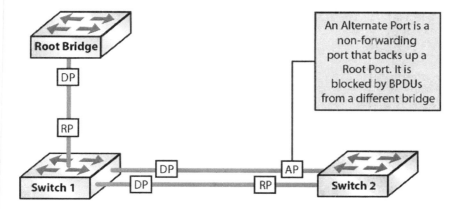

An Alternate Port is a non-forwarding port that backs up a Root Port. It is blocked by BPDUs from a different bridge

FIG 36.2—RSTP Alternate Port

Backup Ports:

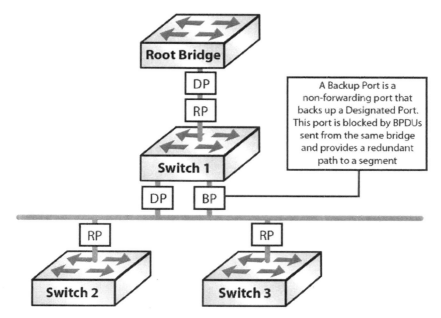

A Backup Port is a non-forwarding port that backs up a Designated Port. This port is blocked by BPDUs sent from the same bridge and provides a redundant path to a segment

FIG 36.3—RSTP Backup Port

RSTP with PVST+

Per VLAN Spanning Tree Plus (PVST+) allows for an individual STP instance per VLAN. Traditional or Normal PVST+ mode relies on the use of the older 802.1D STP for switched network convergence in the event of a link failure.

RPVST+

Rapid Per VLAN Spanning Tree Plus (R-PVST+) allows for the use of 802.1w with PVST+. This allows for an individual RSTP instance per VLAN, whilst providing much faster convergence than would be attained with the traditional 802.1D STP. By default, when RSTP is enabled, R-PVST+ is enabled on the switch.

Configuring RSTP

This can be achieved with one command!

```
Switch#spanning-tree mode rapid-pvst
Switch#show spanning-tree summary
Switch is in rapid-pvst mode
Root bridge for: VLAN0050, VLAN0060, VLAN0070
```

DAY 36 QUESTIONS

1. RSTP is not backward compatible with the original IEEE 802.1D STP standard. True or false?
2. What are the four RSTP port roles?
3. Which command enables RSTP?

DAY 36 LAB—RSTP

Topology

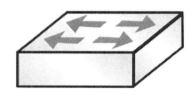

Purpose

Learn the configuration command for RSTP.

Walkthrough

1. Check the Spanning Tree mode on your switch.

    ```
    SwitchA#show spanning-tree summary
    Switch is in pvst mode
    Root bridge for: VLAN0002 VLAN0003
    ```

2. Change the mode to RSTP and check again.

    ```
    SwitchA(config)#spanning-tree mode rapid-pvst
    SwitchA#show spanning-tree summary
    Switch is in rapid-pvst mode
    Root bridge for: VLAN00C2 VLAN00
    ```

DAY 37

IPv6 and Route Summarisation

DAY 37 TASKS

- Read today's theory notes
- Review yesterday's theory notes
- Complete Day 35 STP lab
- Read the ICND2 cram guide
- Spend 15 minutes on the subnetting.org website

Nobody predicted the exponential explosion in the growth of the Internet when it was first developed. Who could have imagined, even just a few years ago, that nearly every household in the world would have a PC in it, or that everyone would require an IP address for their work PCs, home PCs, mobile phones, mobile IP devices, and even remote IP management of such things as home-intruder alarms, cookers, garage doors, and TVs? Experts now agree that estimates of each individual requiring over 250 IP addresses is well within the bounds of possibility.

Today you will learn about the following:

- IPv6 and why we need it
- IPv6 address format
- Migrating from IPv4 to IPv6
- Configuring IPv6 addressing
- Route summarisation
- Applying route summarisation

This lesson maps to the following CCNA syllabus requirements:

- Describe the technological requirements for running IPv6 in conjunction with IPv4 (including protocols, dual stack, tunneling, etc.)
- Describe IPv6 addresses
- Determine the appropriate classless addressing scheme using VLSM and summarisation to satisfy addressing requirements in a LAN/WAN environment

Why We Need IPv6

IPv4 was developed when only large companies required IP addresses. These addresses were cut into blocks, from A to C, with D reserved for multicasting and E for experimental use. The original incarnation of classes created huge wastage; for example, Class A addresses wasted potentially thousands of addresses and Class C addresses forced smaller companies to buy several blocks of network addresses for use in their networks. Often, the addresses were non-contiguous, which added to route summarisation problems.

Work on IPv6 began as soon as the scale of the IPv4 problem was fully realised (1991). At that point, Internet experts argued that the current range of IPv4 addresses would become exhausted somewhere between 2005 and 2015. In addition, because IPv4 is a connectionless protocol, there is no guarantee of data delivery and no facility to mark packets in order to detect or correct errors.

Shortfalls of IPv4

Development of IPv6 allowed many of the shortfalls of IPv4 to be addressed, some of which include the following:

- LAN latency—When IPv4 is used on Ethernet segments, there has to be Layer 3 to Layer 2 mapping. IPv4 uses an ARP broadcast to perform the address resolution. This involves an ARP broadcast packet being sent to and received by all stations on an Ethernet segment. The packet is processed as an interrupt on the Ethernet port.

- Security—IPv4 has no built-in security parameters. This function is left to PC and router firewalls.

- Mobility—IPv4 has no facility to allocate IP addresses to PDAs or other mobile devices.

- Routing—IPv4 addressing can lead to huge routing tables and vast amounts of routing update packets traversing the Internet. Changes made to DNS entries can take up to 48 hours to propagate, leading to network downtime.

Anatomy of an IP Packet

The design of a new IP addressing scheme has given the architects a clean slate and the ability to incorporate a wish list into the design of the IPv6 packet. The requirements were a pure design for the header, with as few fields as possible, which is different from the IPv4 addressing scheme shown below in Figure 37.1:

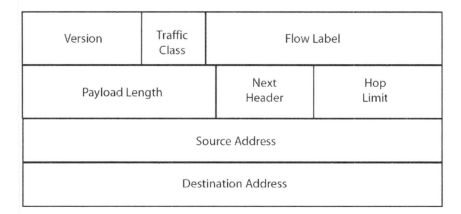

FIG 37.1—IPv4 Header = 20 Octets

IPv4 allows a unique network number to be allocated to every device on the Internet, but IPv6 takes this one step further, as shown in Figure 37.2 below:

Version	Traffic Class	Flow Label	
Payload Length		Next Header	Hop Limit
Source Address			
Destination Address			

FIG 37.2—IPv6 Header = 40 Octets

IPv6 assigns a 128-bit numerical address to each interface on a network. This, of course, will lead to extreme difficulty for network administrators to track which device is which. For this reason, IPv6 will work hand in hand with DNS. There is no requirement for a subnet mask in IPv6; instead, a prefix is used.

IPv6 Address Format

An IPv6 address is comprised of two parts. The first part is the link-layer address (Layer 2), which identifies the host destination within the subnet. The second address is Layer 3 and it identifies the destination network the packet must reach. IPv6 uses the Neighbor Discovery Protocol, not ARP, for Layer 2 to Layer 3 address mapping. The main difference between IPv4 and IPv6 addressing is illustrated in Figure 37.3 below:

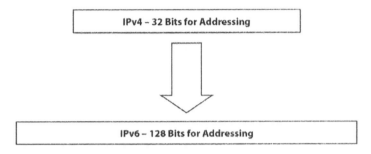

FIG 37.3—IPv6 Address Size

There are 2 to the power of 128 (2^128) addresses available with IPv6, which is exactly 340,282,366 ,920,938,463,374,607,431,768,211,456 addresses. That is over 5 x 10^28 addresses for every person in the world! These addresses are available without the need for private address translation or any other techniques required for address conservation.

RFC 1884 recommends that IPv6 syntax for the 128 bits be represented in eight groups of hexadecimal digits. Each group is divided by a colon, so the syntax is referred to as coloned hex, an example of which is shown below:

EEDE:AC89:4323:5445:FE32:BB78:7856:2022

The addresses can be shortened in the following two ways:

1. Remove leading zeros and double colons to represent successive zeros within colons.
    *   Original address: 3223:0002:3DD2:0000:0667:0000:4CC3:2002
    *   Shortened address: 3223:<u>2</u>:3DD2:0000:0667:0000:4CC3:2002 (the second octet has been shortened to the number 2)

2. Use ONE SET of double colons to replace four consecutive zeros.
    *   Original address: 3223:0002:3DD2:0000:0667:0000:4CC3:2002
    *   Shortened address: 3223:2:3DD2<u>::</u>0667:0000:4CC3:2002 (0000 becomes ::)

NOTE: The reason the second set of four consecutive zeros remains in the address is that the RFC states that only one pair of double colons can be used within an IPv6 address. (You can read more about this at www.rfc-editor.org.)

No Broadcasting

There are three types of IPv6 addresses: unicast, anycast, and multicast. Broadcasting does not exist in IPv6.

1. Unicast—As with IPv4, an IPv6 unicast address is applied to a single interface.
2. Anycast—An IPv6 anycast address is one that can be assigned to a group of interfaces. This can be used in load balancing.
3. Multicast—Much the same as with IPv4, a packet sent to a multicast address is delivered to all the interfaces identified by that address.

In IPv6, broadcasts are replaced by multicasts and anycasts.

Migrating from IPv4 to IPv6

You will not find Internet users all over the world using IPv4 one day and then switching to IPv6 the next. The change will take place over a number of years in a phased approach. Address allocation will take place in batches of addresses using a combination of DNS and DHCP or DHCPv6 auto-configuration scripts. To assign IPv6 addresses manually to nodes on a network would be an almost impossible task. DHCPv6 operation is described in RFC 3736.

The two main methods available to phase IPv6 addressing into networks are dual stack and tunneling, as illustrated in Figures 37.4 and 37.5 below:

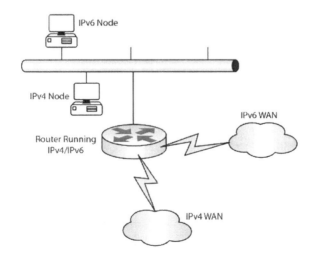

FIG 37.4—Dual Stack

With dual stack, two IP protocol stacks—IPv4 and IPv6—run on a network device simultaneously. The dual-stack method will be the preferred migration method for networks transitioning from IPv4 to IPv6 because it can continue to run both protocols seamlessly while the transition takes place. Dual stack can operate on the same network node interface and chooses which version of IP to use based upon the destination address.

This process has been thoroughly tested by a project team referred to as 6-Bone. The only requirement to implement IPv6 addressing on a network is connectivity to a DNS server.

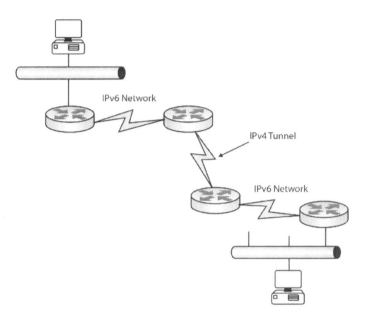

FIG 37.5—Tunneling

Tunneling in internetworking usually refers to one type of packet being encapsulated in another type of packet. In this instance, an IPv6 packet is encapsulated inside an IPv4 packet. In order for tunneling to work, the routers must support dual stack so both IPv4 and IPv6 are running.

IPv6 packets up to 20 bytes can be transmitted because the IPv4 header is 20 bytes in length. The IPv4 header is appended to the packet and removed at the destination router, as illustrated in Figure 37.6 below.

IPv6 tunneling will allow current IPv4 addressing to be used in conjunction with IPv6 addresses, much in the same way that dual protocols can be run on a network that is transitioning from one to another. IPv6 tunneling is defined in RFC 3056 and 2893, among others.

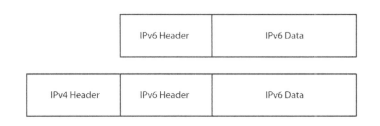

FIG 37.6—IPv4 Header on an IPv6 Packet

IPv6 Interfaces

Each link in an IPv6 network must have a unique Interface Identifier (ID). This is the host portion of the IPv6 address, and it is always 64 bits long, dynamically created, and based on Layer 2 encapsulation. IDs are defined on interface types such as PPP, HDLC, ATM, Frame Relay, Ethernet, and so on.

For Ethernet networking, the ID is based on the MAC address, but the hex number FFFE is inserted into the 48-bit address. For example, 23:80:26:F3:22:E0 would become 23:80:26:**FF:FE**:F3:22:E0, as shown in Figure 37.7 below:

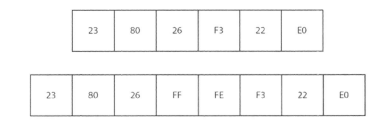

FIG 37.7—IPv6 Host Address

IPv6 and Routing

IPv6 uses the same longest prefix match principle that IPv4 uses. IPv6 currently works with the following:

- Static routing
- New generation RIP
- OSPFv3
- ISIS for IPv6
- EIGRP for IPv6
- MP-BGP4

Configuring IPv6

Cisco IOS supports IPv6 commands in version 12.2(2)'T or later. To implement IPv6 on a Cisco device, simply add an IPv6 configuration to an IPv4 interface and it will run dual stack, as illustrated in the output below:

```
Router#config t
Router(config)#ipv6 unicast-routing
Router(config)#interface fast ethernet 0/0
Router(config-if)#ip address 192.1681.1 255.255.255.0
Router(config-if)#ipv6 address 2eef:c001:b14:2::c12/125
Router(config-if)#exit
Router#show IPv6 interface
FastEthernet0/0 is up, line protocol is down
IPv6 is enabled, link-local address is FE80::20E:83FF:FEF5:FD4F [TENTA-
TIVE]
Global unicast address(es):
2EEF:C001:B14:2::C12, subnet is 2EEF:C001:B14:2::C10/125 [TENTATIVE]
```

Route Summarisation

There are many millions of routes on the Internet. If these routes all had to be stored individually, the Internet would have come to a stop many years ago. Route summarisation, also known as supernetting, was proposed in RFC 1338, which you can read online by clicking on the RFC, or if you have printed this document by visiting www.faqs.org/rfcs/rfc1338.html.

If you want to read a very comprehensive guide to route summarisation, then please grab a hold of Jeff Doyle's excelling Cisco book *Routing TCP/IP Volume 1*, which is in its second edition now.

ZIP Codes

ZIP codes are used by the United States Postal Service to improve routing of letters to addresses within the USA. The first digit represents a group of US states, and the second and third digits represent a region inside that group. The idea is that letters and parcels can be quickly routed by machine or by hand into the correct state and then forwarded to that state. When it reaches the state, it can be routed to the correct region. From there, it can be routed to the correct city and so on, until it is sorted into the correct mailbag for the local postal delivery person.

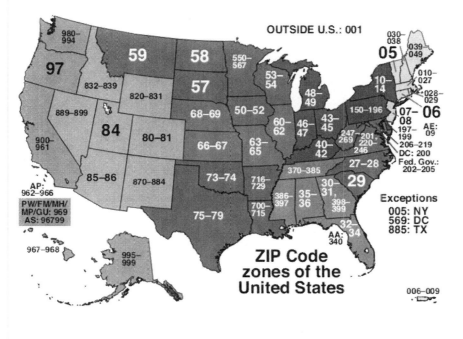

FIG 37.8—ZIP Codes

The system was devised to make routing of mail more accurate and efficient. For example, the sorting office in Atlanta doesn't need to know which street in San Francisco the packet is destined for. Having to store that information would make the sorting process unworkable.

Route Summarisation Prerequisites

In order to use route summarisation on your network, you need to use a classless protocol, such as RIPv2, EIGRP, or OSPF. You also need to design your network in a hierarchical order, which will require careful planning and design. This means that you can't randomly assign networks to various routers or LANs within your network.

Applying Route Summarisation

Let's move on to an example of a network and what the problem will look like on your network if you don't use route summarisation.

In this example, this is how summarisation would work with a range of IP addresses on a network. The router in Figure 37.9 below has several networks attached. The first choice is to advertise all of these networks to the next hop router. The alternative is to summarise these eight networks down to one route and send that summary to the next hop router, which will cut down on bandwidth, CPU, and memory requirements.

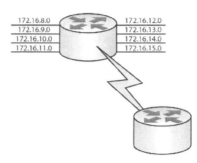

FIG 37.9—An Example of Route Summarisation

The only way to work out a summary route is by converting the IP address into binary (sorry). If you don't do this, then you have no way of knowing whether you are advertising the correct summary route, which will lead to problems on your network.

Firstly, write out all of the network addresses in full and then the binary versions to the right of that, as illustrated below:

172.16.8.0	*10101100.00010000.00001*000.00000000
172.16.9.0	*10101100.00010000.00001*001.00000000
172.16.10.0	*10101100.00010000.00001*010.00000000
172.16.11.0	*10101100.00010000.00001*011.00000000
172.16.12.0	*10101100.00010000.00001*100.00000000
172.16.13.0	*10101100.00010000.00001*101.00000000
172.16.14.0	*10101100.00010000.00001*110.00000000
172.16.15.0	*10101100.00010000.00001*111.00000000
Matching Bits	*10101100.00010000.00001* = 21 bits

I have italicised and underlined the bits in each address that match. You can see that the first 21 bits match on every address, so your summarised route can reflect the following 21 bits:

172.16.8.0 255.255.248.0

One other significant advantage of using route summarisation is that if a local network on your router goes down, the summary network will still be advertised out. This means that the rest of the network will not need to update its routing tables or, worse still, have to deal with a flapping route. I have chosen two exercises dealing with route summarisation for you to work out.

Exercise 1: Write out the binary equivalents for the addresses below, and then determine which bits match. I have written the first two octets for you to save time.

172.16.50.0	*10101100.00010000.*
172.16.60.0	*10101100.00010000.*
172.16.70.0	*10101100.00010000.*
172.16.80.0	*10101100.00010000.*
172.16.90.0	*10101100.00010000.*
172.16.100.0	*10101100.00010000.*
172.16.110.0	*10101100.00010000.*
172.16.120.0	*10101100.00010000.*

What summarised address would you advertise?

I make it 172.16.50.0 255.255.128.0, or /17.

Exercise 2: The company below has three routers connected to their HQ router. They need to summarise the routes advertised from London 1, 2, and 3:

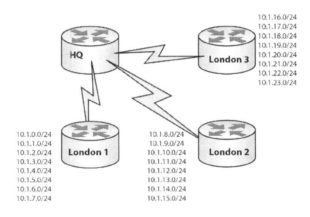

FIG 37.10—Summarised Routes Advertised from London 1, 2, and 3

Let's start with London 1:

10.1.0.0	*00001010.00000001.00000000.00000000*
10.1.1.0	*00001010.00000001.00000001.00000000*
10.1.2.0	*00001010.00000001.00000010.00000000*
10.1.3.0	*00001010.00000001.00000011.00000000*
10.1.4.0	*00001010.00000001.00000100.00000000*
10.1.5.0	*00001010.00000001.00000101.00000000*
10.1.6.0	*00001010.00000001.00000110.00000000*
10.1.7.0	*00001010.00000001.00000111.00000000*

There are 21 common bits, so London 1 can advertise 10.1.0.0/21 to the HQ router.

And for London 2:

10.1.8.0	*00001010.00000001.00001000.00000000*
10.1.9.0	*00001010.00000001.00001001*.00000000
10.1.10.0	*00001010.00000001.00001010*.00000000
10.1.11.0	*00001010.00000001.00001011*.00000000
10.1.12.0	*00001010.00000001.00001100*.00000000
10.1.13.0	*00001010.00000001.00001101*.00000000
10.1.14.0	*00001010.00000001.00001110*.00000000
10.1.15.0	*00001010.00000001.00001111*.00000000

London 2 also has 21 common bits, so it can advertise 10.1.8.0/21 to the HQ router.

And on to London 3:

10.1.16.0	*00001010.00000001.00010000*.00000000
10.1.17.0	*00001010.00000001.00010001*.00000000
10.1.18.0	*00001010.00000001.00010010*.00000000
10.1.19.0	*00001010.00000001.00010011*.00000000
10.1.20.0	*00001010.00000001.00010100*.00000000
10.1.21.0	*00001010.00000001.00010101*.00000000
10.1.22.0	*00001010.00000001.00010110*.00000000
10.1.23.0	*00001010.00000001.00010111*.00000000

London 3 has 21 common bits also, so it can advertise 10.1.16.0/21 upstream to the HQ router.

You will be expected to understand route summarisation for the CCNA exam. If you can quickly work out the common bits, then you should be able to answer the questions quickly and accurately..

Here is the answer to Exercise 1:

00110010.00000000
00111100.00000000
01000110.00000000
01010000.00000000
01011010.00000000
01100100.00000000
01101110.00000000
01111000.00000000

DAY 37 QUESTIONS

1. IPv6 addresses must always be used with a subnet mask. True or false?
2. Name the three types of IPv6 addresses.
3. Name the two ways of using IPv4 with IPv6.
4. Which method encapsulates an IPv6 packet inside the IPv4 packet?
5. Which routing protocols/methods work with IPv6?
6. Which commands enable IPv6 on your router?
7. The 0002 portion of an IPv6 address can be shortened to just 2. True or false?
8. In order to use route summarisation on your network, you need to use what?
9. Write down the subnets 172.16.8.0 to 172.16.15.0, and work out the common bits and what subnet mask you should use as a summary. Don't look in the book before working this out.

DAY 38

Router Security

DAY 38 TASKS

- Read today's theory notes
- Review yesterday's theory notes
- Complete today's lab
- Read the ICND2 cram guide
- Spend 15 minutes on the subnetting.org website

We have covered some network security threats and countermeasures previously. Now it's time to move on to practical steps you can take to secure your router from attempts to log in and reconfigure, either accidentally or maliciously.

Today you will learn about the following:

- Protecting physical access
- Telnet access
- Protecting Enable mode
- Router logging
- SNMP

This lesson maps to the following CCNA syllabus requirement:

- Describe security recommended practises, including initial steps to secure network devices

My first job at Cisco was on the core team. Our role involved helping customers with access lists, IOS upgrades, disaster recovery, and related tasks. One of the first things which struck me is how many engineers didn't lock down their routers with a password. Many of those who did used the password 'password' or 'cisco'—probably two of the most easily guessed, I would imagine!

We are going to look at the basic steps you should take on every network to protect your routers. Please read this module in association with the switch security module, which overlaps it.

Protecting Physical Access

Strange that when you consider the disastrous consequences of losing network access for a business, you often find their router sitting underneath somebody's desk!

Network equipment should be stored in a secure room with keypad access, or at least lock and key access. Cisco routers can be very valuable pieces of equipment, and are attractive targets to thieves. The larger the network, the more valuable the equipment, and the higher the need to protect the data and router configuration files.

Console Access

The console port is designed to give physical access to the router to permit initial configurations and disaster recovery. Anybody having console access can completely wipe or reconfigure the files, so, for this reason, the console port should be protected with a password by adding either a password or a local username and password, as illustrated below:

- Add a password

```
Router(config)#line console 0
Router(config-line)#password cisco
Router(config-line)#login
```

- Or add a local username and password

```
Router(config)#username paul password cisco
Router(config)#line console 0
Router(config-line)#login local
```

Telnet Access

You can't actually telnet into a router unless somebody adds a password to the Telnet or VTY lines. Again, you can put a password under the VTY lines or tell the router to look for a local username and password (in the configuration file), as shown below:

```
Router(config-line)#line vty 0 15
Router(config-line)#password cisco
Router(config-line)#login ← or login local
```

The output below is a Telnet session from one router to another. You can see the hostname change when you get Telnet access. The password will not show as you type it:

```
Router1#telnet 192.168.1.2
Trying 192.168.1.2 ...Open
User Access Verification
Username: paul
Password:
Router2>
```

If you have a security IOS image, you can configure the router to permit only SSH access rather than Telnet. The benefit of this is that all data is encrypted. If you try to telnet after SSH has been enabled, the connection will be terminated:

```
Router1(config)#line vty 0 15
Router1(config-line)#transport input ssh
Router2#telnet 192.168.1.2
Trying 192.168.1.2 ...Open
[Connection to 192.168.1.2 closed by foreign host]
```

Protecting Enable Mode

Enable mode gives configuration access to the router, so you will want to protect this also. You can configure an enable secret or an enable password. In fact, you could have both at the same time, but this is a bad idea.

An enable password is unencrypted, so it can be seen in the router configuration. An enable secret is given level 5 encryption, which is hard to break. You can add the command `service password encryption` to your enable password, but this can be cracked easily because it is level 7 encryption (low security). The following output illustrates this concept:

```
Router(config)#enable password cisco
Router(config)#exit
Router#show run
enable password cisco

Router(config)#enable password cisco
Router(config)#service password-encryption
Router#show run
enable password 7 0822455D0A16

Router(config)#enable secret cisco
Router(config)#exit
Router#show run
enable secret 5 $1$mERr$hx5rVt7rPNoS4wqbXKX7m0
```

Protecting User Access

Cisco IOS gives you the ability to give users individual passwords and usernames and give each of these users access to a restricted list of commands. This would be useful if you have tiers of network support. An example of this is shown in the following output:

```
RouterA#config term
Enter configuration commands, one per line. End with CNTL/Z.
RouterA(config)#username paul password cisco
RouterA(config)#username stuart password hello
RouterA(config)#username davie password football
RouterA(config)#line vty 0 4
RouterA(config-line)#login local
RouterA(config-line)#exit
RouterA(config)#exit
```

You can specify access levels for user accounts on the router. You may want, for example, junior network team members to be able to use only some basic troubleshooting commands. It is also worth remembering that Cisco routers have two modes of password security, User mode (Exec) and Privileged mode (Enable).

Cisco routers have 16 different privilege levels (0 to 15) available to configure, where 15 is full access, as illustrated below:

```
RouterA#conf t
Enter configuration commands, one per line. End with CNTL/Z.
RouterA(config)#username support privilege 4 password soccer
     LINE Initial keywords of the command to modify
RouterA(config)#privilege exec level 4 ping
RouterA(config)#privilege exec level 4 traceroute
RouterA(config)#privilege exec level 4 show ip interface brief
RouterA(config)#line console 0
RouterA(config-line)#password basketball
RouterA(config-line)#login local ←password is needed
RouterA(config-line)#^z
```

The support person logs in to the router and tries to go into configuration mode, but this command and any other command not available are not valid and cannot be seen:

```
RouterA con0 is now available
Press RETURN to get started.
User Access Verification
Username: support
Password:
RouterA#config t ←not allowed to use this command
          ^
% Invalid input detected at '^' marker.
```

Updating the IOS

Admittedly, updating the IOS can sometimes introduce new bugs or problems into your network, so it is best practise to do this on the advice of Cisco if you have a TAC support contract. In general, though, keeping your IOS up to date is highly recommended.

Updating your IOS:

- Fixes known bugs
- Closes security vulnerabilities
- Offers enhanced features and IOS capabilities

We have covered banner messages and CDP in the switch security module, so it won't be repeated here.

Router Logging

Routers offer the ability to log events. They can send the log messages to your screen or a server if you wish. You should log router messages, and there are seven levels of logging severity available, as shown in bold in the output below:

```
logging buffered ?
<0-7>Logging severity level
alerts—Immediate action needed (severity=1)
critical—Critical conditions (severity=2)
debugging—Debugging messages (severity=7)
emergencies—System is unusable (severity=0)
errors—Error conditions (severity=3)
informational—Informational messages (severity=6)
notifications—Normal but significant conditions (severity=5)
warnings—Warning conditions (severity=4)
```

You can send the logging messages to several places:

```
Router(config)#logging ?
  A.B.C.D   IP address of the logging host
  buffered  Set buffered logging parameters
  console   Set console logging parameters
  host      Set syslog server IP address and parameters
  on        Enable logging to all enabled destinations
  trap      Set syslog server logging level
  userinfo  Enable logging of user info on privileged mode enabling
```

Simple Network Management Protocol (SNMP)

SNMP is a service you can use to manage your network remotely. It consists of a central station run by an administrator running the SNMP management software and smaller files (agents) on each of your network devices, including routers, switches, and servers.

Several vendors have designed SNMP software, including HP, Cisco, IBM, and Solarwinds. There are also open source versions available. The software allows you to monitor bandwidth and activity on devices, such as logins and port status.

You can remotely configure or shut down ports and devices using SNMP. You can also configure it to send alerts when certain conditions are met, such as high bandwidth or ports going down.

DAY 38 QUESTIONS

1. Write out the two ways of configuring console passwords. Write the actual commands.
2. Which command will permit only SSH traffic into the VTY lines?
3. Which command will encrypt a password with level 7 encryption?
4. Name the seven levels of logging available on the router.

DAY 38 LAB—BASIC ROUTER SECURITY

Topology

Purpose

Learn some basic steps to take to lock down your router.

Walkthrough

1. Protect Enable mode with an enable secret password. Test this by logging out of Privileged mode and then logging back in.

```
Router#conf t
Enter configuration commands, one per line.  End with CNTL/Z.
Router(config)#enable secret cisco
Router(config)#exit
Router#
%SYS-5-CONFIG_I: Configured from console by console
Router#exi
Router con0 is now available

Press RETURN to get started.
Router>en
Password:
Router#
```

2. Set an enable password and then add service password encryption. This is rarely done on live routers because it is not secure.

```
Router(config)#no enable secret
Router(config)#enable password cisco
Router(config)#service pass
Router(config)#service password-encryption
Router(config)#exit
Router#
%SYS-5-CONFIG_I: Configured from console by console

Router#show run
Building configuration...

Current configuration: 480 bytes
```

```
!
version 12.4
no service timestamps log datetime msec
no service timestamps debug datetime msec
service password-encryption
!
hostname Router
!
enable password 7 0822455D0A16
```

3. Protect the Telnet lines. Set a local username and password and have users enter this when connecting to the router.

```
Router(config)#line vty 0 ?
  <1-15>  Last Line number
  <cr>
Router(config)#line vty 0 15
Router(config-line)#login local
Router(config-line)#exi
Router(config)#username in60days password cisco
Router(config)#
```

You have tested Telnet before, but feel free to add a PC and telnet into the router so you are prompted for a username and password.

4. Protect the console port with a password. Set one directly on the console port.

```
Router(config)#line console 0
Router(config-line)#password cisco
```

You can test this by unplugging and plugging your console lead back into the router. You can also protect the auxiliary port on your router if you have one:

```
Router(config)#line aux 0
Router(config-line)#password cisco
```

5. Protect the Telnet lines by permitting only SSH traffic in. You can also permit only SSH traffic outbound. You will need a security image for this command to work.

```
Router(config)#line vty 0 15
Router(config-line)#transport input ssh
Router(config-line)#transport output ssh
```

6. Add a banner message of the day (MOTD). Set the character which tells the router you have finished with your message as X (the delimiting character).

```
Router(config)#banner motd X
Enter TEXT message.  End with the character 'X'.
Do not use this router without authorization. X

Router(config)#
Router(config)#exit
Router#
%SYS-5-CONFIG_I: Configured from console by console
Exit

Router con0 is now available
Press RETURN to get started.

Do not use this router without authorization.
Router>
```

7. Turn off CDP on the entire router. You could disable it on an interface only with the `no cdp enable interface` command.

```
Router(config)#no cdp run
```

You can test whether this is working by connecting a switch or router to your router before you turn off CDP and issuing the `show cdp neighbor (detail)` command.

8. Set the router to send logging messages to a host on the network.

```
Router#conf t
Enter configuration commands, one per line.  End with CNTL/Z.
Router(config)#logging ?
  A.B.C.D   IP address of the logging host
  buffered  Set buffered logging parameters
  console   Set console logging parameters
  host      Set syslog server IP address and parameters
  on        Enable logging to all enabled destinations
  trap      Set syslog server logging level
  userinfo  Enable logging of user info on privileged mode enabling
Router(config)#logging 10.1.1.1
```

EIGRP

DAY 39 TASKS

- Read today's theory notes
- Review yesterday's theory notes
- Review ACLs or VTP/STP
- Complete today's lab
- Read the ICND2 cram guide
- Spend 15 minutes on the subnetting.org website

Entire books have been written on the subject of Enhanced Interior Gateway Routing Protocol (EIGRP); however, I want to stick to a CCNA-level review of the subject, for obvious reasons.

Today you will learn about the following:

- EIGRP basics
- Configuring EIGRP
- EIGRP operations
- Troubleshooting EIGRP

This lesson maps to the following CCNA syllabus requirement:

- Configure, verify, and troubleshoot EIGRP

EIGRP Basics

EIGRP was developed by Cisco, so it can only be used on Cisco routers. It uses some elements from Distance Vector protocols (such as split horizon) and some from Link State (such as incremental updates). EIGRP runs directly over IP using protocol number 88.

Although IGRP is no longer covered in the CCNA syllabus, EIGRP was developed in order to overcome its limitations. The problems with IGRP included the following:

- Hop limitation
- Full routing table updates
- No VLSM support
- Slow to converge
- Lack of loop prevention

Features of EIGRP include the following:

- It sends updates when topology changes
- A default hop count of 100 (255 max)
- It supports VLSM
- It uses Diffusing Update Algorithm (DUAL) for loop prevention

Configuring EIGRP

EIGRP is a very robust and scalable protocol; however, we won't delve into much more than the basics of configuring it because we would be stepping into CCNP-level subjects.

EIGRP is activated on the router with one simple command:

```
Router eigrp [ASN]
```

You will then need to add network numbers for any networks you wish to take part in the routing process.

The autonomous system number (ASN) can be any number from 1 to 65,535. You can choose any ASN number because they are not reserved or assigned by any specific body, and they can be used unlimited times. Every router you want to communicate with in your routing domain must have the same ASN.

You can see the ASN with the `show ip protocols` command, as illustrated in the output below:

```
R1#show ip protocols
Routing Protocol is "eigrp 150"
  Outgoing update filter list for all interfaces is not set
  Incoming update filter list for all interfaces is not set
  Default networks flagged in outgoing updates
  Default networks accepted from incoming updates
  EIGRP metric weight K1=1, K2=0, K3=1, K4=0, K5=0
  EIGRP maximum hopcount 100
  EIGRP maximum metric variance 1
```

If you add network 10.0.0.0 to your EIGRP routing process, then any network in the 10.x.x.x range would be advertised, as illustrated in the output below:

```
Router(config-router)#router eigrp 20
Router(config-router)#network 10.0.0.0

R1#show ip protocols
Routing Protocol is "eigrp 150"
  Outgoing update filter list for all interfaces is not set
  Incoming update filter list for all interfaces is not set
  Default networks flagged in outgoing updates
EIGRP metric weight K1=1, K2=0, K3=1, K4=0, K5=0
  EIGRP maximum hopcount 100
  EIGRP maximum metric variance 1
  Redistributing: eigrp 150
  EIGRP NSF-aware route hold timer is 240s
  Automatic network summarization is in effect
  Maximum path: 4
  Routing for Networks:
    10.0.0.0
  Routing Information Sources:
    Gateway           Distance       Last Update
Distance: internal 90 external 170
```

EIGRP Operations

EIGRP Topology Table

The Topology Table allows all EIGRP routers to have a consistent view of the entire network. It also allows for rapid convergence in EIGRP networks. Each individual entry in the Topology Table contains the destination network and the neighbour(s) that have advertised the destination network.

Both the Feasible Distance and the Reported Distance are stored in the Topology Table. The EIGRP Topology Table contains the information needed to build a set of distances and vectors to each reachable network. The reported distance is the metric towards a destination network as advertised by an upstream neighbor. An example of this is illustrated in the following output:

```
R1#show ip eigrp topology
IP-EIGRP Topology Table for AS(150)/ID(10.3.3.1)

Codes: P - Passive, A - Active, U - Update, Q - Query, R - Reply,
       r - reply Status, s - sia Status

P 10.3.3.0/24, 1 successors, FD is 128256
        via Connected, Loopback3
P 10.2.2.0/24, 1 successors, FD is 128256
        via Connected, Loopback2
P 10.1.1.0/24, 1 successors, FD is 128256
        via Connected, Loopback1
P 10.0.0.0/24, 1 successors, FD is 128256
        via Connected, Loopback0
```

Routing Subnets

If you want to route specific subnets rather than the entire network range, you can add a wildcard mask to the network, as illustrated in the following output:

```
R1(config)#router eigrp 150
R1(config-router)#network 10.1.1.0 0.0.0.255
R1(config-router)#network 10.3.3.0 0.0.0.255
R1(config-router)#exit
R1#show ip protocols
Routing Protocol is "eigrp 150"
  Automatic network summarization is in effect
  Maximum path: 4
  Routing for Networks:
    10.1.1.0/24
    10.3.3.0/24
  Routing Information Sources:
    Gateway          Distance       Last Update
  Distance: internal 90 external 170
```

EIGRP Metrics

EIGRP uses a composite metric, which includes different variables. These variables are referred to as the K values. The K values are constants that are used to distribute weight to different path aspects, which may be included in the composite EIGRP metric. The default values for the K values are $K1 = K3 = 1$ and $K2 = K4 = K5 = 0$. In other words, K1 and K3 are set to a default value of 1, whilst K2, K4, and K5 are set to a default value of 0.

Assuming the default K value settings, the complete EIGRP metric can be calculated using the following mathematical formula:

[K1 * bandwidth + (K2 * bandwidth) / (256 - load) + K3 * delay] * [K5 / (reliability + K4)]

However, given that only K1 and K3 have any positive values by default, the default EIGRP metric calculation is performed using the following mathematical formula:

$[(10^7/\text{least bandwidth on path}) + (\text{sum of all delays})] \times 256$

This essentially means that, by default, EIGRP uses the minimum bandwidth on the path to a destination network and the total delay to compute routing metrics.

Neighbour Discovery

Dynamic neighbour discovery is performed by sending EIGRP Hello packets to the destination multicast group address 224.0.0.10. This is performed as soon as the `network` command is used when configuring EIGRP on the router. In addition, as stated earlier, EIGRP packets are sent directly over IP using protocol number 88.

To populate the Topology Table, EIGRP runs the Diffusing Update Algorithm (DUAL). This is at the crux of the EIGRP routing protocol. DUAL looks at all routes received from neighbour routers, compares them, and then selects the lowest metric (best), loop-free path to the destination network, which is the Feasible Distance (FD), resulting in the Successor route. The FD includes both the metric of a network, as advertised by the connected neighbour, plus the cost of reaching that particular neighbour.

Troubleshooting EIGRP

For the CCNA exam, when you see neighbours not forming, look to the following possible causes:

- Mismatched K values
- ASNs don't agree
- Passwords don't agree (if used)
- Neighbour not on a common subnet
- Neighbour interface down (no shut or missing clock rate)

DAY 39 QUESTIONS

1. You can see the ASN with the `show ip _____` command.

2. Every router you want to communicate with in your routing domain must have a different ASN. True or false?

3. What is the purpose of the EIGRP Topology Table?

4. By default, EIGRP uses the _____ bandwidth on the path to a destination network and the total _____ to compute routing metrics.

5. Dynamic neighbour discovery is performed by sending EIGRP Hello packets to the destination multicast group address _____.

6. EIGRP packets are sent directly over IP using protocol number _____.

7. To populate the Topology Table, EIGRP runs the _____ algorithm.

8. The _____ _____ includes both the metric of a network as advertised by the connected neighbour, plus the cost of reaching that particular neighbour.

9. Name the most common causes of neighbours not forming for EIGRP.

DAY 39 LAB—EIGRP

Topology

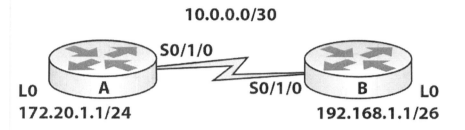

10.0.0.0/30

S0/1/0

LO   A   S0/1/0   B   LO

172.20.1.1/24   192.168.1.1/26

Purpose

Learn how to configure basic EIGRP.

Walkthrough

1. Configure all IP addresses on the topology above. Make sure you can ping across the Serial link.

2. Configure EIGRP with AS 30 on each router.

```
RouterA(config)#router eigrp 30
RouterA(config-router)#net 172.20.0.0
RouterA(config-router)#net 10.0.0.0
RouterA(config-router)#^Z
RouterA#

RouterB#conf t
Enter configuration commands, one per line.  End with CNTL/Z.
RouterB(config)#router eigrp 30
RouterB(config-router)#net 10.0.0.0
%DUAL-5-NBRCHANGE: IP-EIGRP 30: Neighbor 10.0.0.1 (Serial0/1/0) is up: new
adjacency
RouterB(config-router)#net 192.168.1.0
```

3. Check the routing table on each router.

```
RouterA#sh ip route
Codes: C - connected, S - static, I - IGRP, R - RIP, M - mobile, B - BGP
       D - EIGRP, EX - EIGRP external, O - OSPF, IA - OSPF inter area
       N1 - OSPF NSSA external type 1, N2 - OSPF NSSA external type 2
       E1 - OSPF external type 1, E2 - OSPF external type 2, E - EGP
       i - IS-IS, L1 - IS-IS level-1, L2 - IS-IS level-2, ia - IS-IS inter
area
       * - candidate default, U - per-user static route, o - ODR
       P - periodic downloaded static route
```

```
Gateway of last resort is not set

     10.0.0.0/8 is variably subnetted, 2 subnets, 2 masks
D       10.0.0.0/8 is a summary, 00:01:43, Null0
C       10.0.0.0/30 is directly connected, Serial0/1/0
     172.20.0.0/16 is variably subnetted, 2 subnets, 2 masks
D       172.20.0.0/16 is a summary, 00:01:43, Null0
C       172.20.1.0/24 is directly connected, Loopback0
D    192.168.1.0/24 [90/20640000] via 10.0.0.2, 00:00:49, Serial0/1/0
RouterA


RouterB#show ip route
[output truncated]
     10.0.0.0/8 is variably subnetted, 2 subnets, 2 masks
D       10.0.0.0/8 is a summary, 00:01:21, Null0
C       10.0.0.0/30 is directly connected, Serial0/1/0
D    172.20.0.0/16 [90/20640000] via 10.0.0.1, 00:01:27, Serial0/1/0
     192.168.1.0/24 is variably subnetted, 2 subnets, 2 masks
D       192.168.1.0/24 is a summary, 00:01:21, Null0
C       192.168.1.0/26 is directly connected, Loopback0
RouterB#
```

4. Check to ensure each router is auto-summarising each network. Then turn off auto-summary on Router B.

```
RouterB#show ip protocols
Routing Protocol is "eigrp  30"
  Outgoing update filter list for all interfaces is not set
  Incoming update filter list for all interfaces is not set
  Default networks flagged in outgoing updates
  Default networks accepted from incoming updates
  EIGRP metric weight K1=1, K2=0, K3=1, K4=0, K5=0
  EIGRP maximum hopcount 100
  EIGRP maximum metric variance 1
Redistributing: eigrp 30
  Automatic network summarization is in effect
  Automatic address summarization:
    192.168.1.0/24 for Serial0/1/0
      Summarizing with metric 128256
    10.0.0.0/8 for Loopback0
      Summarizing with metric 20512000
  Maximum path: 4
  Routing for Networks:
    10.0.0.0
    192.168.1.0
  Routing Information Sources:
    Gateway         Distance      Last Update
    10.0.0.1        90            496078
```

```
  Distance: internal 90 external 170

RouterB(config)#router eigrp 30
RouterB(config-router)#no auto-summary
```

5. Check the routing table on Router A.

```
RouterA#show ip route
[output truncated]
Gateway of last resort is not set

      10.0.0.0/8 is variably subnetted, 2 subnets, 2 masks
D        10.0.0.0/8 is a summary, 00:00:04, Null0
C        10.0.0.0/30 is directly connected, Serial0/1/0
      172.20.0.0/16 is variably subnetted, 2 subnets, 2 masks
D        172.20.0.0/16 is a summary, 00:00:04, Null0
C        172.20.1.0/24 is directly connected, Loopback0
      192.168.1.0/26 is subnetted, 1 subnets
D        192.168.1.0 [90/20640000] via 10.0.0.2, 00:00:04, Serial0/1/0
RouterA#
```

DAY 40

OSPF

DAY 40 TASKS
- Read today's theory notes
- Review yesterday's theory notes
- Complete today's lab
- Read the ICND2 cram guide
- Spend 15 minutes on the subnetting.org website

As with EIGRP, we could discuss OSPF over several days, but we need to stick to what you need to know for your exam. Even CCNA-level OSPF knowledge wouldn't be sufficient to design and deploy it on most networks.

Today you will learn about the following:

- OSPF operations
- DR and BDR
- Configuring OSPF
- Troubleshooting OSPF

This lesson maps to the following CCNA syllabus requirement:

- Configure, verify, and troubleshoot OSPF

OSPF Operations
OSPF is an open standard Link State protocol which sends network Hello messages to find other links. It uses incremental updates and operates over IP protocol 89.

Features of OSPF include the following:

- It uses multicasts for updates
- It supports authentication
- It supports VLSM
- It divides the networks into areas (subdomains)
- Link State Advertisements are sent inside the area

OSPF is a hierarchical routing protocol that logically divides the network into subdomains referred to as areas. This logical segmentation is used to limit the scope of Link State Advertisements (LSAs) flooding throughout the OSPF domain. LSAs are special types of packets sent by routers running OSPF. Different types of LSAs are used within an area and between areas. By restricting the propagation of certain types of LSAs between areas, the OSPF hierarchical implementation effectively reduces the amount of routing protocol traffic within the OSPF network.

If you have only one OSPF area, then it must be Area 0, which is referred to as the backbone. If you add another area, then it must directly connect to Area 0 (because that is the backbone). Any router which connects to Area 0 and another area is referred to as an area border router (ABR). This concept is illustrated in Figure 40.1 below:

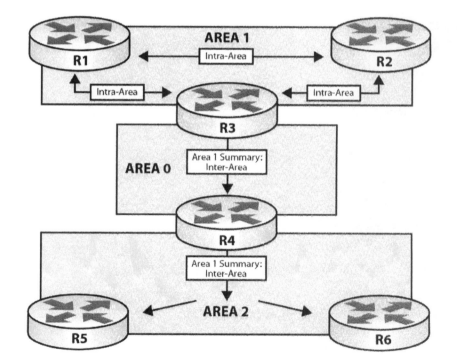

FIG 40.1—All Areas Must Connect to Area 0

OSPF uses different default network types for different media. These network types are as follows:

- Non-broadcast
- Point-to-point
- Broadcast
- Point-to-multipoint

Non-broadcast networks are network types that do not support natively broadcast or multicast traffic. The most common example of a non-broadcast network type is Frame Relay. Non-broadcast network types require additional configuration to allow for both broadcast and multicast support. On such networks, OSPF elects a Designated Router (DR) and/or a Backup Designated Router (BDR). These two routers will be described later in this lesson.

In Cisco IOS software, OSPF-enabled routers send Hello packets every 30 seconds on non-broadcast network types. If a Hello packet is not received in four times (i.e., the Hello interval of 120 seconds), the neighbour router is considered 'dead.' The following shows the output of the show ip ospf interface command on a Frame Relay Serial interface:

```
R2#show ip ospf interface serial 0/0
Serial0/0 is up, line protocol is up
  Internet Address 150.1.1.2/24, Area 0
  Process ID 2, Router ID 2.2.2.2, Network Type NON_BROADCAST, Cost: 64
  Transmit Delay is 1 sec, State DR, Priority 1
  Designated Router (ID) 2.2.2.2, Interface address 150.1.1.2
  Backup Designated router (ID) 1.1.1.1, Interface address 150.1.1.1
  Timer intervals configured, Hello 30, Dead 120, Wait 120, Retransmit 5
    oob-resync timeout 120
    Hello due in 00:00:00
  Supports Link-local Signaling (LLS)
  Index 2/2, flood queue length 0
  Next 0x0(0)/0x0(0)
  Last flood scan length is 2, maximum is 2
  Last flood scan time is 0 msec, maximum is 0 msec
  Neighbor Count is 1, Adjacent neighbor count is 1
    Adjacent with neighbor 1.1.1.1  (Backup Designated Router)
  Suppress hello for 0 neighbor(s)
```

A point-to-point connection is simply a connection between only two endpoints. Examples of point-to-point connections include physical WAN interfaces using HDLC and PPP encapsulation, and Frame Relay and ATM point-to-point subinterfaces. No DR or BDR is elected on OSPF point-to-point network types. By default, OSPF sends Hello packets out every 10 seconds on point-to-point network types. The 'dead' interval on these network types is four times the Hello interval, which is 40 seconds. The following shows the output of the show ip ospf interface command on a point-to-point link:

```
R2#show ip ospf interface serial 0/0
Serial0/0 is up, line protocol is up
  Internet Address 150.1.1.2/24, Area 0
  Process ID 2, Router ID 2.2.2.2, Network Type POINT_TO_POINT, Cost: 64
  Transmit Delay is 1 sec, State POINT_TO_POINT
  Timer intervals configured, Hello 10, Dead 40, Wait 40, Retransmit 5
    oob-resync timeout 40
    Hello due in 00:00:03
  Supports Link-local Signaling (LLS)
  Index 2/2, flood queue length 0
  Next 0x0(0)/0x0(0)
  Last flood scan length is 1, maximum is 1
  Last flood scan time is 0 msec, maximum is 0 msec
  Neighbor Count is 1, Adjacent neighbor count is 1
    Adjacent with neighbor 1.1.1.1
  Suppress hello for 0 neighbor(s)
```

Broadcast network types are those that natively support broadcast and multicast traffic, the most common example being Ethernet. As is the case with non-broadcast networks, OSPF also elects a DR and/or a BDR on broadcast networks. By default, OSPF sends Hello packets every 10 seconds on these network types, and a neighbour is declared 'dead' if no Hello packets are received within four times the Hello interval, which is 40 seconds. The following shows the output of the show ip ospf interface command on a FastEthernet interface:

```
R2#show ip ospf interface fastethernet 0/0
FastEthernet0/0 is up, line protocol is up
  Internet Address 192.168.1.2/24, Area 0
  Process ID 2, Router ID 2.2.2.2, Network Type BROADCAST, Cost: 64
  Transmit Delay is 1 sec, State BDR, Priority 1
  Designated Router (ID) 192.168.1.3, Interface address 192.168.1.3
  Backup Designated router (ID) 2.2.2.2, Interface address 192.168.1.2
  Timer intervals configured, Hello 10, Dead 40, Wait 40, Retransmit 5
    oob-resync timeout 40
    Hello due in 00:00:04
  Supports Link-local Signaling (LLS)
  Index 1/1, flood queue length 0
  Next 0x0(0)/0x0(0)
  Last flood scan length is 1, maximum is 1
  Last flood scan time is 0 msec, maximum is 0 msec
  Neighbor Count is 1, Adjacent neighbor count is 1
    Adjacent with neighbor 192.168.1.3  (Designated Router)
  Suppress hello for 0 neighbor(s)
```

The point-to-multipoint network type is a non-default OSPF network type. In other words, this network type must be manually configured using the ip ospf network point-to-multipoint [non-broadcast] interface configuration command. By default, the command defaults to a broadcast point-to-multipoint network type. This default network type allows OSPF to use multicast packets to discover neighbour routers dynamically. In addition, there is no DR/BDR election held on broadcast point-to-multipoint network types.

The [non-broadcast] keyword configures the point-to-multipoint network type as a non-broadcast point-to-multipoint network. This requires static OSPF neighbour configuration, as OSPF will not use multicast to discover neighbour routers dynamically. Additionally, this network type does not require the election of a DR and/or a BDR router for the designated segment. The primary use of this network type is to allow neighbour costs to be assigned to neighbours instead of using the interface assigned cost for routes received from all neighbours.

The point-to-multipoint network type is typically used in partial-mesh hub-and-spoke non-broadcast multi-access networks. However, it should also be noted that this network type could also be specified for other network types, such as broadcast multi-access networks (e.g., Ethernet). By default, OSPF sends Hello packets every 30 seconds on point-to-multipoint networks. The default dead interval is four times the Hello interval, or 120 seconds.

The following shows the output of the show ip ospf interface command on a Frame Relay Serial interface that has been manually configured as a point-to-multipoint network:

```
R2#show ip ospf interface serial 0/0
Serial0/0 is up, line protocol is up
  Internet Address 150.1.1.2/24, Area 0
 Process ID 2, Router ID 2.2.2.2, Network Type POINT_TO_MULTIPOINT, Cost:
64
  Transmit Delay is 1 sec, State POINT_TO_MULTIPOINT
  Timer intervals configured, Hello 30, Dead 120, Wait 120, Retransmit 5
    oot-resync timeout 120
    Hello due in 00:00:04
  Supports Link-local Signaling (LLS)
  Index 2/2, flood queue length 0
  Next 0x0(0)/0x0(0)
  Last flood scan length is 1, maximum is 2
  Last flood scan time is 0 msec, maximum is 0 msec
  Neighbor Count is 1, Adjacent neighbor count is 1
    Adjacent with neighbor 1.1.1.1
  Suppress hello for 0 neighbor(s)
```

The primary reason that OSPF requires that the network type be the same on both routers is because of the timer values. As illustrated in the examples above, different network types use different Hello and Dead timer intervals. In order for an OSPF adjacency to be successfully established, these values must match on both routers.

DR and BDR

As stated in the previous section, OSPF elects a Designated Router and/or a Backup Designated Router on broadcast and non-broadcast network types. It is important to understand that the BDR is not a mandatory component on these network types. In fact, OSPF will work just as well if only a DR is elected and there is no BDR; however, there will be no redundancy if the DR fails, and the OSPF routers will need to go through the election process again to elect a new DR.

On the segment, each individual non-DR/BDR router establishes an adjacency with the DR, and, if one has also been elected, the BDR, but not with any other non-DR/BDR routers on the segment. The DR and BDR routers are fully adjacent with each other and all other routers on the segment. The non-DR/BDR routers send messages and updates to the AllDRRouters multicast group address 224.0.0.6. Only the DR/BDR routers listen to multicast messages sent to this group address. The DR then advertises messages to the AllSPFRouters multicast group address 224.0.0.5. This allows all other OSPF routers on the segment to receive the updates.

In order for a router to be the DR or BDR for the segment, the router must be elected. This election is based on the following:

- The highest router priority value
- The highest router ID

By default, all routers have a default priority value of 1. This value can be adjusted using the `ip ospf priority <0-255>` interface configuration command. The higher the priority, the greater the likelihood the router will be elected as the DR for the segment. The router with the second-highest priority will then be elected the BDR. If a priority value of 0 is configured, the router will not participate in the DR/BDR election process.

When determining the OSPF router ID, Cisco IOS selects the highest IP address of configured Loopback interfaces. If no Loopback interfaces are configured, the software uses the highest IP address of all configured physical interfaces as the OSPF router ID. Cisco IOS software also allows administrators to specify the router ID manually using the `router-id [address]` router configuration command. This is illustrated in the output below:

```
R3#show ip protocols
Routing Protocol is "ospf 1"
  Outgoing update filter list for all interfaces is not set
  Incoming update filter list for all interfaces is not set
  Router ID 4.4.4.4
  Number of areas in this router is 0. 0 normal 0 stub 0 nssa
  Maximum path: 4
```

```
Routing for Networks:
Reference bandwidth unit is 100 mbps
 Routing Information Sources:
   Gateway         Distance       Last Update
 Distance: (default is 110)
```

It is important to remember that with OSPF, once the DR and the BDR have been elected, they will remain as DR/BDR routers until a new election is held. For example, if a DR and a BDR exist on a multi-access network and a router with a higher priority or IP address is added to the same segment, the existing DR and BDR routers will not change.

If the DR fails, the BDR will assume the role of the DR, not the new router with the higher priority or IP address. Instead, a new election will be held and that router will most likely be elected as the BDR. In order for that router to become the DR, the BDR must be removed or the OSPF process reset, forcing a new DR/BDR election. Once elected, OSPF uses the DR and BDR routers as follows:

- To reduce the number of adjacencies required on the segment
- To advertise the routers on the multi-access segment
- To ensure that updates are sent to all routers on the segment

Configuring OSPF

Basic OSPF can be enabled on the router with one line of configuration, and then by adding the network you wish to advertise:

```
Router ospf 9 ←  locally significant number
network 10.0.0.0 0.255.255.255 area 0
```

OSPF won't become active until at least one interface is up/up, and remember that at least one area must be Area 0. A Sample OSPF network is illustrated in Figure 40.2 below:

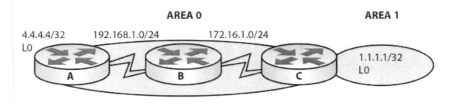

FIG 40.2—A Sample OSPF Network

Router A configuration:

```
router ospf 20
network 4.4.4.4 0.0.0.0 area 0
network 192.168.1.0 0.0.0.255 area 0
Router ID 4.4.4.4
```

Router B configuration:

```
router ospf 22
network 172.16.1.0 0.0.0.255 area 0
network 192.168.1.0 0.0.0.255 area 0
Router ID 192.168.1.2
```

Router C configuration:

```
router ospf 44
network 1.1.1.1 0.0.0.0 area 1
network 172.16.1.0 0.0.0.255 area 0
Router ID 1.1.1.1

RouterC#show ip route
Gateway of last resort is not set
      1.0.0.0/32 is subnetted, 1 subnets
C        1.1.1.1 is directly connected, Loopback0
      4.0.0.0/32 is subnetted, 1 subnets
O        4.4.4.4 [110/129] via 172.16.1.1, 00:10:39, Serial0/0/0
      172.16.0.0/24 is subnetted, 1 subnets
C        172.16.1.0 is directly connected, Serial0/0/0
O     192.168.1.0/24 [110/128] via 172.16.1.1, 00:10:39, Serial0/0/0
```

Troubleshooting OSPF

At the CCNA-level, look to the following four possible causes of OSPF routing issues:

- Is Area 0 configured?
- Is there an active interface (up/up)?
- Are the correct networks advertised?
- Is the correct IP address and subnet mask on your interface?

DAY 40 QUESTIONS

1. OSPF uses _____ updates and operates over IP protocol _____.

2. OSPF does NOT support VLSM. True or false?

3. Any router which connects to Area 0 and another area is referred to as an _____ _____ router or _____.

4. If you have a DR, you must always have a BDR. True or false?

5. The DR/BDR election is based upon which two factors?

6. By default, all routers have a default priority value of _____. This value can be adjusted using the _____ _____ _____ <0-255> interface configuration command.

7. When determining the OSPF router ID, Cisco IOS selects the highest IP address of configured Loopback interfaces. True or false?

8. What roles do the DR and BDR carry out?

9. What command would put network 10.0.0.0/8 into Area 0 on a router?

10. What command would set the router ID to 1.1.1.1?

11. Name the common troubleshooting issues for OSPF.

DAY 40 LAB—OSPF

Topology

10.0.0.0/30

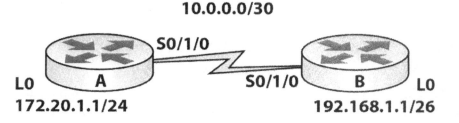

LO   **A**   **S0/1/0**   **B**   LO
172.20.1.1/24   **192.168.1.1/26**

Purpose

Learn how to configure basic OSPF.

Walkthrough

1. Configure all IP addresses on the topology above. Make sure you can ping across the Serial link.

2. Add OSPF to Router A. Put the network on Loopback 0 into Area 1 and the 10 network in Area 0.

```
RouterA(config)#router ospf 4
RouterA(config-router)#network 172.20.1.0 0.0.0.255 area 1
RouterA(config-router)#network 10.0.0.0 0.0.0.3 area 0
RouterA(config-router)#^Z
RouterA#
%SYS-5-CONFIG_I: Configured from console by console

RouterA#show ip protocols

Routing Protocol is "ospf 4"
  Outgoing update filter list for all interfaces is not set
  Incoming update filter list for all interfaces is not set
  Router ID 172.20.1.1
  Number of areas in this router is 2. 2 normal 0 stub 0 nssa
  Maximum path: 4
  Routing for Networks:
    172.20.1.0 0.0.0.255 area 1
    10.0.0.0 0.0.0.3 area 0
  Routing Information Sources:
    Gateway         Distance      Last Update
    172.20.1.1          110       00:00:09
  Distance: (default is 110)
```

3. Add OSPF on Router B. Put the Loopback network into OSPF Area 40.

```
RouterB(config)#router ospf 2
RouterB(config-router)#net 10.0.0.0 0.0.0.3 area 0
RouterB(config-router)#
00:22:35: %OSPF-5-ADJCHG: Process 2, Nbr 172.20.1.1 on Serial0/1/0 from
LOADING to FULL, Loading Done

RouterB(config-router)#net 192.168.1.0 0.0.0.63 area 40
RouterB(config-router)#^Z

RouterB#show ip protocols

Routing Protocol is "ospf 2"
  Outgoing update filter list for all interfaces is not set
  Incoming update filter list for all interfaces is not set
  Router ID 192.168.1.1
  Number of areas in this router is 2. 2 normal 0 stub 0 nssa
  Maximum path: 4
  Routing for Networks:
    10.0.0.0 0.0.0.3 area 0
    192.168.1.0 0.0.0.63 area 40
  Routing Information Sources:
    Gateway          Distance      Last Update
    172.20.1.1          110        00:01:18
    192.168.1.1         110        00:00:44
  Distance: (default is 110)
```

4. Check the routing table on your routers. Look for the OSPF advertised network. You will see an IA, which means IA - OSPF inter-area. You will also see the AD for OSPF, which is 110.

```
RouterA#sh ip route
[output truncated]

     10.0.0.0/30 is subnetted, 1 subnets
C       10.0.0.0 is directly connected, Serial0/1/0
     172.20.0.0/24 is subretted, 1 subnets
C       172.20.1.0 is directly connected, Loopback0
     192.168.1.0/32 is subnetted, 1 subnets
O IA    192.168.1.1 [110/65] via 10.0.0.2, 00:01:36, Serial0/1/0
RouterA#
```

5. Issue some of the available OSPF commands on either router.

```
RouterA#sh ip ospf ?
  <1-65535>       Process ID number
  border-routers  Border and Boundary Router Information
  database        Database summary
```

```
interface       Interface information
neighbor        Neighbor list
```

NOTE: OSPF is a huge subject to cover, but for the CCNA exam, you only need to know the very basic configuration commands.

DAY 41

Frame Relay

DAY 41 TASKS

- Read today's theory notes
- Review yesterday's theory notes
- Complete today's lab
- Read the ICND2 cram guide
- Spend 15 minutes on the subnetting.org website

Frame Relay was an important part of the CCNA to CCIE syllabus for several years; however, its popularity has waned recently due to the wide availability of DSL connections for businesses and the price of leased lines becoming more affordable. We cover it here because it is included in the CCNA syllabus.

Today you will learn about the following:

- Frame Relay operations
- Configuring Frame Relay
- Troubleshooting Frame Relay

This lesson maps to the following CCNA syllabus requirement:

- Configure and verify Frame Relay on Cisco routers

Frame Relay Operations

Frame Relay is a Layer 2 WAN protocol based upon an older protocol called X.25, which is still used by ATMs due to its extensive error-checking capabilities. Frame Relay is comprised of one physical circuit upon which many logical circuits can form. Connections are made on an as-needed basis. An example of a Frame Relay network is illustrated below:

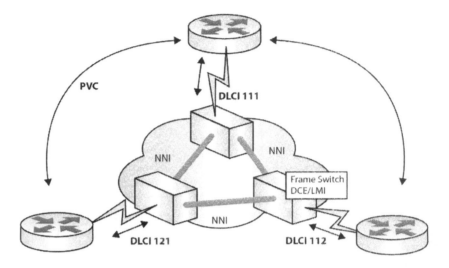

FIG 41.1—A Frame Relay Network

Common Frame Relay Terms

LMI

Local management interface (LMI) is a keepalive which runs from the Frame Relay switch. This switch belongs to your service provider and is located at their premises. You will need to specify the LMI type on your router, unless the CISCO default is used. The three types of LMIs available are as follows:

- CISCO
- ANSI
- Q933a

LMIs are illustrated in Figure 41.2 below:

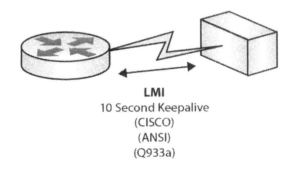

LMI
10 Second Keepalive
(CISCO)
(ANSI)
(Q933a)

FIG 41.2—LMI Types

If you have a fault with your Frame Relay connection, then debugging the LMI messages would be one of your troubleshooting steps, as illustrated in the output below:

```
RouterA#debug frame-relay lmi
00:46:58: Serial0(in): Status, myseq 55
00:46:58: RT IE 1, length 1, type 0
00:46:58: KA IE 3, length 2, yourseq 55, myseq 55
00:46:58: PVC IE 0x7 , length 0x6 , dlci 100, status 0x2 , bw 0
```

An LMI is sent every 10 seconds, and every sixth message is a full status update. As above, you want it to report status 0x2, which is an active link.

PVC

A permanent virtual circuit (PVC) is the logical end-to-end connection formed from one end of your Frame Relay network to the other, as illustrated in Figure 41.3 below. Each endpoint is given a DLCI number (see next section) to identify it.

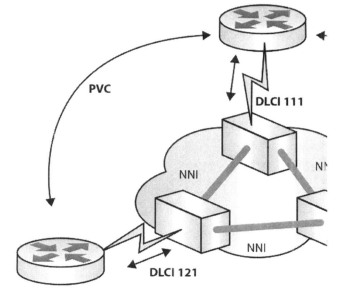

FIG 41.3—A PVC

DLCI

The Data Link Connection Identifier (DLCI) is a locally significant number used to identify your connection to the Frame Relay switch, as illustrated in Figure 41.4 below. The number can be anything from 10 to 1007, inclusive.

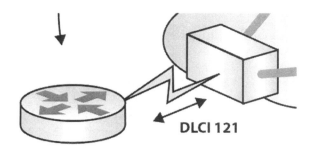

FIG 41.4—DLCI Identifies Your Router to the Telco

Often, when troubleshooting Frame Relay links, the issue lies with either the customer or the provider using the wrong DLCI number on their configuration.

When your DLCI is active, an end-to-end connection forms in the following order:

1. Active DLCI sends inverse ARP request
2. DLCI waits for reply with network address
3. Map created of remote router address
4. DLCI status of Active/Inactive/Deleted

NNI

The Network-to-Network Interface is the connection between frame relay switches.

Configuring Frame Relay

Unfortunately, it can be somewhat tricky to configure Frame Relay, and this is because different network types require different commands. This is to overcome how network addresses resolve over the WAN and how routing protocols operate. The steps to configure Frame Relay are as follows:

1. Set encapsulation
2. Set LMI type (optional)
3. Configure static/dynamic address mapping
4. Address protocol-specific problems

You will not be expected to know how to configure a telco Frame Relay switch in the CCNA exam. You would only want to know how to do this if you are setting up your own Frame Relay connection on a home or remote lab.

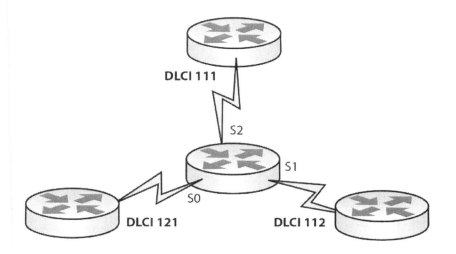

FIG 41.5—Frame Relay Network

For the network topology above, you would configure the following on the Frame Relay switch in the middle. Please only use this information for reference, as you won't need it for the exam:

```
Router#conf t
Router(config)#frame-relay switching
Router(config)#int s0
Router(config-if)#clock rate 64000
Router(config-if)#encapsulation frame-relay
Router(config-if)#frame-relay intf-type dce
Router(config-if)#frame-relay route 121 interface s1 112
Router(config-if)#frame-relay route 121 interface s2 111
Router(config-if)#no shut
Router(config-if)#int s1
Router(config-if)#clock rate 64000
Router(config-if)#encapsulation frame-relay
Router(config-if)#frame-relay intf-type dce
Router(config-if)#frame-relay route 112 interface s0 121
Router(config-if)#frame-relay route 112 interface s2 111
Router(config-if)#int s2
Router(config-if)#clock rate 64000
Router(config-if)#encapsulation frame-relay
Router(config-if)#frame-relay intf-type dce
Router(config-if)#frame-relay route 111 interface s0 121
Router(config-if)#frame-relay route 111 interface s1 112
Router(config-if)#no shut
Router#show frame-relay route
```

Troubleshooting Frame Relay

As stated earlier, often the telco gets the mapping information wrong when they map your DLCI to the wrong port or get the number wrong. You will need to prove that they are at fault before calling them or logging a ticket, using the following commands:

```
show frame-relay pvc
show frame-relay lmi
Show frame-relay map
debug frame-relay pvc
debug frame-relay lmi
```

Frame Relay Errors

Annoyingly, in the exam they sometimes like to ask you about errors on the Frame Relay link, so here is what you need to know:

- Backward-explicit congestion notification (BECN): Frames in the direction opposite of the frame transmission experienced congestion
- Forward-explicit congestion notification (FECN): Congestion was experienced in the direction of the frame transmission

DAY 41 QUESTIONS

1. Frame relay is based upon which older protocol?
2. What are the three types of LMIs available?
3. An LMI is sent every _____ seconds, and every _____ message is a full status update.
4. The DLCI number is only locally significant, so you could have a different one for the other end of your Frame Relay connection. True or false?
5. Explain the difference between BECNs and FECNs.

DAY 41 LAB—FRAME RELAY

Topology

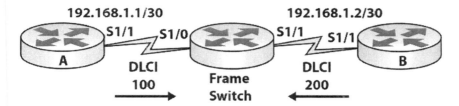

Purpose

Learn to configure basic Frame Relay.

Walkthrough

1. Configure the Frame Relay switch first. You will never have to do this in the CCNA exam. Also, add the IP addresses to the serials on Router A and B.

```
Router#conf t
Enter configuration commands, one per line.  End with CNTL/Z.
Router#hostname FrameSwitch
FrameSwitch(config)#frame-relay switching
FrameSwitch(config)#int s1/0
FrameSwitch(config-if)#encap frame-relay
FrameSwitch(config-if)#frame-relay intf-type dce
FrameSwitch(config-if)#clock rate 64000
FrameSwitch(config-if)#frame-relay route 100 int s1/1 200
FrameSwitch(config-if)#no shut
*May 10 04:28:13.275: %LINK-3-UPDOWN: Interface Serial1/0, changed state
to up
*May 10 04:28:29.275: %LINEPROTO-5-UPDOWN: Line protocol on Interface Se-
rial1/0, changed state to up
FrameSwitch(config-if)#int s1/1
FrameSwitch(config-if)#encap frame
FrameSwitch(config-if)#frame-relay intf-type dce
FrameSwitch(config-if)#clock rate 64000
FrameSwitch(config-if)#frame route 200 int s1/0 100
FrameSwitch(config-if)#no shut
FrameSwitch(config-if)#^Z

FrameSwitch#show frame route
Input Intf     Input Dlci    Output Intf   Output Dlci  Status
Serial1/0      100           Serial1/1     200          inactive
Serial1/1      200           Serial1/0     100          inactive
FrameSwitch#
```

2. Configure Frame Relay on Router A.

```
RouterA(config)#interface s0/1/0
RouterA(config-if)#encap frame-relay
RouterA(config-if)#frame-relay interface-dlci 100
RouterA(config-if)#no shut
```

3. Copy these commands on Router B, but your DLCI number is 200.

4. Ping across the Frame Relay link to test whether it has come up.

```
RouterB#ping 192.168.1.1
Type escape sequence to abort.
Sending 5, 100-byte ICMP Echos to 192.168.1.1, timeout is 2 seconds:
!!!!!
Success rate is 100 percent (5/5), round-trip min/avg/max = 12/17/20 ms
RouterB#
```

5. Check the Frame Relay PVC and mapping.

```
RouterB#show frame-relay pvc

PVC Statistics for interface Serial1/1 (Frame Relay DTE)

              Active      Inactive      Deleted       Static
  Local         1            0             0             0
  Switched      0            0             0             0
  Unused        0            0             0             0

DLCI = 200, DLCI USAGE = LOCAL, PVC STATUS = ACTIVE, INTERFACE = Serial1/1

   input pkts 1            output pkts 1           in bytes 34
   out bytes 34            dropped pkts 0          in pkts dropped 0
   out pkts dropped 0           out bytes dropped 0
   in FECN pkts 0         in BECN pkts 0           out FECN pkts 0
   out BECN pkts 0        in DE pkts 0             out DE pkts 0
   out bcast pkts 1       out bcast bytes 34
   5 minute input rate 0 bits/sec, 0 packets/sec
   5 minute output rate 0 bits/sec, 0 packets/sec
   pvc create time 00:00:26, last time pvc status changed 00:00:26
RouterB#

RouterB#show frame map
Serial1/1 (up): ip 192.168.1.1 dlci 200(0xC8,0x3080), dynamic,
               broadcast, status defined, active
RouterB#
```

6. Debug Frame Relay LMI exchanges. When you see the status 0x2 tag, issue an undebug all command to turn off debugs.

```
Router3#debug frame-relay lmi
Frame Relay LMI debugging is on
Displaying all Frame Relay LMI data
Router3#
*May 10 04:42:48.311: Serial1/1(out): StEnq, myseq 24, yourseen 23, DTE up
*May 10 04:42:48.311: datagramstart = 0xF1A6FCC4, datagramsize = 13
*May 10 04:42:48.311: FR encap = 0xFCF10309
*May 10 04:42:48.311: 00 75 01 01 01 03 02 18 17
*May 10 04:42:48.311:
*May 10 04:42:48.319: Serial1/1(in): Status, myseq 24, pak size 13
*May 10 04:42:48.319: RT IE 1, length 1, type 1
*May 10 04:42:48.319: KA IE 3, length 2, yourseq 24, myseq 24
Router3#
*May 10 04:42:58.311: Serial1/1(out): StEnq, myseq 25, yourseen 24, DTE up
*May 10 04:42:58.311: datagramstart = 0xF1A73AFC, datagramsize = 13
*May 10 04:42:58.311: FR encap = 0xFCF10309
*May 10 04:42:58.311: 00 75 01 01 00 03 02 19 18
*May 10 04:42:58.311:
*May 10 04:42:58.319: Serial1/1(in): Status, myseq 25, pak size 21
*May 10 04:42:58.319: RT IE 1, length 1, type 0
*May 10 04:42:58.319: KA IE 3, length 2, yourseq 25, myseq 25
*May 10 04:42:58.319: PVC IE 0x7, length 0x6, dlci 200, status 0x2, bw 0
Router3#un all
```

Point-to-Point Protocol

DAY 42 TASKS

- Read today's theory notes
- Review yesterday's theory notes
- Complete today's lab
- Read the ICND2 cram guide
- Spend 15 minutes on the subnetting.org website

Point-to-Point Protocol (PPP) is very widely used by many production networks all over the world, and is used to connect many home broadband/DSL users to their ISP.

Today you will learn about the following:

- PPP operations
- Configuring PPP
- PPP authentication
- Troubleshooting PPP

This lesson maps to the following CCNA syllabus requirement:

- Configure and verify a PPP connection between Cisco routers

PPP Operations

PPP is considered an Internet-friendly protocol due to the following factors:

- It supports data compression
- Authentication is built in (PAP and CHAP)
- Network layer address negotiation
- Error detection

You can use PPP over several connection types, including the following:

- DSL
- ISDN
- Synchronous and asynchronous links
- HSSI

PPP can be broken down into the following sublayers:

- NCP—establishes network layer protocols
- LCP—establishes, authenticates, and tests link quality
- HDLC—encapsulates datagrams over the link

Knowing the above may well come in handy during your CCNA exam!

Configuring PPP

PPP is very easy to configure, as shown in Figure 42.1 and the following output below. You can also add authentication, which will be demonstrated in a moment.

FIG 42.1—A PPP Connection

```
R1#conf t
R1(config)#interface s0
R1(config-if)#ip add 192.168.1.1 255.255.255.0
R1(config-if)#clock rate 64000
R1(config-if)#encapsulation ppp
R1(config-if)#no shut
```

```
R2#conf t
R2(config)#interface s0
R2(config-if)#ip add 192.168.1.2 255.255.255.0
R2(config-if)#encapsulation ppp
R2(config-if)#no shut
```

PPP Authentication

PPP has built-in authentication in the form of Password Authentication Protocol (PAP) or Challenge Handshake Authentication Protocol (CHAP). PAP sends the passwords over the link in clear text, which poses a security risk, whereas CHAP sends a hashed value using MD5 security.

Here is a CHAP configuration:

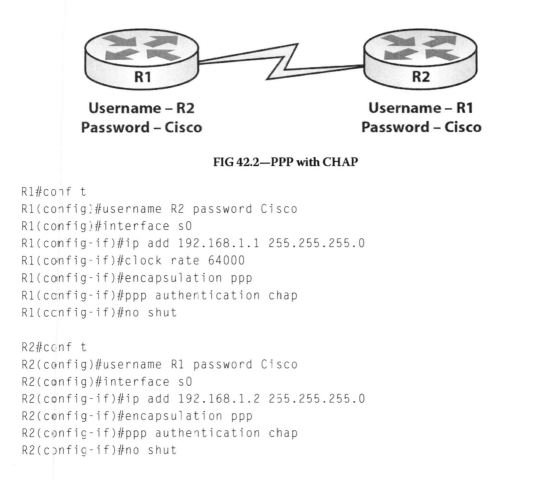

Username – R2
Password – Cisco

Username – R1
Password – Cisco

FIG 42.2—PPP with CHAP

```
R1#conf t
R1(config)#username R2 password Cisco
R1(config)#interface s0
R1(config-if)#ip add 192.168.1.1 255.255.255.0
R1(config-if)#clock rate 64000
R1(config-if)#encapsulation ppp
R1(config-if)#ppp authentication chap
R1(config-if)#no shut

R2#conf t
R2(config)#username R1 password Cisco
R2(config)#interface s0
R2(config-if)#ip add 192.168.1.2 255.255.255.0
R2(config-if)#encapsulation ppp
R2(config-if)#ppp authentication chap
R2(config-if)#no shut
```

To configure PAP, you would replace the [chap] keyword in the configuration above with the [pap] keyword.

Troubleshooting PPP

Issue a `show interface serial 0/0` command, or the relevant interface number, to display the IP address, interface status, and the encapsulation type, as illustrated in the output below:

```
RouterA#show interface serial 0/0

Serial0 is up, line protocol is up
  Hardware is HD64570
  Internet address is 192.168.1.1/30
  MTU 1500 bytes, BW 1544 Kbit, DLY 20000 usec,
    reliability 255/255, txload 1/255, rxload 1/255
  Encapsulation PPP, loopback not set
  Keepalive set (10 sec)
```

If you are using CHAP, then check to ensure the username matches that of the router you are calling, and bear in mind that the hostnames are case sensitive.

DAY 42 QUESTIONS

1.   PPP does not include data compression or error detection. True or false?
2.   Name the PPP sublayers.
3.   Write out the command to configure CHAP with PPP.
4.   Which command will show you the encapsulation type on your Serial interface?

DAY 42 LAB—PPP WITH CHAP

Topology

10.0.0.0/30

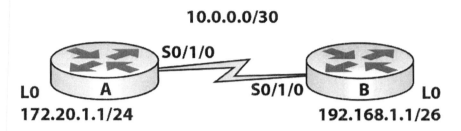

LO   **A**   **S0/1/0**   **B**   LO

172.20.1.1/24   **192.168.1.1/26**

Purpose

Learn how to configure PPP and CHAP.

Walkthrough

1. Configure IP addresses and hostnames as per the topology above.

2. Set the encapsulation on each side to PPP. Here is the command for Router A:

```
RouterA(config)#interface s0/1/0
RouterA(config-if)#encapsulation ppp
```

3. Set CHAP on each router. You will set the hostname of the opposite router and the password 'cisco.'

```
RouterA(config)#username RouterB password cisco
RouterA(config-if)#ppp authentication chap
RouterA(config-if)#exit

RouterB(config)#username RouterA password cisco
RouterB(config-if)#ppp authentication chap
RouterB(config-if)#exit
```

4. Ping across the link to ensure it is up.

```
RouterB#ping 10.0.0.1

Type escape sequence to abort.
Sending 5, 100-byte ICMP Echos to 10.0.0.1, timeout is 2 seconds:
!!!!!
Success rate is 100 percent (5/5), round-trip min/avg/max = 31/31/32 ms

RouterB#
```

5. Break the connection by changing the hostname on Router A to Router C. You will also want to turn on PPP debugs and shut/no shut the interface to open negotiation again. You will have to be quick to type undebug all. If you are at the interface prompt, then type do undebug all.

```
RouterA#conf t
Enter configuration commands, one per line.  End with CNTL/Z.
RouterA(config)#hostname RouterC
RouterC(config)#exi
RouterC#
RouterC#debug ppp neg
PPP protocol negotiation debugging is on
RouterC#debug ppp auth

RouterC#config t
RouterC(config)#int s0/1/0
RouterC(config-if)#shut

Serial0/1/0 LCP: State is Open
Serial0/1/0 PPP: Phase is AUTHENTICATING

Serial0/1/0 IPCP: O CONFREQ [Closed] id 1 len 10 ← Router won't authenticate

RouterC(config-if)#do undebug all

RouterC#sh int s0/1/0
Serial0/1/0 is up, line protocol is down (disabled)
```

DAY 43

Review 1

DAY 43 TASKS
- Take the exam below
- Complete the challenge lab
- Review NAT
- Read the ICND2 cram guide (and the CCENT cram guide, if taking the CCNA exam)
- Spend 15 minutes on the subnetting.org website

DAY 43 EXAM
1. How do you turn off CDP on a router interface?
2. Write down a NAT pool, and then the command to overload the pool. What about the ACL?
3. Write down all the administrative distances and TCP ports you remember.
4. What are the two available PPP authentication types? How do you configure them?
5. What are the OSI data-link sublayers of PPP?

DAY 43 LAB—PPP AND NAT

Topology

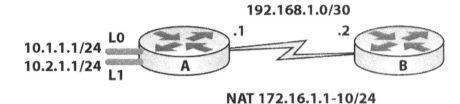

192.168.1.0/30

10.1.1.1/24 L0

10.2.1.1/24 L1

.1   A   .2   B

NAT 172.16.1.1-10/24

Instructions

Connect two routers together with a serial or crossover cable:

1. Add IP addresses to the routers and a Loopback interface on Router A, according to the diagram
2. Turn on debug ppp negotiation and debug ppp authentication
3. Configure PPP authentication CHAP for the WAN connection
4. Designate NAT inside and outside interfaces
5. Add a static route on Router B to send all traffic back to Router A
6. Ping between Router A and Router B to test the Serial line (remember clock rates)
7. Turn off all debugging with undebug all
8. Create a NAT pool of 172.16.1 to 10, inclusive
9. Create two access list lines to permit the Loopback networks (/24) for NAT
10. Turn on NAT debugging
11. Source two extended pings, one each from L0 and L1 from A to B
12. Check the NAT translation table

DAY 44

Review 2

DAY 44 TASKS

- Take the exam below
- Review ACLs
- Complete the challenge lab
- Read the ICND2 cram guide (and the CCENT cram guide if taking the CCNA exam)
- Spend 15 minutes on the subnetting.org website

DAY 44 EXAM

1. Write down the syntax for standard, extended, and named ACLs.
2. Write down the syntax for applying an ACL to an interface and console port.
3. Write down the syntax to create a static NAT.
4. Write down a NAT pool. How do you overload this pool?

DAY 44 LAB—PPP AND ACL

Topology

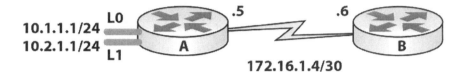

10.1.1.1/24 L0
10.2.1.1/24 L1
A
.5   .6
B
172.16.1.4/30

Instructions

Connect two routers together with a serial or crossover cable:

1. Add IP addresses to the routers and loopback interfaces on Router A, according to the diagram
2. Turn on debug ppp negotiation and debug ppp authentication
3. Configure PPP authentication CHAP for the WAN connection
4. Add a static route on Router B to send all traffic back to Router A
5. Ping between Router A and Router B to test the Serial line (remember clock rates)
6. Turn off all debugging with undebug all
7. Permit telnetting to Router A and add a local login
8. Create an extended ACL on Router A; it should block all Telnet traffic, unless it is destined for 10.2.1.1
9. Test by telnetting from Router B to the Serial and L0 addresses first; it should be blocked
10. Telnet to L1; this should be permitted
11. Issue a show ip access-lists command

DAY 45

Review 3

DAY 45 TASKS

- Take the exam below
- Complete the challenge lab
- Review all switching
- Read the ICND2 cram guide (and the CCENT cram guide if taking the CCNA exam)
- Spend 15 minutes on the subnetting.org website

DAY 45 EXAM

1. Write down the commands to create a VLAN, and put an interface into a VLAN on a switch.
2. Write down the syntax to create a trunk link.
3. Which two ways can you force a switch to become the Root Bridge for STP?
4. Which command configures RSTP on a switch?

DAY 45 LAB—NAMED ACL

Topology

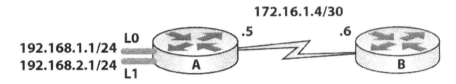

172.16.1.4/30

192.168.1.1/24 L0 .5 .6

192.168.2.1/24 L1 A B

Instructions

Connect two routers together with a serial or crossover cable:

1. Add IP addresses to the routers and a Loopback interface on Router A, according to the diagram
2. Add a static route on Router B to send all traffic back to Router A
3. Ping between Router A and Router B to test the Serial line (remember clock rates)
4. Create a local username and password for the router
5. Permit connections to the Telnet (VTY) lines on the router and login local
6. Permit only SSH traffic into the VTY lines on Router A
7. Create a named ACL on Router A; it should block all ping traffic, unless it is destined for 192.168.1.1; and, of course, apply the ACL to the Serial interface on Router A
8. Test by pinging the Serial and other Loopback addresses
9. Issue a `show ip access-lists` command

Review 4

DAY 46 TASKS

- Take the exam below
- Complete the challenge lab
- Review switching
- Read the ICND2 cram guide (and the CCENT cram guide if taking the CCNA exam)
- Spend 15 minutes on the subnetting.org website

DAY 46 EXAM

1. What is the default STP priority on a switch?
2. Write down the port costs for STP connections for all the bandwidths from 4Mbps to 10Gbps.
3. Explain the purpose of Port Fast, BPDU Guard, BPDU Filter, Uplink Fast, and Backbone Fast.
4. Which command configures the Spanning Tree cost on a port?

DAY 46 LAB—VLANS AND STP

Topology

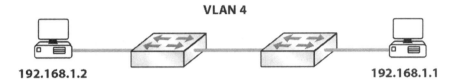

VLAN 4

192.168.1.2   192.168.1.1

Instructions

Connect to the switch using a console connection. Connect a PC to each switch, or connect the switch to the FastEthernet port on a router:

1. Add IP addresses to the PCs or router Ethernet interfaces
2. Create VLAN 4 on the switches
3. Set the ports the PCs connect to as access ports (default, but do it anyway)
4. Put the two switch ports into VLAN 4
5. Configure the link between the switches as trunk ports and no shut them
6. Wait about 30 seconds, at most, and then ping from PC to PC.
7. Check which switch is the Root Bridge with the `show spanning-tree vlan 4` command
8. Set the other switch as the Root Bridge with the `spanning-tree vlan 4 priority 0` command
9. Now check to see whether the switch has become the Root Bridge
10. Remove the `spanning-tree vlan 4 priority 0` command to reset the original switch as the Root Bridge (put `no` in front of the command)
11. Now set the other switch as the Root Bridge with the `spanning-tree vlan 4 root primary` command

DAY 47

Review 5

DAY 47 TASKS

- Take the exam below
- Complete the challenge lab
- Review OSPF
- Read the ICND2 cram guide (and the CCENT cram guide if taking the CCNA exam)
- Spend 15 minutes on the subnetting.org website

DAY 47 EXAM

1. How does EIGRP calculate the best path (which metrics)?
2. How do you prevent EIGRP from sending a summary of a network when you are using VLSM?
3. Can you name the administrative distances for all routing protocols?

DAY 47 LAB—EIGRP AND ACL

Topology

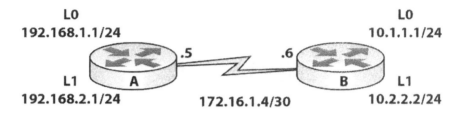

LO
192.168.1.1/24

LO
10.1.1.1/24

.5   .6

L1   A   B   L1
192.168.2.1/24   172.16.1.4/30   10.2.2.2/24

Instructions

Connect two routers together with a serial or crossover cable:

1. Add IP addresses to the routers and a Loopback interface on Router A and Router B, according to the diagram
2. Ping between Router A and Router B to test the Serial line (remember clock rates)
3. Configure EIGRP 30 on both routers
4. Add all routes and add wildcard masks
5. Check the routing table. Were the routes summarised?
6. Now add `no auto-summary` to the EIGRP process
7. Ping all routes
8. Now add a named ACL on Router B; only Telnet to 10.2.2.2 should be permitted
9. Make sure you have enabled Telnet and have added a username/password
10. Test the ACL by attempting to connect to 172.16.1.6 first, and then 10.2.2.2

If EIGRP is no longer working, why would that be and how do you fix the issue?

DAY 48

Review 6

DAY 48 TASKS

- Take the exam below
- Complete the challenge lab
- Review EIGRP
- Read the ICND2 cram guide (and the CCENT cram guide if taking the CCNA exam)
- Spend 15 minutes on the subnetting.org website

DAY 48 EXAM

1. What are the two ways of integrating IPv6 with IPv4?
2. How can IPv6 addresses be shortened?
3. Which command enables IPv6 on a router?
4. You want to block a ping. Which service do you configure on your access list?
5. Which service command encrypts all router passwords to level 7?
6. What is the configuration to configure a banner message of the day (MOTD) on the router?

DAY 48 LAB—OSPF

Topology

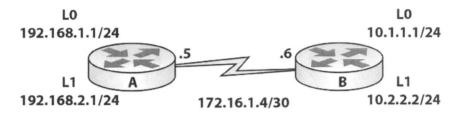

LO
192.168.1.1/24

LO
10.1.1.1/24

.5   .6

L1   A
192.168.2.1/24   172.16.1.4/30

B   L1
10.2.2.2/24

Instructions

Connect two routers together with a serial or crossover cable:

1. Add IP addresses to the routers and a Loopback interface on Router A and Router B, according to the diagram
2. Ping between Router A and Router B to test the Serial line (remember clock rates)
3. Configure OSPF on both routers
4. Ensure you add all correct wildcard masks
5. Double-check the WAN wildcard mask and subnet: it ISN'T 172.16.1.0 0.0.0.3!!
6. Put all networks into an area, but put 192.168.2.0/24 into Area 1 and 10.2.2.0 into Area 2
7. Check the routing table
8. Check the router ID for each router
9. How would you change the router ID for each router?

Review 7

DAY 49 TASKS

- Take the exam below
- Complete the challenge lab
- Review IPv6/OSPF/NAT/EIGRP
- Read the ICND2 cram guide (and the CCENT cram guide if taking the CCNA exam)
- Spend 15 minutes on the subnetting.org website

DAY 49 EXAM

1. What service and port does DNS use?
2. How would you block EIGRP with an access list?
3. Does EIGRP and OSPF offer a way of sending route updates securely?
4. Where do switches get their base MAC address from? How would you find it?
5. Does PPP work with asynchronous links, or just synchronous?
6. How would you join OSPF Area 2 to the OSPF domain if it was connected only to Area 1?

DAY 49 LAB—OSPF AND ACL

Topology

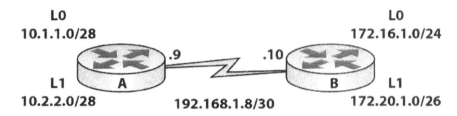

LO
10.1.1.0/28

L1
10.2.2.0/28

.9

A

192.168.1.8/30

.10

B

LO
172.16.1.0/24

L1
172.20.1.0/26

Instructions

Connect two routers together with a serial or crossover cable:

1. Add IP addresses to the routers and a Loopback interface on Router A and Router B, according to the diagram
2. Ping between Router A and Router B to test the Serial line (remember clock rates)
3. Configure OSPF on both routers
4. Ensure you add all correct wildcard masks (which subnet is the WAN link in?)
5. Put all networks into an area, but put 172.20.1.0/26 into Area 1 and 10.2.2.0/28 into Area 20
6. Check the routing table and ping all IP addresses
7. Configure an extended ACL on Router B
8. Block www traffic into Router B destined for the 172.20.1.0/26 network. Permit all other IP traffic
9. You can only test this if you have a web server behind the router OR on live routers by adding the `ip http server` command to the router and telnetting on port 80:
10. `RouterA#telnet 172.20.1.0 80` **[this won't work on Packet Tracer]**

Review 8

DAY 50 TASKS

- Take the exam below
- Complete the challenge lab
- Review the subjects of your choice
- Read the ICND2 cram guide (and the CCENT cram guide if taking the CCNA exam)
- Spend 15 minutes on the subnetting.org website

DAY 50 EXAM

1. Can a router in area 0 running OSPF process ID 2 swap LSAs with a router in area 0 running OSPF process ID 10?
2. What is the port cost for a FastEthernet interface in STP? What about 1Gigabit?
3. What is the difference between `enable secret cisco` and `enable password cisco`?
4. List the five Cisco enhancements to STP and explain what they do.
5. Name the three LMI Frame Relay encapsulation types.
6. What does a DLCI do?
7. Is it true that the DLCI number must be the same across the entire Frame Relay circuit?

DAY 50 LAB—EIGRP WITH PPP AND ACL

Topology

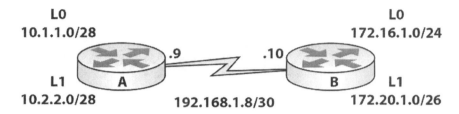

LO
10.1.1.0/28

LO
172.16.1.0/24

.9   .10

L1   A   B   L1
10.2.2.0/28   192.168.1.8/30   172.20.1.0/26

Instructions

Connect two routers together with a serial or crossover cable:

1. Add IP addresses to the routers and a Loopback interface on Router A and Router B, according to the diagram
2. Ping between Router A and Router B to test the Serial lines (remember clock rates)
3. Now set the Serial lines to use PPP but with no authentication required
4. Configure EIGRP on both routers; add wildcard masks and turn off `auto summary`
5. Check the routing table and ping all IP addresses
6. Configure an extended ACL on Router A
7. Block Telnet traffic to the router, unless destined for the 10.2.2.0/28 subnet
8. Configure Telnet access on the VTY lines for Router A, and do a login and password under the VTY line (not username and password)
9. Test the ACL by telnetting to 10.1.1.1 (the IP address for Loopback 0) from Router B
10. Test it works by telnetting to 10.2.2.1

DAY 51

Review 9

DAY 51 TASKS

- Complete the challenge labs
- Review the subject of your choice
- Read the ICND2 cram guide (and the CCENT cram guide if taking the CCNA exam)
- Spend 15 minutes on the subnetting.org website

DAY 51 LAB 1—STP AND VLANS

Topology

VLAN 20

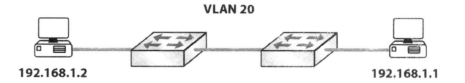

192.168.1.2   192.168.1.1

Instructions

Connect to the switch using a console connection. Connect a PC to each switch, or connect the switch to the FastEthernet port on a router:

1. Add IP addresses to the PCs or router Ethernet interfaces
2. Create VLAN 20 on the switch
3. Set the ports the PCs connect to as access ports (default, but do it anyway)
4. Put the two switch ports into VLAN 20
5. Check which switch is the Root Bridge
6. Force the other switch to become the Root Bridge
7. Hard-set the switch ports to the PCs to 100Mbps and full duplex
8. Wait 30 seconds and test a ping

DAY 51 LAB 2—VLANS

Topology

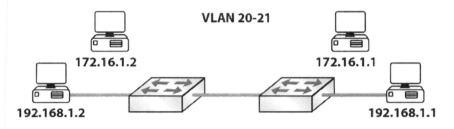

Instructions

Connect to the switch using a console connection. Connect two PCs to each switch, or connect the switch to the FastEthernet port on two routers:

1. Add IP addresses to the PCs or router Ethernet interfaces
2. Create VLAN 20 and 21 on the switch
3. Set the ports the PCs connect to as access ports (default, but do it anyway)
4. Put two switch ports into VLAN 20 and two switch ports into VLAN 21; you can choose which subnets go into which VLANS.
5. Check which switch is the Root Bridge
6. Force the other switch to become the Root Bridge for VLAN 21 only
7. Ping from 172.16.1.1 to 172.16.1.2, and then from 192.168.1.1 to 192.168.1.2; you won't be able to ping between subnets, as there is no router involved

Review 10

DAY 52 TASKS

- Follow the exam tasks below
- Complete the challenge lab
- Review the subject of your choice
- Read the ICND2 cram guide (and the CCENT cram guide if taking the CCNA exam)
- Spend 15 minutes on the subnetting.org website

DAY 52 EXAM

- Spend some extra time on www.subnetting.org.
- Write out the cram guide(s) from memory.

DAY 52 LAB—OSPF AND ROUTER SECURITY

Topology

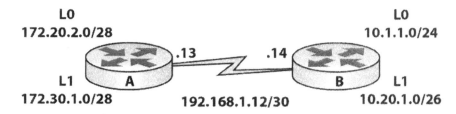

LO
172.20.2.0/28

LO
10.1.1.0/24

.13   .14

L1   A
172.30.1.0/28

B   L1
10.20.1.0/26

192.168.1.12/30

Instructions

Connect two routers together with a serial or crossover cable.

1.   Add IP addresses to the routers and a Loopback interface on Router A and Router B, according to the diagram
2.   Ping between Router A and Router B to test the Serial lines (remember clock rates)
3.   Now set the Serial lines to use PPP with CHAP (also set usernames and passwords)
4.   Configure OSPF on both routers and place one Loopback network in another area
5.   Lock down both routers with enable secret passwords and Telnet passwords
6.   Turn CDP off one router and off the interface of the other router
7.   Add a banner message on one router
8.   Issue a `service password-encryption` command on one router
9.   Check the routing tables

Review 11

DAY 53 TASKS

- Follow the exam task below
- Complete the challenge lab
- Review the subject of your choice
- Read the ICND2 cram guide (and the CCENT cram guide if taking the CCNA exam)
- Spend 15 minutes on the subnetting.org website

DAY 53 EXAM

- Write out the syntax for standard, extended, and named access lists, and how to apply them to interfaces and ports, such as VTY and console.

DAY 53 LAB—EIGRP AND ACL

Topology

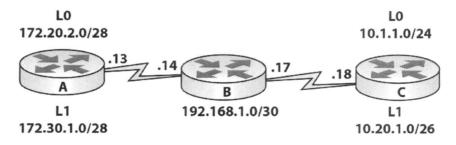

LO
172.20.2.0/28

LO
10.1.1.0/24

.13   .14   .17   .18

A   B   C

L1
172.30.1.0/28

192.168.1.0/30

L1
10.20.1.0/26

Instructions

Connect three routers together with a serial or crossover cable:

1. Add IP addresses to the routers and Loopback interfaces on Routers A, B, and C, according to the diagram
2. Ping between Routers A and B and between Routers B and C to test the Serial lines (remember clock rates)
3. Now set the Serial lines to use PPP with CHAP (also set usernames and passwords)
4. Configure EIGRP 40 on all routers
5. Check the routing tables and make sure you include both of the 192.168.1.x networks
6. Set an access list to Router A. Telnet should be permitted from the Router C Serial address, but not from Router B; permit Telnet on Router A first, of course.

DAY 54

Review 12

DAY 54 TASKS

- Take the exam below
- Complete the challenge lab
- Review the subject of your choice
- Read the ICND2 cram guide (and the CCENT cram guide if taking the CCNA exam)
- Spend 15 minutes on the subnetting.org website

DAY 54 EXAM

1. What is the default priority number for STP on switches?
2. What are the states STP ports transition through (in the correct order)?
3. What are the timers for the port transition states?
4. The STP Bridge ID is made from what?
5. What does IEEE 802.1w refer to?
6. Name the RSTP port roles.

DAY 54 LAB—OSPF AND ACL

Topology

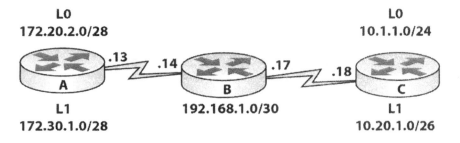

LO
172.20.2.0/28

LO
10.1.1.0/24

.13   .14   .17   .18

A   B   C

L1   192.168.1.0/30   L1
172.30.1.0/28   10.20.1.0/26

Instructions

Connect three routers together with a serial or crossover cable:

1. Add IP addresses to the routers and Loopback interfaces on Routers A, B, and C, according to the diagram
2. Ping between Routers A and B and between Routers B and C to test the Serial lines (remember clock rates)
3. Now set the Serial lines to use PPP with CHAP (also set usernames and passwords)
4. Configure OSPF on all routers; put one Loopback on either end in a non-zero area
5. Check the routing tables and make sure you include both of the 192.168.1.x networks
6. Set a named access list to Router A; DNS traffic should be permitted into Router A only if it comes from Router C. All other IP traffic should be permitted (excluding DNS!)

You won't be able to test this ACL unless you have a DNS service running behind the router, or have live equipment and can telnet on the correct port. Post on the study page if you get stuck.

Review 13

DAY 55 TASKS

- Complete the challenge lab
- Review the subject of your choice
- Write out the ICND2 cram guide (and the CCENT cram guide if taking the CCNA exam) from memory
- Spend 15 minutes on the subnetting.org website

DAY 55 LAB—OSPF AND NAT

Topology

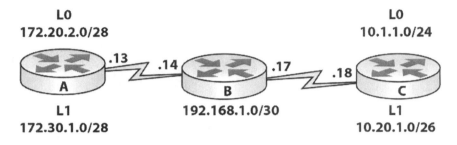

L0
172.20.2.0/28

L0
10.1.1.0/24

.13   .14   .17   .18

A   **B**   **C**

L1
172.30.1.0/28

192.168.1.0/30

L1
10.20.1.0/26

Instructions

Connect three routers together with a serial or crossover cable:

1. Add IP addresses to the routers and Loopback interfaces on Routers A, B, and C, according to the diagram
2. Ping between Routers A and B and between Routers B and C to test the Serial lines (remember clock rates)
3. Now set the Serial lines to use PPP with CHAP (also set usernames and passwords)
4. Configure OSPF on all routers. Put one Loopback on either end in a non-zero area, but do not add 172.30.1.0 to OSPF
5. Check the routing tables and make sure you include both of the 192.168.1.x networks
6. Create a NAT pool of 192.168.2.1 to 10/24, inclusive, on Router A; set an access list to match the 172.30.1.0/28 subnet
7. Set a static route for traffic to go from 192.168.2.0/24 to 192.168.1.13 on Router B
8. Turn on NAT debugging on Router A, and do an extended ping from 172.30.1.1 to Router B

DAY 56

Review 14

DAY 56 TASKS

- Complete the challenge labs
- Review the subject of your choice
- Write out the ICND2 cram guide (and the CCENT cram guide if taking the CCNA exam) from memory
- Spend 15 minutes on the subnetting.org website

DAY 56 LAB

Repeat the following three challenge labs, each in 10 minutes, without looking at the configuration guide:

- OSPF with NAT
- OSPF with ACL
- VLANs and STP

DAY 57

Review 15

DAY 57 TASKS

- Complete the challenge labs
- Review the subject of your choice
- Write out the ICND2 cram guide (and the CCENT cram guide if taking the CCNA exam) from memory
- Spend 15 minutes on the subnetting.org website

DAY 57 LABS

Repeat the previous three challenge labs:

- PPP and NAT
- VLANs
- VLANs and STP

DAY 58

Review 16

DAY 58 TASKS

Check the entire list of exam topics for your exam (ICND2 or CCNA). Mark them out of 10 for how well you understand them. Anything less than an 8, review today.

Review 17

DAY 59 TASKS

Review any areas of your choice.

Review 18

DAY 60 TASKS

Exam day for you (or tomorrow).

Nothing else I can teach you or recommend. You know your weak areas, so good luck.

When you pass the exam, please drop me a line at help@howtonetwork.net, along with a photo of you holding your CCNA certificate.

APPENDIX A

CCENT Cram Guide

The complete contents of this guide MUST be committed to memory before attempting the exam. This cram guide is NOT a brain dump, so there is no way of knowing what exactly you are going to be asked about in the exam. We have done our best to condense down everything you need to know in the CCNA syllabus.

OSI MODEL

Layer	Encapsulation	Function	Services	Device
7. Application	Data	Establishes availability of resources	FTP, SMTP, Telnet, POP3	
6. Presentation	Data	Compression, encryption, and decryption	JPEG, GIF, MPEG, ASCII	
5. Session	Data	Establishes, maintains, and terminates sessions	NFS, SQL, RPC	
4. Transport	Segment	Establishes end-to-end connection; uses virtual circuits, buffering, windowing, and flow control	TCP, UDP, SPX	
3. Network	Packet	Determines best path for packets to take	IP, IPX	Router
2. Data Link (LLC, MAC)	Frame	Transports data across a physical connection; error detection	Frame Relay, PPP, HDLC	Switch/Bridge
1. Physical	Bits	Puts data onto the wire		Hub/Repeater/ Concentrator/ MAU

Layers: <u>A</u>ll <u>P</u>eople <u>S</u>eem <u>T</u>o <u>N</u>eed <u>D</u>ata <u>P</u>rocessing. **Data formats:** <u>D</u>on't <u>S</u>ome <u>P</u>eople <u>F</u>ry <u>B</u>acon.

7. Application Layer

Provides services to lower layers. Enables program-to-program communication and determines whether sufficient resources exist for communication. Examples are e-mail gateways (SMTP), TFTP, FTP, and SNMP.

6. Presentation Layer

Presents information to the Application Layer. Compression, data conversion, encryption, and standard formatting occur here. Contains data formats JPEG, MPEG, MIDI, and TIFF.

5. Session Layer

Establishes and maintains communication 'sessions' between applications (dialogue control). Sessions can be simplex (one direction only), half duplex (one direction at a time), or full duplex (both ways simultaneously). Session Layer keeps different applications data separate from other applications. Protocols include NFS, SQL, X Window, RPC, ASP, and NetBios Names.

4. Transport Layer

Responsible for end-to-end integrity of data transmissions and establishes a logical connection between sending and receiving hosts via 'virtual circuits.' Windowing works at this level to control how much information is transferred before acknowledgement is required. Data is segmented and reassembled at this layer. Port numbers are used to keep track of different conversations crossing the network at the same time. Supports TCP, UDP, SPX, and NBP. Segmentation works here (Segments) and error correction (not detection).

3. Network Layer

Routes data from one node to another and determines the best path to take. Routers operate at this level. Network addresses are used here, which are used for routing (Packets). Routing tables, subnetting, and control of network congestion occur here. Routing protocols, regardless of which protocol they run over, reside here: IP, IPX, ARP, IGRP, and Appletalk.

2. Data Link Layer

Sometimes referred to as the LAN layer. Responsible for the physical transmission of data from one node to another. Error detection occurs here. Packets are translated into frames here and hardware address is added. Bridges and switches operate at this layer.

Logical Link Control sublayer (LLC) 802.2: Manages communications between devices over a single link on a network. Uses Service Access Points (SAPs) to help lower layers talk to the Network Layer.

Media Access Control sublayer (MAC) 802.3: Builds frames from the 1s and 0s that the Physical Layer (address = 6 byte/48 bit) picks up from the wire as a digital signal and runs a Cyclic Redundancy Check (CRC) to assure no bits were lost or corrupted.

1. Physical Layer

Puts data onto the wire and takes it off. Physical Layer specifications, such as the connectors, voltage, physical data rates, and DTE/DCE interfaces. Some common implementations include Ethernet/IEEE 802.3, FastEthernet, and Token Ring/IEEE 802.5.

CISCO HIERARCHICAL MODEL

Core Layer—Purpose is to switch traffic as quickly as possible. Fast transport to enterprise services (Internet, etc.). No packet manipulation, VLANs, access-lists. High-speed access required, such as FDDI and ATM.

Distribution Layer—Time-sensitive manipulation, such as routing, filtering, and WAN access. Broadcast/multicast, media translations, security.

Access Layer—Switches and routers; segmentation occurs here, as well as workgroup access. Static (not dynamic) routing.

TCP/IP

Port Numbers

These are used to connect to various services and applications, and piggyback onto IP addresses. Common port numbers are as follows:

20—File Transfer Protocol—Data (TCP)

21—File Transfer Protocol—Control (TCP) (Listens on this port)

22—SSH (TCP)

23—Telnet (TCP)

25—Simple Mail Transfer Protocol (TCP)

53—Domain Name Service (TCP/UDP)

69—Trivial File Transfer Protocol (UDP)

80—HTTP/WWW (TCP)

110—Post Office Protocol 3 (TCP)

119—Network News Transfer Protocol (TCP)

123—Network Time Protocol (UDP)

161/162—Simple Network Management Protocol (UDP)

443—HTTP over Secure Sockets Layer (HTTPS) (TCP)

TCP—(Protocol 6) Reliable, sequenced, connection-oriented delivery, 20-byte header.

UDP—(Protocol 17) Connectionless, unsequenced, best-effort delivery, 8-byte header. Sends data but does not check to see whether it is received.

Telnet—Used to connect to a remote device (TCP). A password and username is required to connect. Telnet tests all seven layers of the OSI model.

FTP—Connection-orientated (TCP) protocol used to transfer large files.

TFTP—Connectionless (UDP) protocol used for file transfer.

SNMP—Allows remote management of network devices.

ICMP—Supports packets containing error, control, and informational messages. Ping uses ICMP to test network connectivity.

ARP—Used to map an IP address to a physical (MAC) address. A host wishing to obtain a physical address broadcasts an ARP request onto the TCP/IP network. The host replies with its physical address.

DNS—Resolves hostnames to IP addresses (not the other way around). To configure the router to use a host on the network, use the command ROUTER(config)#ip name-server 4.2.2.2, and to configure DNS, use the command ip name-server (usually already turned on for the router configuration by default). If you want hosts on the network to use the router as a proxy DNS server, put the command Router(config)#ip dns server onto the router.

DHCP—Involves a central server, or devices, which relays TCP information to hosts on a network. You can configure a router to be a DHCP server with the configuration below. You must have hosts on the same LAN as the router interface:

```
Router(config)#ip dhcp pool E00_DHCP_Pool
Router(dhcp-config)#network 10.10.10.0 255.255.255.0
Router(dhcp-config)#dns-server 24.196.64.39 24.196.64.40
Router(dhcp-config)#domain-name mydomain.com
Router(dhcp-config)#default-router 10.10.10.254
Router(dhcp-config)#lease 1
```

Cisco IOS

Six Modes

1. User EXEC: Router>
2. Privileged EXEC: Router#
3. Global Configuration: Router(config)#
4. ROM Monitor: > or rommon>
5. Setup: series of questions
6. RXBoot: Router<boot>

Editing Commands

Ctrl+W—Erases a word

Ctrl+U—Erases a line

Ctrl+A—Moves cursor to beginning of line

Ctrl+E—Moves cursor to end of line

Ctrl+F (or right arrow)—Moves forward one character

Ctrl+B (or left arrow)—Moves back one character

Ctrl+P (or up arrow)—Recalls previous commands from buffer

Ctrl+N (or down arrow)—Returns to more recent commands in buffer

Esc+B—Moves back one word

Esc+F—Moves forward one word

Tab—Completes a command you have started

```
Router# copy ru ← press Tab key after the 'u'
Router# copy running-configuration
```

'?' gives you the command options:

```
Router#copy ?
flash:            Copy from flash: file system
ftp:              Copy from ftp: file system
nvram:            Copy from nvram: file system
running-config    Copy from current system configuration
startup-config    Copy from startup configuration
system:           Copy from system: file system
tftp:             Copy from tftp: file system
[truncated]
```

...or the commands beginning with the letters you have typed:

```
Router#a?
access-enable   access-profile   access-template
```

Router Elements

DRAM—Working area for router. Contains routing tables, ARP cache, packet buffers, IOS, and running configuration. Some routers run the IOS from DRAM.

show version—Shows information about IOS in RAM and displays how much physical memory is installed. Also shows the configuration register setting.

show process—Shows information about programs running in DRAM.

show running-configuration—Shows active configuration in DRAM.

show memory/stacks/buffers—Command used to view tables and buffers.

NVRAM—Stores router's startup configuration. Does not lose data when powered off due to a battery power source:

```
show startup-configuration
erase startup-configuration
copy running-configuration startup-configuration (copy run start)
```

Configuration register 0x2142 skips startup configuration file in NVRAM (for password recovery).

Configuration register 0x2102 loads startup configuration files from NVRAM.

Flash—EEPROM or PCMCIA card holds the compressed operating system image (IOS). This is where software upgrades are stored:

```
show flash
dir flash:
```

ROM—Contains power on diagnostics, a bootstrap program, and a mini-IOS (rommon). You can specify which file the routers boots from if you have more than one in flash memory:

```
Router(config)#boot system flash {IOS filename}
```

Or you can specify that it boots from a TFTP server if, for example, the image is too large to fit in flash:

```
Router(config)#boot system tftp {IOS filename}{tftp address}
```

You can also backup the flash image for emergency use:

```
Router(config)#copy flash tftp
```

Cabling

	Hub	Switch	Router	Workstation
Hub	Crossover	Crossover	Straight	Straight
Switch	Crossover	Crossover	Straight	Straight
Router	Straight	Straight	Crossover	Crossover
Workstation	Straight	Straight	Crossover	Crossover

Pinouts

Crossover	
1	3
2	6
3	1
4	4
5	5
6	2
7	7
8	8

Straight	
1	1
2	2
3	3
4	4
5	5
6	6
7	7
8	8

Console	
1	8
2	7
3	6
4	5
5	4
6	3
7	2
8	1

Two types of crosstalk can occur on twisted-pair cables:
Near-end Crosstalk (NEXT) and Far-end Crosstalk (FEXT)

Router Management

Console port—A PC connected to the console port via a rollover cable. Used for initial configuration or disaster recovery.

Virtual terminals—Normally accessed by telnetting to the router. Five lines available, numbered 0 to 4 (more lines possible, depending on the Router/Switch model).

Auxiliary port—Normally a modem connected to this port.

TFTP server—The router can get its configurations or IOS from a server (a PC, for example) running TFTP software and holding the necessary files.

NMS—Network management station. Uses SNMP to manage the router normally via a web-style interface.

CDP

Cisco Discovery Protocol (proprietary) runs only on Cisco devices; it allows you to gather information about other routers and switches. It is enabled by default.

```
Router#show cdp neighbors (NOTE: Cisco uses US spelling conventions)
```

This command displays the neighbouring router or switch's hostname, hardware platform, port identifier, and capabilities list:

```
Router#show cdp neighbors detail
```

This command displays more detail than the previous one. You can view the IP address, the IOS release, and the duplex setting.

To turn off CDP on an interface, use the following command:

```
Router(config-if)#no cdp enable
```

To turn off CDP on your entire router or switch, use the following command:

```
Router(config)#no cdp run
```

LAN Switching

A LAN switch has three primary functions:

1. Address learning—Maintains a table (CAM—Content Addressable Memory) of addresses and on which port they can be reached.
2. Forward/filter decision—Forwards frames only out of the relevant port.
3. Loop avoidance—STP.

Broadcast frames are forwarded out of all ports. Because all Ethernet hosts can transmit at the same time, this can lead to collisions, thus slowing down the network considerably.

Transmitting Frames through a Switch

Store-and-Forward—The switch copies the entire frame into its buffer and computes the CRC. The frame is discarded if there is an error. High latency.

Cut-through—Reads only the destination address (first 6 bytes after preamble), looks up address, and forwards frame. Lower latency.

Fragment-free—The switch reads the first 64 bytes before forwarding the frame. Collisions normally occur within the first 64 bytes.

Bridging/Switching

Bridges are primarily software-based and have one Spanning Tree instance per bridge. Normally 16 ports per bridge. LAN switches are primarily hardware-based. There are many Spanning Tree instances per switch and up to 100 ports.

Common Switching Commands

This is not a sample configuration but, rather, a demonstration of commands you need to know:

```
Switch(config)#ip default-gateway 192.168.1.1  ← switch default gateway
Switch#show mac-address-table dynamic  ← shows mac table (dynamic)
Switch(config)#interface fast 0/1
Switch(config-if)#switchport port-security  ← enable port security
Switch(config-if)#switchport port-security violation shutdown
Switch(config-if)#switchport port-security maximum 4  ← only 4 MACs
Switch(config-if)#switchport port-security mac-address xxx  ← hard codes
Switch #show port-security  ← you can add 'interface fast 0/1'
```

Please visit the free IOS commands page at www.howtonetwork.net/public/department98.cfm for further explanation of the commands and more context.

The switch must be in transparent mode to add higher numbered VLANs (1006 to 4096).

IP ADDRESSING AND SUBNETTING

Class	Format/Default Mask	Leading Bit Pattern	Network Address Range	Max Networks	Max Hosts/ Nodes
A	N.H.H.H 255.0.0.0	0	0 to 126	126	16,777,214
B	N.N.H.H 255.255.0.0	10	128 to 191	16,384	65,534
C	N.N.N.H 255.255.255.0	110	192 to 223	2,097,152	254
D	N/A	1110	224 to 239	Multicast	N/A
E	N/A	11110	240 to 255	Experimental	N/A

Network number 127 is reserved for Loopback testing (127.0.0.1 local Loopback)

Subnetting

Max # of Subnets = 2(to the power of masked bits)

Max # of Hosts (per subnet) = 2(to the power of unmasked bits)—2

Easy Subnetting

What network is host 172.16.5.68 255.255.255.240 in?

256 - 240 = 16, so you have the subnets going up in increments of 16, starting with zero (if subnet zero is permitted in the exam). Each subnet will need to have a subnet and a broadcast number, so this leaves 14 hosts per subnet. The subnets start at 0,16,32,48, 64, 80...224, 240 (the 0 and 240 are valid only if subnet zero is allowed).

Subnet	First Host	Last Host	Broadcast
172.16.5.0	1	14	15
172.16.5.16	17	30	31
172.16.5.32	33	62	63
172.16.5.64*	65	78	79

Looking at the 172.16.5.<u>68</u> host address, you are clearly looking to find the host on the fourth octet because this is where the non-zero mask is (255.255.255.<u>240</u>). Just keep adding 16 until you find the range that the host number 68 is in. In this case, 172.16.5.<u>64,</u> as indicated by the asterisk (*).

The Super Subnetting Chart™ will also provide the answers for you very quickly. To get to the 240 mask, tick down four subnet numbers on the left column and then tick four along the top row to get the subnet increment (i.e., 16).

	Bits	128	64	32	16	8	4	2	1
Subnets		✔	✔	✔	✔				
128	✔								
192	✔								
224	✔								
240	✔								
248									
252									
254									
255									
Powers of Two	Subnets	Hosts -2							
2									
4									
8									
16									
32									
64									
128									
256									

Super Subnetting Chart™ © Paul Browning 2005-2012

If you see a slash address, such as 192.168.1.2/26, then you simply have to convert that 26 into a subnet mask. Using the Super Subnetting Chart™ is the easiest way, or you can simply count up in octets, remembering that 255 is 8 in binary bits. To reach 26 binary bits, you know that 255.255.255.0 is 8 + 8 + 8 binary bits, giving you 24. To get to 26, you need to add another 2 binary bits, which is a tick in the 128 and 192 (128 + 64 = 192) boxes in the left column.

To work out the subnet increment, simply tick two along the top row (or take 192 away from 256).

	Bits	128	64	32	16	8	4	2	1
Subnets		✔	✔						
128	✔								
192	✔								
224									
240									
248									
252									
254									
255									
Powers of Two	Subnets	Hosts -2							
2									
4									
8									
16									
32									
64									
128									

Super Subnetting Chart™ © Paul Browning 2005-2012

128 + 64 gives you 192, so the /26 mask gives you 255.255.255.192, which is 26 binary bits. You can tick two across the top row to reveal the subnet increments (i.e., multiples of 64).

Working out how many subnets is also a simple process. If you have the IP address 192.168.1.0 with the default /24 mask ,and the client wants five subnets created out of that, you simply tick down the Powers of Two numbers until you get to the required amount of subnets.

In the exam, you *should* be permitted to use subnet zero, so you will not have to take two away from the subnets, but you still need to take two away from the hosts.

	Bits	128	64	32	16	8	4	2	1
Subnets									
128	✔								
192	✔								
224	✔								
240									
248									
252									
254									
255									
Powers of Two	Subnets	Hosts -2							
2	✔	✔							
4	✔	✔							
8	✔	✔							
16		✔							
32		✔							
64									
128									

Super Subnetting Chart™ © Paul Browning 2005-2012

Ticking down three rows gives you 8. I know that the requirement is five subnets, but this is the closest you can get for the client. Taking 3 bits from the hosts leaves 5 remaining host bits (8 - 3 = 5). Tick down five boxes in the Hosts-2 column and take two away (for the subnet and broadcast) to give you 30 hosts per subnet. Voila!

If you want to know the subnet mask, tick down three (for the subnet bits stolen) in the left column in the top of the chart, giving you 224, or in full, 255.255.255.224, which is 8 + 8 + 8 + 3, or /27 masked bits.

To view several free subnetting videos on YouTube, visit the link below:

www.youtube.com/user/paulwbrowning

IP Routing

Routers must have some means of learning networks to which they are not directly connected.

Static routing:

```
Router(config)#ip route {destination network}{mask}{next hop address}
e.g. ip route 172.16.5.2 255.255.255.0 172.16.12.8
```

Dynamic addressing uses a routing protocol:

for RIP v2

```
Router(config)#router rip
Router(config-router)#version 2
Router(config-router)#network 172.16.0.0
Router(config-router)#no auto-summary ← optional
```

Facts

RIP v2

- Uses UDP port 520
- Classless
- Max hop count is 15
- Multicasts route updates to 224.0.0.9
- Supports authentication
- Update timer, 30 seconds
- Invalid, 90 seconds
- Hold down, 180 seconds
- Flush, 270 seconds

Distance Vector

Distance Vector protocols understand the direction and distance to any given network connections. Algorithms calculate the cost to reach the connection and pass this information to every neighbour router. Examples are RIP and IGRP. Problems with Distance Vector protocols include routing loops and counting to infinity. To overcome these problems, the following can be implemented:

- Define a maximum number of hops—15 for RIP and 255 for IGRP.
- Split horizon—If the router learns a route on an interface, do not advertise it out of the same interface.
- Route poisoning—Information passed out of an interface is marked as unreachable by setting the hop count to 16 (for RIP).

- Hold Down timers—Ignores new routing updates until a determined time has passed.
- Triggered updates—Instead of routing updates being sent at the default intervals, a triggered update is sent every time to indicate a change in the routing table.

Link State

These have a picture of the entire network from Link State Advertisements (LSAs) and Link State Packets (LSPs). Once these have all been passed, only changes to the network are sent out, reducing network traffic.

Link State protocols do require a lot of CPU time and bandwidth when LSAs are flooded out. Examples are OSPF and ISIS.

Routers use administrative distances to determine how believable the route learned is depending upon the protocol it learns from the router.

Source	Default Distance
Directly Connected Interface	0
Static Hop to Next Router	1
EIGRP Summary	5
External BGP	20
EIGRP (Internal)	90
OSPF	110
IS-IS	115
RIP	120
Exterior Gateway Protocol (EGP)	140
External EIGRP	170
Internal BGP	200
Unknown	255

An administrative distance of 0 is most preferred. For example, a router running RIP and OSPF will prefer the OSPF routes most and install these in the routing table.

Routing protocols maintain a table of hosts and which interface they can be reached by. Examples include RIP and OSPF.

BGP is an exterior gateway protocol. It is used to connect autonomous systems together.

Routed protocols are used to transport traffic from source to destination. Examples: IP, IPX, and Appletalk.

When a packet traverses the network from device to device (hop to hop), the IP address remains constant, but the hardware (MAC) address changes.

NAT

Network Address Translation will convert an address from the inside of your network to another address on the outside of your network, and vice versa. It is most commonly used to convert a non-routable address to a routable address.

For all configurations, you must specify which interfaces are internal for NAT and which are external:

```
Router(config-if)#ip nat inside/outside
```

Static NAT—Maps one address to one address, such as 192.168.1.1 to 200.1.1.1:

```
Router(config)#ip nat inside source static 192.168.1.1 200.1.1.1
```

Dynamic NAT—Maps a number of internal addresses to a pool of external addresses. The configuration below creates a pool of 10 addresses with a mask (prefix length) of 255.255.255.0 and the name 'ad_team.' The hosts that will go through NAT are on the 192.168.1.0 network. The access list (source list) tells the router which addresses to translate:

```
Router(config)#ip nat pool ad_team 10.0.0.1 10.0.0.10 prefix-length 24
Router(config)#ip nat inside source list 1 pool ad_team out
Router(config)#access-list 1 permit 192.168.1.0 0.0.0.255
```

Overload NAT (or PAT)—Maps private internal addresses to one or more external addresses using port numbers. The configuration below creates a pool of 10 addresses (more are possible), and the command `overload` tells the router to use port address translation (PAT):

```
Router(config)#ip nat pool ad_team 10.0.0.1 10.0.0.10 prefix-length 24
Router(config)#ip nat inside source list 1 pool ad_team out overload
Router(config)#access-list 1 permit 192.168.1.0 0.0.0.255
```

Wireless Networking

Wireless Basics

Wireless clients connect to access points. The two wireless modes are ad-hoc and infrastructure. Ad hoc is similar to peer-to-peer networking, where nodes connect directly to each other. They must have the same SSID and channel for this to work. In infrastructure mode, the clients connect to the access point via basic service set (BSS—one access point and multiple clients) or extended service set (ESS—two or more BSSs).

Wireless Security

The two methods for wireless authentication are open system and shared key. In the open-system method, the host sends an association request to the wireless access point and it will be sent a success or failure message. With the shared-key method, a key or pass phrase is configured on both the host and the access point. There are three types of shared-key authentication—WEP, WPA, and WPA2.

WEP is an encryption algorithm built in the 802.11 standard. It uses RC4 40-bit or 104-bit keys and a 24-bit initialisation vector.

WPA uses dynamic key management, adds a stronger encryption cipher, and is built on the EAP/802.1X mechanism. It uses Temporal Key Integrity Protocol (TKIP), and the Initialization Vector is increased to 48-bit (more than 500 trillion key combinations). It is used with RADIUS in the enterprise.

WPA2 is the next generation in wireless security. It uses even stronger encryption than WPA and this is achieved by using the Advanced Encryption Standard (AES). In addition, WPA2 creates a new key for every new association. This is a benefit over WPA in that the client's keys are unique and specific to that client.

Switch and Router Security

Passwords (the `service password-encryption` command encrypts all passwords):

Enable—Used to get from User Exec mode to Privileged Exec mode. Not encrypted.

```
Router(config)#enable password {password}
```

Enable secret—Encrypts password (only use enable or enable secret, not both):

```
Router(config)#enable secret {password}
```

VTY—Needed if Telnet access is required:

```
Router(config)#line vty 0 4
Router(config-line)#password cisco
Router(config-line)#login
```

If you want to permit SSH into the router or switch Telnet lines, then you need to add the command `transport input ssh` to the VTY lines.

Auxiliary—Allows modem access to the auxiliary port:

```
Router(config)#line aux 0
Router(config-line)#password cisco
Router(config-line)#login
```

Console—Used to allow console access:

```
Router(config)#line console 0
Router(config-line)#password cisco
Router(config-line)#login
```

Protect the Ports
```
Switch1(config)#int fast 0/1
Switch1(config-if)#switchport port-security
Switch1(config-if)#switchport port-security ?
  mac-address  Secure mac address
  maximum      Max secure addresses
  violation    Security violation mode
  <cr>
```

Violation action
```
Switch1(config-if)#switchport port-security violation ?
  protect   Security violation protect mode
  restrict  Security violation restrict mode
  shutdown  Security violation shutdown mode
```

VTP Password:

```
Switch1(config)#vtp password cisco
```

Restrict VLANs passing on ports:

```
Switch1(config-if)#switchport trunk allowed vlan 7-12
```

Protecting the Network

Firewalls divide your network into three zones—trusted, semi-trusted, and un-trusted.

A VPN allows information to be sent securely over an insecure medium (e.g., the Internet). A VPN can be site-to-site (e.g., WAN) or access (e.g., home worker).

SUPER SUBNETTING CHART™

	Bits	128	64	32	16	8	4	2	1
Subnets									
128									
192									
224									
240									
248									
252									
254									
255									
Powers of Two	Subnets	Hosts -2							
2									
4									
8									
16									
32									
64									
128									
256									
512									
1024									
2048									
4096									
8192									
16384									

Super Subnetting Chart™ © Paul Browning 2005-2012

APPENDIX B

VLSM

VLSM is the process whereby you take a major network address and then break it down into different subnets, with different subnet masks at various points. In the exam, you may well be faced with a scenario where you are required to design an IP addressing scheme to fit certain requirements. It is best to illustrate with the following example, illustrated in Figure B.1 below:

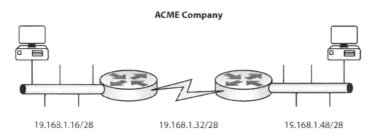

ACME Company

19.163.1.16/28   19.168.1.32/28   19.168.1.48/28

FIG B.1—ACME Company with No VLSM

You may have spotted a few problems with the addressing scheme above. The most important issue is the breach of the conservation of IP addresses. If you are using RFC 1918 addresses (non-routable, such as 10.x.x.x), then perhaps you may not be worried about address wastage, but this is very bad practise, and for Cisco exams, you will be expected to conserve IP addresses.

With a /28 mask, or 255.255.255.240, you have 14 hosts per subnet. This may be fine for your LAN on either end but for your WAN connection, you only need two IP addresses, meaning you are wasting 12 addresses! You could change the masks to /30, or 255.255.255.252, but then for your LANs, you will obviously need more than two hosts.

The first workaround is to buy a separate network address for each network (two LANs and one WAN), but this would prove expensive and unnecessary. The other alternative is to break down your subnet further using VLSM, which is actually what it was designed to do!

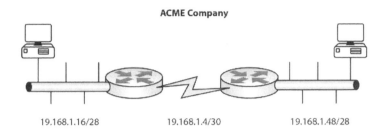

FIG B.2—ACME Company with VLSM

In Figure B.2 above, you can see that the WAN link now has a /30 mask, which gives you two usable hosts. In addition, you have a tighter addressing allocation. Should ACME expand (as companies do), you can easily allocate further WAN links and LANs.

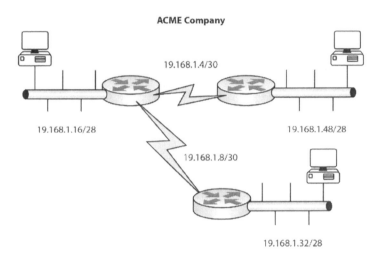

FIG B.3—ACME with a New Office

In Figure B.3 above, you can see that ACME has now grown and has added a remote office. Because you have taken the time to plan and allocate a carefully thought out VLSM scheme, you can simply allocate the next block of IP addresses.

But won't the IP addresses clash? This is a very common question and it's very valid. Let's say you have address 19.16.1.1/28 for one of your LANs; you will not, therefore, be able to use the IP address 19.16.1.1 with any other subnet mask. The IP address can be used only once, no matter which subnet mask is attached to it.

It is a bit of a head scratcher for people who are new to networking or subnetting, but it does work. Feel free to think on it some more, or just accept that with VLSM (RFC 950), it is not possible to reuse IP addresses.

VLSM IN THE EXAM

You may be asked to address a network using VLSM and allocate the correct masks to the WAN and LAN links. The following, as an example, is a network you have been asked to design an addressing scheme for:

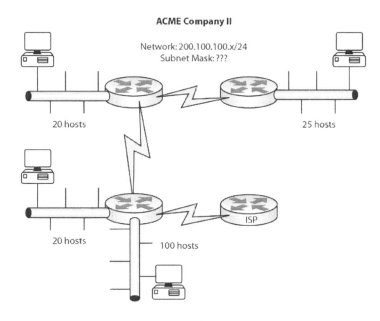

FIG B.4—ACME II Company

In Figure B.4, ACME II company has been allocated the network 200.100.100.x, with a default mask of 255.255.255.0. If you keep the standard mask, you are left with one network with 254 usable hosts. If you want to check this for yourself, please use the Subnetting Secrets Chart©. Visit the book updates page to download.

If you use the bottom part of the Subnetting Secrets Chart©, you can tick down eight places in the left column and see that you have one subnet with 256 - 2 hosts, giving you 254. I don't want to dwell on that part of the calculations because that is covered very well earlier in this book.

Your challenge is this then. You have three Serial connections and each requires only two usable host addresses. You have four LANs that need anything from 20 to 100 hosts. If you just design a mask to give you anything from 20 to 100 hosts, you are going to be wasting a lot of addresses. To get 100 hosts (using the Subnetting Secrets Chart©), tick down seven places in the Hosts-2 column, giving you a mask of 255.255.255.128 (because you only have 1 bit left to tick down for the subnets portion). This gives you 126 hosts (128 - 2). You would then have two networks, one starting 200.100.100.0 and one starting 200.100.100.128. Not great, to be honest. You need seven subnets (three WAN and four LAN) and some only require 20 hosts, so why waste 108 addresses? What you need to do is refer to the Subnetting Secrets Chart©.

If you use the bottom portion and tick down until you find a number close enough to give you the 100 hosts, the only number you can use is 128, which is seven ticks down. You are stealing 7 bits from the host portion, leaving you 1 bit for subnetting.

Powers of 2	Subnets	Hosts -2
2	✔	✔
4		✔
8		✔
16		✔
32		✔
64		✔
128		✔
256		
512		

If you use the upper portion of the Subnetting Secrets Chart©, then you will tick down one place to reveal the subnet mask of 128.

Subnets	
128	✔
192	
224	
240	
248	
252	
254	
255	

When we use the 128 subnet with ACME II company's IP address, you get subnet 200.100.100.0 and subnet 200.100.100.128, both with a mask of /25, or 255.255.255.128. For your network needing 100 hosts, you can use the 200.100.100.128 subnet. For the first host, you will use 200.100.100.129 and so on, up to 200.100.100.229. So now you have the following:

Large LAN Hosts

200.100.100.128/25—LAN (hosts 129 to 254)

200.100.100.0/25—Available for use or for VLSM

You need to allocate hosts to three remaining LAN networks and three WANs. The other three LANs all need anything from 20 to 30 hosts. If you tick down five in the Hosts-2 column, you will get to 32, and taking 2 away gives you 30 hosts. If you steal 5 bits from the host portion, you are left with 3 bits for the subnet (because there are 8 bits in every octet).

Powers of 2	Subnets	Hosts -2
2	✔	✔
4	✔	✔
8	✔	✔
16		✔
32		✔
64		
128		
256		
512		

Tick down three places on the lower Subnet section to reveal a subnet mask of 224. This mask will give you eight subnets (you only need three for the LANs), and each subnet will have up to 30 available host addresses. Can you see how this will fit ACME II's requirements?

Subnets	
128	✔
192	✔
224	✔
240	
248	
252	
254	
255	

If you tick across three places on the top row, you will see that your subnets go up in increments of 32. Your subnets will be 0, 32, 64, and 96, and you can't use 128 because this is used for the large LAN.

Bits	128	64	32	16	8	4	2	1
	√	√	√					

So now you have the following:

LAN Hosts

200.100.100.0/27—(Let's reserve this for the WAN links)

200.100.100.32/27—LAN 1 (hosts 33 to 62)

200.100.100.64/27—LAN 2 (hosts 65 to 94)

200.100.100.96/27—LAN 3 (hosts 96 to 126)

Next, you need IP addresses for three WAN connections. WAN IP addressing is fairly easy because you only ever need two IP addresses if it is a point-to-point link. On the Hosts-2 column, tick down two places to get 4 and take 2 away to get 2 hosts. This leaves 6 bits for the subnet.

Powers of 2	Subnets	Hosts -2
2	√	√
4	√	√
8	√	
16	√	
32	√	
64	√	
128		
256		
512		

Tick down six places on the lower Subnets column to get 252 as your subnet mask.

Subnets	
128	√
192	√
224	√
240	√
248	√
252	√
254	
255	

As a network administrator, you would keep a record of used IP addresses and subnets. So far, you will have allocated the addresses as follows:

WAN Links

200.100.100.0 /30—WAN link 1 (hosts 1 to 2)

200.100.100.4 /30—WAN link 2 (hosts 5 to 6)

200.100.100.8/30—WAN link 3 (hosts 9 to 10)

LAN Hosts

200.100.100.32/27—LAN 1 (hosts 33 to 62)

200.100.100.64/27—LAN 2 (hosts 65 to 94)

200.100.100.96/27—LAN 3 (hosts 96 to 126)

Large LAN Hosts

200.100.100.128/25—LAN (hosts 129 to 254)

VLSM principles will let you take a network and slice it down into smaller chunks. Those chunks can then be sliced into smaller chunks, and so on. You will reach the limit only when you get to the mask 255.255.255.252, or /30, because this gives you two usable hosts, which is the minimum you would need for any network.

Let's take network 200.100.100.0/24, for example. If you change the mask from /24 to /25, the following happens:

Original Mask (Last Octet)	00000000	1 Subnet	254 Hosts
New Mask (Subnet 1)	00000000	200.100.100.0—Subnet 1	126 Hosts
New Mask (Subnet 2)	10000000	200.100.100.128—Subnet 2	126 Hosts

Now you have two subnets. If you take the new Subnet 2 of 200.100.100.128 and break it down further by changing the mask from /25 to /26, you get the following:

Original Mask (Last Octet)	10000000	1 Subnet	126 Hosts
New Mask (Subnet 1)	10000000	200.100.100.128—Subnet 1	62 Hosts
New Mask (Subnet 2)	11000000	200.100.100.192—Subnet 2	62 Hosts

If you take the second subnet and break it down further by changing the mask from /26 to /28 (for example), you get the following:

Original Mask (Last Octet)	11000000	1 Subnet	62 hosts
New Mask (Subnet 1)	11000000	200.100.100.192 (Subnet 1)	14 hosts
New Mask (Subnet 2)	11010000	200.100.100.208 (Subnet 2)	14 hosts
New Mask (Subnet 3)	11100000	200.100.100.224 (Subnet 3)	14 hosts
New Mask (Subnet 4)	11110000	200.100.100.240 (Subnet 4)	14 hosts

Summary

I hope this has helped you to understand a bit more about VLSM. It is no mystery really. Please take time to go over the examples above again, and then have a go at the challenge illustrated in Figure B.5 below:

ACME Company II has been allocated the address below. It requires you to design an addressing system so that hosts can be given IP addresses and the WAN links can be addressed with no wastage.

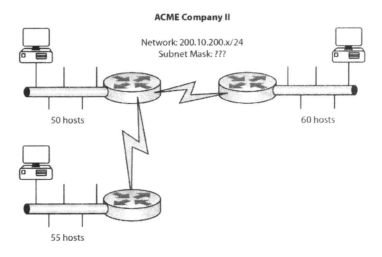

FIG B.5—ACME Company II

APPENDIX C

ICND2 Cram

LAN SWITCHING

Spanning Tree Protocol (STP) IEEE 802.1d

STP is a link management protocol that provides path redundancy whilst preventing undesirable loops in the network. For communication to work correctly on an Ethernet network, there can be only one path between two destinations. STP uses Bridge Protocol Data Units (BPDUs) received by all switches to determine the Spanning Tree topology. A port on a switch is either in Forwarding or Blocking state. Forwarding ports provide the lowest path cost to the Root Bridge. A port will remain in Blocking state from startup if the Spanning Tree determines there is a better path.

You can force a particular switch to become a Root Bridge by manually configuring the priority (in increments of 4096) as follows:

```
Switch(config)#spanning-tree vlan 2010 priority 8192
Or
Switch(config)#spanning-tree vlan 2010 root primary
```

Rapid Spanning Tree Protocol (RSTP) IEEE 802.1w

STP takes up to 50 seconds to converge to a stable network, whereas RSTP takes 2 seconds. RSTP port roles are Root Port, Designated Port, Backup Port, Alternate Port, and Disabled. Most implementations of RSTP use Per VLAN Spanning Tree+ (PVST+). Here, multiple instances of Spanning Tree are running so the load on the CPU is higher, but you can load share over the links. To enable RSTP for each VLAN in your switched network, use the following command:

```
Switch(config)#spanning-tree mode rapid-pvst
```

Bridging/Switching

Bridges are primarily software-based and have one Spanning Tree instance per bridge, normally, 16 ports per bridge. LAN switches are primarily hardware-based. There are many Spanning Tree instances per switch and up to 100 ports.

Virtual LAN (VLAN)

A VLAN is a switched network that consists of logically segmented communities, without regard to physical location. Each port on a switch can belong to a VLAN. VLAN ports share broadcasts. A router is needed to route traffic between VLANs because Layer 2 devices do not use IP addresses. This reduces administrative costs, and allows for tighter security and better control of broadcasts.

Common Switching Commands

This is not a sample configuration but, rather, a demonstration of commands you need to know:

```
Switch(config)#vlan 2 ← creates VLAN 2
Switch(config-vlan)#name SALES ← names VLAN
Switch(config)#interface fast 0/1
Switch(config-if)#switchport access vlan 2 ← puts interface into VLAN 2
Switch(config-if)#switchport mode trunk ← sets interface to trunk
Switch(config)#vtp mode transparent/client/server ← sets switch mode
Switch(config)#vtp domain howtonetwork.net ← sets VTP domain name
Switch(config)#spanning-tree portfast ← sets Port Fast
Switch(config)#ip default-gateway 192.168.1.1 ← switch default gateway
Switch#show vlan brief ← shows summary of VLAN info
Switch#show vtp status ← shows various VTP information, including mode/version
Switch#show interfaces trunk ← shows trunk interfaces
Switch#show mac-address-table dynamic ← shows mac table (dynamic)
Switch(config)#interface fast 0/1
Switch(config-if)#switchport port-security ← enables port security
Switch(config-if)#switchport port-security violation shutdown
Switch(config-if)#switchport port-security maximum 4 ← only 4 MACs
Switch(config-if)#switchport port-security mac-address xxx ← hard codes
Switch #show port-security ← you can add interface fast 0/1
```

The switch must be in transparent mode to add higher numbered VLANs (1006-4096).

IPv6

An IPv6 address consists of 128 bits represented in hexadecimal format and separated into eight parts (e.g., EEDE:AC89:4323:5445:FE32:BB78:7856:2022). There are no broadcast packets, only anycast, multicast, and unicast.

The two methods of migrating from IPv4 to IPv6 are dual stack and tunneling. Cisco IOS supports IPv6 commands in version 12.2(2)T and later.

Configure IPv6:

```
Router#config t
Router(config)#ipv6 unicast-routing
Router(config)#interface fast ethernet 0/0
Router(config-if)#ip address 192.1681.1 255.255.255.0
Router(config-if)#ipv6 address 2eef:c001:b14:2::c12/125
Router(config-if)#exit
Router#show IPv6 interface

FastEthernet0/0 is up, line protocol is down
IPv6 is enabled, link-local address is FE80::20E:83FF:FEF5:FD4F [TENTA-
TIVE]
Global unicast address(es):
2EEF:C001:B14:2::C12, subnet is 2EEF:C001:B14:2::C10/125 [TENTATIVE]
```

Route Summarisation

You need to be able to work this out for the exam. It is basically advertising out on as few routes as possible from your network. You can only work out a summary route by converting the IP address into binary (sorry). If you don't do this, then you have no way of knowing if you are advertising the correct summary route, which will lead to problems on your network.

Firstly, write out all of the network addresses in full, and then the binary versions to the right of that:

172.16.8.0	*10101100.00010000.00001*000.00000000
172.16.9.0	*10101100.00010000.00001*001.00000000
172.16.10.0	*10101100.00010000.00001*010.00000000
172.16.11.0	*10101100.00010000.00001*011.00000000
172.16.12.0	*10101100.00010000.00001*100.00000000
172.16.13.0	*10101100.00010000.00001*101.00000000
172.16.14.0	*10101100.00010000.00001*110.00000000
172.16.15.0	*10101100.00010000.00001*111.00000000
Matching Bits	*10101100.00010000.00001* = 21 bits

I have italicised the bits in each address which match. You can see that the first 19 bits match on every address, so your summarised route can reflect these 21 bits:

172.16.8.0 255.255.248.0

IP Routing

Routers must have some means of learning networks to which they are not directly connected.

Static routing:

```
Router(config)#ip route {destination network}{mask}{next hop address}
(e.g., IP route 172.16.5.2 255.255.255.0 172.16.12.8)
```

Dynamic addressing uses a routing protocol:

For EIGRP:

```
Router(config)# router eigrp 20
Router(config-router)#network 172.16.0.0
Router(config-router)#no auto-summary ← optional
```

For OSPF:

```
Router(config)#router ospf 20
Router(config-router)#network 172.16.0.0 0.0.255.255 area 0
```

Facts

EIGRP:

Uses IP protocol 88

Classless

Hybrid of Distance Vector and Link State

Multicasts updates to 224.0.0.10

Uses feasible successors to determine alternative routes to networks

The feasible successor is a backup route based upon the Topology Table

OSPF:

Uses IP protocol 89

Classless

Uses Dijkstra's shortest path algorithm (SFP)

Router ID is the highest IP address, but Loopback address is used if present

Backbone area is Area 0

All non-backbone areas must connect directly to Area 0

Areas can be numbered from 0 to 65,535

Multicasts on 224.0.0.5

OSPF uses cost as a metric (see below: * indicates the most common)

Interface	Cost (10^8/Bandwidth)
ATM, FastEthernet, GigabitEthernet, FDDI (> 100Mbps)	1
HSSI (45Mbps)	2

16Mbps Token Ring	6
10Mbps Ethernet	10
4Mbps Token Ring	25
T1 (1.544 Mbps)*	64
DS-0 (64k)*	1562
56k	1785

Network Security

Access Lists

Access lists are a set of conditions that permit or deny access to or through a router's interface.

Range	Usage
1 to 99	IP Standard
1300 to 1999	IP Standard (Expanded Range)
100 to 199	IP Extended
2000 to 2699	IP Extended (Expanded Range)

Standard Access Lists

Standard IP access lists check only the source address of the packet, and permit or deny the entire TCP/IP suite. You cannot choose a particular port or application to block. Cisco recommends that they are placed as close to the destination as possible:

```
Router(config)#access-list{number 1-99}{permit/deny}{source address}
access-list 10 permit 172.16.5.2 ← address can be a host or a network
```

Extended Access Lists

These allow for a lot more granularity when filtering IP traffic. They can filter packets based upon source or destination, a particular IP protocol, and a port number. Cisco recommends that they are placed as close to the source as possible:

```
Router(config)#access-list {number 100-99}{permit/ceny}{protocol} {source}
{destination}{port}
access-list 112 permit tcp host 172.16.5.2 host 172.16.10.2 eq www
```

Named Access Lists

```
Router(config)#ip access-list {standard/extended} name
Router(config)#ip access-list extended no_ftp
```

Access lists applied to inbound interfaces save the router from having to process the packet; denied packets will be dropped at the interface. Outbound access lists will be processed by the router and then dropped at the outbound interface if they match the access list.

Access lists can be applied to multiple interfaces, but there can be only one access list per protocol per direction per interface.

Use the term access-class if applying to console/auxiliary/VTY lines:

```
show ip access-lists
show access-list 1
```

Packets are processed by the access list and then routed.

Wildcard Masks

Wildcard masks tell the router which parts of the address to look at and which to disregard.

```
access-list 12 permit 172.16.5.0 0.0.0.255
```

The above would permit any host on network 172.16.5.x. In order to work out a wildcard mask, simply write out the mask in full and then take that number away from 255.

Number	255	255	255	255
- Mask	255	255	192	0
Equals	0	0	63	255

Access lists are applied to interfaces:

```
Router(config)#access-list 1 permit 172.16.5.2
Router(config)#interface e0
Router(config-if)#ip access-group 1 in
```

Passwords (the service password-encryption command encrypts all passwords):

Enable—Used to get from User Exec mode to Privileged Exec mode. Not encrypted:

```
Router(config)#enable password {password}
```

Enable Secret—Encrypts password (use only enable or enable secret, not both):

```
Router(config)#enable secret {password}
```

VTY—Needed if Telnet access is required:

```
Router(config)#line vty 0 4
Router(config-line)#password cisco
Router(config-line)#login
```

Auxiliary—Allows modem access to the auxiliary port:

```
Router(config)#line aux 0
Router(config-line)#password cisco
Router(config-line)#login
```

Console—Used to allow console access:

```
Router(config)#line console 0
Router(config-line)#password cisco
Router(config-line)#login
```

WAN Protocols and Services

HDLC—Cisco default on serial WAN connections. No authentication available.

PPP—Data link. Uses PAP (clear text) and CHAP (secure hash) authentication. Authentication is optional. Use PPP if connecting a Cisco router to a non-Cisco router:

```
Router(config)#hostname paul password cisco ← case sensitive
Router(config)#interface serial 0
Router(config-if)#encapsulation ppp
Router(config-if)# ppp authentication chap
```

Frame Relay

Based upon x.25 protocol, but with less error checking so it's quicker. Normally 56k to 2Mb, so it's ideal for SMEs. Works at the Physical and Data Link Layers. DLCIs are used to identify the circuit. Each router uses LMIs for keepalives on the line between the Router and Frame Relay switch. LMI type is Cisco by default. You must use another type, such as ANSI, if connecting to a non-Cisco router.

```
Router(config-if)#encapsulation frame-relay
Router(config-if)#frame-relay map ip 2.2.2.2 100
```

In the output above, the router is told to get to IP address 2.2.2.2 (use DLCI 100). Frame Relay problems include the following:

- Incorrect LMI setting
- Incorrect DLCI
- Split horizon preventing routing updates leaving interface

Use Frame Relay subinterfaces if point-to-point or multipoint connection is needed. IP address is applied to subinterfaces for these, NOT the main interface.

Frame Relay uses backwards explicit congestion notification (BECN) on returning frames to warn of congestion, and forward explicit congestion notification (FECN) is set by the DCE end to warn of congestion from the sending end.

Troubleshooting

Always use a systematic and methodical approach to troubleshooting.

The first command to issue is `show ip interface brief` to establish whether the interfaces are down or up. There are only a handful of ways to break any network in the exam.

Layer 1

Ensure that there is a clock rate on the DCE interface (use the `show controllers serial X` command—where X is the Serial interface number—to see what type of cable is attached).

Ensure that the `no shut` command has been applied to the interface.

Layer 2

Ensure that the correct encapsulation type is on the interface (i.e., HDLC, PPP, etc.) (use the `show interface serial X` command to check).

If it is not the correct encapsulation type, then go into Interface Configuration mode and change it.

Layer 3

Ensure that the correct IP address AND subnet mask is applied to the interface.

Ensure that the correct networks are being advertised by the routing protocol (`show ip protocols`).

Always ensure that you can ping across directly connected router interfaces BEFORE applying routing protocols and access lists. <u>You have been warned</u>.

APPENDIX D

Bonus CCENT Labs

I've mixed up various aspects of CCENT-level subjects for the following multi-technology labs. Have some fun playing with them. Work on your speed and the important configuration commands involved. When you configure the labs, change up the topology and IP addresses so you don't get too used to the same ones; otherwise, you will be fazed in the actual exam.

LAB 1—STATIC ROUTING

Topology

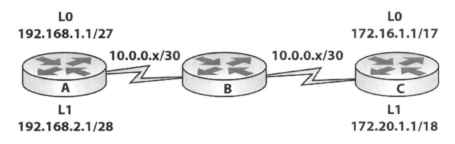

LO
192.168.1.1/27

LO
172.16.1.1/17

10.0.0.x/30   10.0.0.x/30

A   B   C

L1
192.168.2.1/28

L1
172.20.1.1/18

Configuration

I'm not going to walk you through this lab because you have done it before.

Configure static routes on each router so it can ping every network on every other router. Router A will have three routes, for example.

Hints

You are using VLSM here, so the networks using the WAN links take up only two IP addresses. This is best practise, but you need to bear in mind that these are different networks. The IP addresses are as follows:

    A—10.0.0.1/30
    B—10.0.0.2/30 (towards A)

And

    B—10.0.0.5/30 (towards C)
    C—10.0.0.6/30

LAB 2—RIPV2

Topology

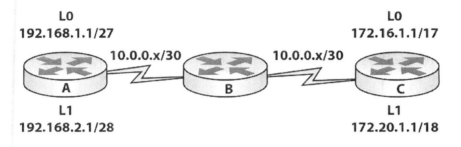

LO
192.168.1.1/27

LO
172.16.1.1/17

10.0.0.x/30   10.0.0.x/30

A   B   C

L1
192.168.2.1/28

L1
172.20.1.1/18

Configuration

Configure RIPv2 routes on each router so it can ping every network on every other router. Router A will have three routes, for example.

Hints

If you have more than one network on the 10 network, then you should use auto-summarisation. This would be more important if you had a 10 network with a non-standard mask at either end of the topology.

LAB 3 –STATIC NAT AND RIPV2

Topology

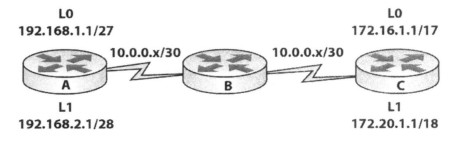

LO
192.168.1.1/27

LO
172.16.1.1/17

10.0.0.x/30   10.0.0.x/30

A   B   C

L1
192.168.2.1/28

L1
172.20.1.1/18

Configuration

Configure RIPv2 on the network above. Check the routing tables on all routers.

Configure NAT on ROUTER A so the 192.168.2.1 address is translated to 192.168.200.200. Test the NAT configuration with an extended ping.

Hints

Remember that you will need a static route for the 192.168.200.0 network on Router B; otherwise, the packet will be dropped, as the router won't know where to send it.

LAB 4—STATIC ROUTES WITH TELNET

Topology

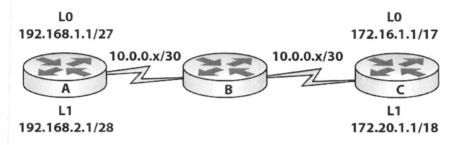

LO
192.168.1.1/27

LO
172.16.1.1/17

10.0.0.x/30

10.0.0.x/30

A

B

C

L1
192.168.2.1/28

L1
172.20.1.1/18

Configuration

Configure static routes on all networks so you can ping every IP address from every router.

Add a Telnet password to Router C so you can telnet to it. Make sure you are challenged for a username and password.

Issue a show cdp neighbor detail command on Router B. Now turn off CDP on the interface only on Router C. Turn off CDP on the entire router on Router A.

Hints

Easy enough. Make sure you don't peek at the earlier labs unless you get really stuck.

LAB 5—NAT POOL

Topology

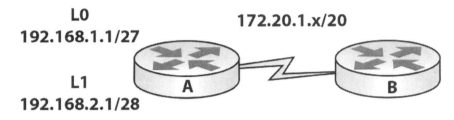

L0
192.168.1.1/27

172.20.1.x/20

L1
192.168.2.1/28

A

B

Configuration

Configure the IP addresses above. Choose the last two valid IPs for your WAN link in the 172.20.1.x/20 network.

Add a static route on Router B to send any traffic for any network back to Router A.

Configure a NAT pool on Router A. The pool should be 10.1.1.1 to 10.1.1.10, inclusive. Add an access list to ensure that any traffic from the 192.160.1.x and 192.168.2.x networks is matched for NAT.

Test the NAT pool by sourcing pings from L0 and L1 on Router A to Router B.

Hints

Your ACL will require two lines for this to work.

LAB 6—NAT OVERLOAD

Topology

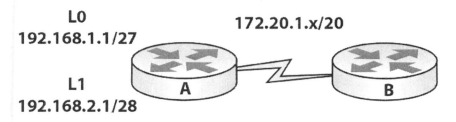

LO
192.168.1.1/27

172.20.1.x/20

L1
192.168.2.1/28

A   B

Configuration

Configure the IP addresses above. Choose the last two valid IPs for your WAN link in the 172.20.1.x/20 network.

Add a static route on Router B to send any traffic for any network back to Router A.

Configure a NAT pool on Router A. The pool should be 172.16.1.1 only. Add an access list to ensure that any traffic from the 192.160.1.x and 192.168.2.x networks is matched for NAT.

Test the NAT pool by sourcing pings from L0 and L1 on Router A to Router B.

Hints

Your ACL will require two lines for this to work.

Your pool needs one address only, but you still need to specify the start and end address for the pool:

```
ip nat pool internet_out 172.16.1.1 172.16.1.1 prefixlength 24
or
ip nat pool internet_out 172.16.1.1 172.16.1.1 netmask 255.255.255.0
```

Remember that you need to add another line of configuration to reference the pool and overload it.

LAB 7—DHCP

Topology

Configuration

Configure the IP address 172.16.1.1 on the Ethernet port of the router. Connect a PC or laptop with a crossover cable.

Configure a pool of DHCP addresses on the router of 172.16.0.0 and add excluded addresses of 172.16.1.1 to 172.16.1.10, inclusive. Add a DNS IP address and default router address to allocate to hosts.

Set the PC to obtain an address via DHCP and then look at the IP configuration to check address allocation.

Hints

No hints here.

Bonus ICND2 Labs

LAB 1—EIGRP

Topology

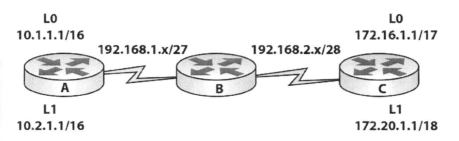

L0
10.1.1.1/16

L0
172.16.1.1/17

192.168.1.x/27

192.168.2.x/28

A

B

C

L1
10.2.1.1/16

L1
172.20.1.1/18

Configuration

Configure the IP addresses on the network above.

Configure EIGRP 20 on all routers, but set Router C as EIGRP 30. Leave auto-summarisation on for now. Then ensure that the routing tables contain all the correct networks.

Fix the issue of the wrong AS on Router C. You will encounter similar problems when tested in the exam.

Turn off auto-summary on Router C only. Check the routes on Router B and Router A to see whether they are different. If they are, why would that be and how would you fix this issue?

Hints

No hints here.

LAB 2—OSPF

Topology

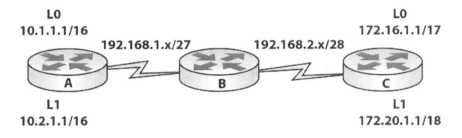

L0
10.1.1.1/16

192.168.1.x/27   192.168.2.x/28

L0
172.16.1.1/17

A   B   C

L1
10.2.1.1/16

L1
172.20.1.1/18

Configuration

Configure the IP addresses on the network above.

Configure OSPF on all routers. Put the 172.20 network on Router C into Area 100. Put the 10.2 network on Router A into Area 10.

Hints

You really need to ensure your wildcard masks are correct on your OSPF network statements because, unlike EIGRP, OSPF will not overcome user configuration errors.

LAB 3—STANDARD ACL

Topology

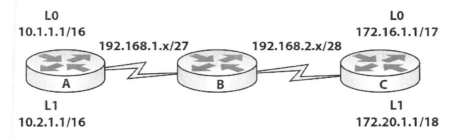

LO
10.1.1.1/16

192.168.1.x/27   192.168.2.x/28

LO
172.16.1.1/17

A   B   C

L1
10.2.1.1/16

L1
172.20.1.1/18

Configuration

Configure the IP addresses on the network above.

Set a standard ACL on Router C. Deny host address 10.1.1.1 and deny network 10.2.0.0 incoming on your Serial interface.

Test this by pinging the Serial of Router B via both Loopbacks on Router A and this should work. Pings to the Serial interface on Router C should fail.

Hints

No hints here.

LAB 4—EXTENDED ACL

Topology

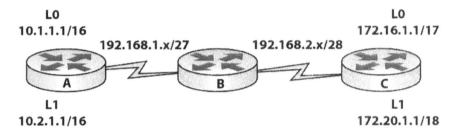

LO
10.1.1.1/16

192.168.1.x/27

192.168.2.x/28

LO
172.16.1.1/17

A

B

C

L1
10.2.1.1/16

L1
172.20.1.1/18

Configuration

Configure the IP addresses on the network above.

Set an extended ACL on Router A.

Block Telnet (after you have enabled Telnet) to 10.1.1.1 if it comes from Router B (Serial IP address). Telnet should work from any other IP address.

You can test this by telnetting from Router C.

Add an ACL on router C. Permit pings from Router A but deny all other pings incoming. You need to permit other IP traffic, though; otherwise, your Telnet test to Router A may not work.

Hints

Which service does ICMP use?

Your ACL on Router C needs to have three lines in it. One needs to permit the pings from the Serial interface on Router A. One needs to deny all other ping traffic. One needs to permit all other IP traffic.

LAB 5—EIGRP WITH PPP AND NAMED ACL

Topology

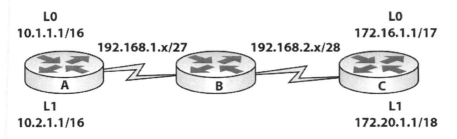

LO
10.1.1.1/16

192.168.1.x/27

LO
172.16.1.1/17

192.168.2.x/28

A

B

C

L1
10.2.1.1/16

L1
172.20.1.1/18

Configuration

Configure the IP addresses on the network above.

Set a PPP as the WAN protocol between all routers.

Add EIGRP 40 to all routers, and then ensure all routes are working.

Set a named ACL on Router C. Permit Telnet only from host address 10.2.1.1. Permit pings from network 192.168.1.x/27 only. No other Telnet or pings should work. Live IOS routers do permit you to telnet from a source interface or IP address - `telnet 192.168.1.4 /source-interface FastEthernet0`

Hints

Did the ACL break your routing? Whoops!

ACLs block everything that isn't permitted, so you need to permit EIGRP in your ACL for your routing to work. If only this book told you how to do that. Or maybe it does somewhere!

LAB 6—VLANS AND TRUNKING

Topology

Configuration

Configure the trunk link between Switch A and Switch B. Do not leave either side in negotiate mode.

Configure VLAN 10 on both switches and set the ports your PCs are connected to as VLAN access ports in VLAN 10.

Permit only VLAN 10 to pass over the trunk link. Check this with the `show interface trunk` command.

Hints

Should be easy enough!

LAB 7—STP ELECTION

Topology

Configuration

Configure VLANs 10 and 20 on both switches. Set the trunk interface between both switches and ensure they are hard-set as trunk interfaces.

Permit only VLANs 10 and 20 across the trunk.

Check which switch has been designated as the Root Bridge for both VLANs. Change the Root Bridge to the other switch, first by changing the priority and then by designating it as the primary Root Bridge.

Hints

All of the commands have been covered in earlier labs.

LAB 8—VTP

Topology

Configuration

Configure VLANs 100 and 200 on both switches. Set the trunk interface between both switches and ensure they are hard-set as trunk interfaces.

Permit only VLANs 100 and 200 across the trunk.

Set a VTP domain on both switches called 'in60days.' Set a VTP password of 'cisco.' Set Switch B to be a VTP client.

Hints

Check out the configuring VTP notes.